WHITE TERROR

RUSSELL MEEUF

WHITE TERROR

THE HORROR FILM FROM OBAMA TO TRUMP

INDIANA UNIVERSITY PRESS

This book is a publication of

Indiana University Press
Office of Scholarly Publishing
Herman B Wells Library 350
1320 East 10th Street
Bloomington, Indiana 47405 USA

iupress.org

Chapter 6, "Motor City Gothic: White Youth and Economic
Anxiety in *It Follows* and *Don't Breathe*" by Russell Meeuf and
Benjamin James originally appeared in *Dark Forces at Work:
Essays on Social Dynamics and Cinematic Horrors* (Lexington
Books, 2019) and is reprinted with permission.

This book is printed on acid-free paper.

Manufactured in China

First printing 2022

Cataloging information is available from the Library of Congress.
ISBN 978-0-253-06037-2 (hardback)
ISBN 978-0-253-06038-9 (paperback)
ISBN 978-0-253-06039-6 (ebook)

CONTENTS

ACKNOWLEDGMENTS

THIS PROJECT WAS ORIGINALLY A collaboration with my amazing friend and colleague Ben James, a screenwriter with a keen interest in horror storytelling. Ben and I developed the concept for this book together while co-teaching a freshman seminar on US horror films. We wanted to write an accessible book to help students, scholars, and horror fans grapple with the role of race and White racial anxieties in contemporary US horror films. Ben was pulled away from the project by his creative work (writing and directing a short horror film about corruption in rural White communities, appropriately enough), but this project has been informed by his insights and ideas from the very start.

My editor at Indiana University Press, Allison Chaplin, was also instrumental in supporting this project, and her suggestions along the way about how to create a scholarly book that is accessible and engaging to general audiences have been immensely helpful. The readers who supplied feedback on the project also provided invaluable suggestions.

I was also supported by a wonderful network of friends and colleagues who suggested great readings on horror and other topics, watched and discussed horror films with me, and generally provided moral support while I spent much of my professional life ensconced in a world of haunted houses, demonic possession, and creepy children: Jon Hegglund, Chad Burt, Zach Turpin, Dylan Champagne, Kevin Lewallen, Doug Heckman, Jenn Ladino, Erin James, and others. My department at the University of Idaho also supported my work here over the past several years, especially Kenton Bird, Pat Hart, Robin Johnson, Katie Blevins, Caitlin Cieslik-Miskimen, and Kyle Howerton. Special thanks to Carter Soles for sharing some of his recommendations on horror research and to Johanna Gosse for recommending some amazing research on race and surveillance culture that informs chapter 7. Chris Holmlund also provided support, suggestions, and a friendly ear as I finished the project.

The Society for Cinema and Media Studies Horror Studies Scholarly Interest Group was also invaluable, especially the folks who participated in the Facebook group and helped answer many queries over the years. Many thanks to Murray Leeder for his leadership with that group.

A version of chapter 6 appeared in the book *Dark Forces at Work: Essays on Social Dynamics and Cinematic Horrors*, edited by Cynthia J. Miller and A. Bowdoin Van Riper and published by Lexington Books. Many thanks to the editors of the collection for their suggestions on that chapter.

And, as always, the biggest thanks go to Ryanne, my partner and best friend, who can't watch horror movies but cheerfully discussed them with me while helping me raise three (hopefully non-creepy) children. During the time it took me to write this book, Alden went from being a little boy who couldn't get through the first jump scares of a horror movie to a teenager who doesn't think they are scary enough; Will has slowly graduated to watching PG-13 horror films, only needing to cover his eyes occasionally; and Fern (no surprise) has decided that nothing can possibly scare her.

WHITE TERROR

INTRODUCTION

Whiteness, Politics, and Horror

IN THE FIRST YEARS OF Donald Trump's presidency, activists and critics turned to the imagery of horror to encapsulate what was, to them, the nightmare of a President Trump. Chicago artist Mitch O'Connell began creating and circulating images of Trump in the style of the secret alien overlords in John Carpenter's *They Live* (1988); when seen with special glasses, the faces are revealed to be horrific, blue-tinged skulls (see fig. I.1). O'Connell created the images early in the presidential campaign and raised money for "Trump Lives!" billboards after the election.

Meanwhile, a trypophobia-inducing picture of Trump's head, pocked with holes containing Steve Bannon's face, made the rounds on Reddit and other social-media outlets. And when Melania Trump unveiled the somewhat unorthodox Christmas decor for the White House in 2017, internet Photoshoppers took the liberty of drawing connections to classic horror movies (see fig. I.2), a theme repeated in 2018, when she unveiled a hallway of blood-red Christmas trees.

For many Americans, the spectacle of horror became a fitting lens through which to view the political realities of a blustering, often-vulgar president who embraced deception and race-baiting. As the Trump presidency became mired in a never-ending series of scandals and crass tweets in its first years, the grim and unsettling worldview of horror mirrored our eroding political norms. American politics has, of course, long abandoned the pretense of civil discourse, but for many people, the ascendency of Trump created a horrific bizarro world. Ideal political norms, even if rarely achieved, were turned on their heads. Policy debates were replaced with bluster. Careful analysis was

Fig. I.1. Mitch O'Connell's rendering of Trump as an alien overlord from 1988's *They Live*, using the lens of horror to express the political horrors of Trumpism.

Fig. I.2. *Left*: An image of Trump's face filled with holes containing Steve Bannon that circulated on Reddit in 2017. *Right*: A meme that placed Jack Torrance from *The Shining* into Melania Trump's Christmas decor in 2017.

replaced with "alternative facts." The rhetoric of respect gave way to explicit sexism and xenophobia. In the age of Trump, US political culture didn't even pretend to valorize traditional norms; with the veil of tradition cast aside, it was revealed to be a farce, behind which stood only opportunism, corruption, and hate.

The uncanny media coverage of a president who is anything but presidential lent itself well to the uncanny world of horror, where everything that should be life-affirming and reassuring—family, home, religion, social institutions—is a grim inversion of its ideal form, marked by decay, immorality, and death.

At the same time, a series of overtly political horror stories reinforced the idea that horror would become a key mode of political critique early in the Trump era. Jordan Peele's *Get Out* (2017) scored several rare Oscar nominations for a horror film by addressing the terror of White liberalism's racial condescension and won Peele the Oscar for best original screenplay. Peele's film inspired waves of criticism and discussion about race in Trump's America and how to escape the culture's racial "sunken place."[1] The seventh season of the horror anthology TV program *American Horror Story* (2017), meanwhile, addressed Trump directly, focusing on a Trump-inspired extremist cult seeking to consolidate political power in a small town in Michigan. These stories made it big at the box office and in the ratings, demonstrating the appetite for critical, politically aware horror stories.[2]

For *LA Times* film critic Justin Chang, horror stories in 2017 were quickly becoming the "signature genre of the present moment."[3] Tracing the political awareness of recent horror from *Get Out* to the indie thriller *It Comes at Night* (2017) and the sci-fi horror *Life* (2017), Chang suggests that horror may see a political resurgence harkening back to the work of Tobe Hooper and George Romero. Meanwhile, in *Marie Claire* in 2018, Anne T. Donahue extolled the power of horror to help audiences cope with the political darkness of the contemporary US.[4] And on CNN, critic Brandon Tensley declared in 2019 that horror films are now the "best political commentary of our times."[5]

The idea that horror functions as a form of social critique has long been promoted by theorists and scholars. For Robin Wood, whose writings on the genre have been hugely influential, horror films are natural sites for political critique. Wood argues that horror stories revolve around a powerful vision of monstrosity that is both appalling and appealing. Horror monsters are ostensibly evil scapegoats that can represent ideas and people on the margins of patriarchal capitalist culture: racial and ethnic groups, women, political dissidents, the young. And yet these monsters allow repressed ideas to bubble to the surface and burst out in violent protest against social norms. As a genre, horror fixates on the moral decay of a society's institutions (family life, the church, the government, and consumerism, among others), all while offering grotesque images that subvert bourgeois norms around the body, death, and violence.[6] For scholars such as Christopher Sharrett, "There is no genre more subversive, more innately critical of the values of White bourgeois patriarchal society, than the horror film."[7]

Horror's reputation for political critique was cemented in the 1960s and 1970s in a cultural moment similar to the Trump years. Against the backdrop of a conservative president elected to office despite widespread protests and calls for progressive changes, low-budget horror filmmakers in the late 1960s and 1970s created a wave of gritty, gory films that exposed the violence, brutality, and depravity of the bourgeois mainstream. These films included Romero's foundational zombie films, *Night of the Living Dead* (1968) and *Dawn of the Dead* (1978), Tobe Hooper's *The Texas Chainsaw Massacre* (1974), Wes Craven's *Last House on the Left* (1972) and *The Hills Have Eyes* (1977), and others. These films gave voice to the fears and angst of the Richard Nixon era, telling stories of depraved White families and corrupt White institutions capable of horrific violence. Given this historical parallel, it is no wonder US culture turned to horror in the Trump era as our culture's moral decay and violence began bubbling to the surface.

Wood, however, is careful to note the core ambivalence of horror. In particular historical moments, horror may provide a grotesque spectacle that challenges social norms, but horror also affirms the core fear of the powerful: that Others are lurking around every corner, attempting to dismantle traditional institutions. After all, the political engagement of the 1970s horror film led to less overtly political horror films in the '80s and '90s. And for Sharrett, the stark conservatism of the second Bush administration saw a reactionary turn in the genre away from its radical political roots.

So while some horror today may critically explore the Trumpian nightmare envisioned by the political left, mainstream horror in the US has always been more than willing to explore the very fears that helped propel Trump to office in 2016: fears of outsiders disrupting the sanctity of the (almost always White) family, fears of evil forces or transgressive ideas transforming loved ones, fears of young people turning against the traditions of the older generation, fears that the world and its technology are moving too fast. As a popular genre, horror bends just as much to conservative fears around a changing world as it does to a liberal critique of social power. Mainstream horror, in fact, mostly operates somewhere in the gory middle of these two trends, mirroring the often-contradictory fears of a deeply divided and changing culture in a given historical moment. Recognizing that the election of Trump represented a failure of voters to compassionately imagine "a vision of genuine human progress," Chang reiterates the old notion that "in life, as in art, we get the horrors we deserve."[8]

The future may hold a golden age for critical horror exploring a nightmare of conservative politics, but this book looks back at the horror we deserved in the lead-up to the election of Trump in 2016. What fears dominated the horror of the Barack Obama era? What major cycles or trends proliferated in the horror film? And how did these films reflect the cultural fears that would lead slightly less than half of the voting public (but a majority of the Electoral College) to cast their vote for a candidate who so openly embodied xenophobia and sexism?

The horror of the Obama era wallowed in the anxieties of White Americans struggling with a perceived loss of social and economic standing in a postrecession America overseen by a Black president. Acknowledging that US horror is a predominantly White genre centered on the fears and privileges of White people, this book traces the contours of White fear in the Obama years, seeing the contemporary horror film as a key reflection of the racial terrors that would lead the US into the presidency of Trump.

FEAR AND THE WHITENESS OF HORROR

The top-grossing horror film of 2008 was actually released late in 2007, in the early days of the US presidential campaign: the Will Smith vehicle *I Am Legend*. In retrospect, the film proved to be a prophetic vision of the Obama years. Adapted from the 1954 Richard Matheson novel of the same name, the film stars Smith as Robert Neville, a US Army doctor who led the government's efforts to contain a viral outbreak that transformed the population into pale rage-filled zombies who only come out at night. Neville's efforts, however, were a total failure. He appears to be the only survivor of the outbreak, living a lonely life in a postapocalyptic New York, his only companion a German shepherd named Sam. By day, Neville hunts the wildlife that have reclaimed the city, talks to a series of mannequins he has rigged up to provide him company, and tries to trap specimens of the zombies in order to study them (see fig. I.3). He still hopes to find a cure by comparing their blood to his own, which is resistant to the virus. By night, he barricades himself into his apartment while the zombies wreak havoc outside his doors.

The casting of Smith as the lead provides an interesting racial reworking of the novel for the Obama era. The film tells the story of a smart, professional Black man, once lauded as a hero, who works relentlessly and without reward trying to save an angry horde of pale White folks who would much rather destroy him than be helped by him. Neville appears in flashbacks as a figure who inspired hope and salvation, like Obama (Neville still keeps on his fridge a picture of himself on the cover of *Time* magazine with the word *Savior* next to his image, a hand-drawn question mark debating the veracity of that claim). But, like Obama, Neville is overwhelmed by the rage of those he tries to help.

The pale-faced zombies of the film serve as a particularly appropriate metaphor for the waves of racial resentment that would wash over the US as a result of the election of the first Black president. The reality of an intelligent, sophisticated Black man in the Oval Office may have briefly inspired hopes of a postracial culture in America, but starting in the dark corners of right-wing media, feelings of White terror and rage swelled. In the end, Neville is overwhelmed and nobly sacrifices himself, but not before he finds a way to pass along his research, which may someday restore the humanity of the zombies that hate him.[9]

While the filmmakers couldn't have known precisely how prophetic their vision of Black heroism and White rage would become over the next eight years, their film certainly tapped into a set of resonant tensions around race, leadership, and the fears of social collapse.

Fig. I.3. Will Smith as Robert Neville, a Black scientist who tries to cure angry pale zombies in *I Am Legend* (Warner Bros., 2007).

These tensions, however, would fade to the background as star-driven big-budget horror movies like *I Am Legend* were replaced in the Obama era by more traditional horror subgenres, like the haunted house film and the possession film. Quelling fears that the creativity of American horror filmmakers was mired in the splatter films that proliferated after 9/11 or that US filmmakers were only capable of regurgitating Americanized versions of innovative international horror remakes, the horror of the Obama era yielded more critical and commercial success by returning to classic horror fare. Ghostly mansions, evil demons, and occult curses helped rejuvenate the genre in major franchises such as *The Conjuring* cinematic universe, the *Paranormal Activity* series, and the *Insidious* films.

The popular cycles of the Obama years typically centered on White families under siege from demonic forces, tapping into narratives of White victimization and loss of social standing. So why did these cycles of horror reemerge at this moment in US history? Why did these stories resonate with the culture, and what is their appeal? Why are the structures of horror in this moment so bound up with debates about race and power?

Critics and scholars have long discussed the appeal of horror, if you can call one's responses to horror appealing at all. For many, horror's appeal is rooted in deep-seated anxieties about the very essence of humanity. One scholar claims that horror explores "fundamental questions about the nature of human existence, questions that, in some profound ways, go beyond culture and society as these are organized in any period or form."[10] In this school of thought, horror taps into universal fears of human existence—death, threats to the sanctity of the body, the breakdown of trust and social bonds—and allows humanity to explore the foundational elements of human life. Other scholars are more focused on the psychology of horror, especially the ways that horror plays out the psychological dynamics of gender, sexuality, and identity.[11] Still others turn their attention to history and culture, arguing that horror films resonate because they "reflect the desires and anxieties of the time and place in which they are made" (a concept that this book relies on heavily).[12] More recently, scholars have turned toward cognitive and affective understandings of horror in an attempt to comprehend the mental and emotional processes of horror viewing.[13]

Whatever lens these scholars use to understand the appeal of horror, however, one variable is often missing: race—or, more specifically, Whiteness. Most discussions of horror make some reference to the genre's universality, its engagement with seemingly essential human concepts like death and violence or gender and sexuality. But Euro-American horror, in particular, doesn't simply offer a meditation on death and the body; it provides a meditation on death from the vantage of those with relative power and privilege, most often from the vantage of Whiteness. Death, bodily decay, violence, sex, and emotion may be universal parts of the human experience, but the ways that humans engage with such phenomenon are always filtered through social identities like race.[14]

In other words, US horror cinema fixates on anxious and terrified White people. In what ways, then, are the terrors of horror reflections of not simply the Other, but also a meditation on Whiteness and privilege?[15]

Whiteness, after all, has been at the core of Euro-American horror storytelling since its inception. The eighteenth- and nineteenth-century Gothic tradition that still informs horror today, for example, centers on White people in a particular colonial moment reacting with terror to cultural, economic, and technological change. As the Industrial Revolution and mass culture began to transform day-to-day life in the UK and then the US, Gothic literature dramatized the tensions of this tumultuous process. Gothic storytelling from this period features uncanny supernaturalism (haunted castles, spirits and ghosts, Machiavellian villains) in an era of increasing rationality and secularism. Such tales inevitably focus on the fears of privileged Whites—largely the withering family trees of the old nobility—who discover that, even in an age of so-called progress, the horrific past continues to impinge on the present. In fact, the Whiteness of its subjects is precisely at stake. Set against the shifting conceptions and definitions of race in the colonial era, Gothic storytelling in both the UK and the US exploits the nagging fear in a White supremacist culture that Whiteness itself is not as discrete or sacred as the culture assumes.[16]

These fears would only be magnified in the deeply racialized contexts of the US, where "stolen indigenous lands minus indigenous peoples plus black (and, in other ways, Asian) labor equals white property," according to Dixa Ramírez D'Oleo. For D'Oleo, horror stories are the natural outcome of this racialized equation, as they ritualistically enact the fears that beleaguer not just White folks but specifically the "property-owning white man."

D'Oleo writes, "The message of much of US horror storytelling is that no world is more terrifying for a white man than the one that decenters him, and, as such, destroys him."[17]

These racial preoccupations would also spawn the modern horror film in the US and Europe, centering Whiteness and the racial fears of Whites in these cinematic traditions. Mainstream US horror cinema fundamentally poses questions about the boundaries and significance of Whiteness in the modern world, especially today. Horror is not an incidentally White genre produced by a predominately White film industry, but rather a genre that, at its core, addresses the intrinsic fears of Whiteness in traditionally White supremacist cultures. Despite the popular assertions that horror stories tap into somehow universal fears built into all human experience, the fears explored in most horror stories reflect the fears of those with just enough social power and prestige that they might be afraid of losing it. In the context of the US, this tends to mean middle-class White people.

This isn't to ignore that people of color in the US have long embraced the horror film, both as audiences and as filmmakers who reimagine the White horror tradition to speak to the terrors of racism. A film like *Get Out* clearly demonstrates the flexibility of horror to explore the fears of Black folks amid continuing White supremacy in America (although, at its core, *Get Out* is intrinsically about the insecurity of Whiteness). Robin Means Coleman offers a detailed accounting of the ways that Blackness has informed horror storytelling and how Black folks in the US have attempted to create a Black horror cinema in films such as *Blacula* (1972) or *Def by Temptation* (1990).[18] Moreover, this is not to ignore the varied and vibrant global horror cinemas that emerged, especially after World War II, in places like Japan, South Korea, Nigeria, and many others.[19] Clearly, a range of horror traditions has been taken up globally and across racial and ethnic borders.

But as a storytelling tradition, contemporary US horror continues to be dominated by the trials and tribulations of middle-class White folks. Of the 147 mainstream US horror films released between 2008 and 2016 that are examined in this book, a respectable sixty-one (41.4%) featured people of color in significant roles, but only eleven of those films featured people of color as central characters in lead roles—a measly 7.4 percent. The trope of the ethnic side character who dies early in the narrative is still alive and well in this period of horror filmmaking. Additionally, of the eleven films with lead characters of color, three were parodies of horror filmmaking (*Meet the Blacks* [2016], *Boo! A Madea Halloween* [2016], and the New Zealand/US coproduction *What We Do in the Shadows* [2014]). Another three featured mixed-race or Latinx actors known for playing White or ambiguously ethnic characters in roles without any significant reference to their character's race or ethnicity (Jay Hernandez in *Quarantine* [2008], Jessica Alba in *The Eye* [2008], and Jesse Williams in *The Cabin in the Woods* [2012]). That leaves a total of five serious horror films in that period that clearly center on people of color, representing only 3.4 percent of the films. By comparison, according to UCLA's annual Hollywood Diversity Report, minorities had leading roles in 13.9 percent of all Hollywood films in 2018, although even that is a fairly dismal percentage in a country where people of color represent around 40 percent of the population.[20] When it comes to telling horror stories in the US, we still primarily tell stories about terrified White people, for a variety of industrial and cultural reasons.[21]

WHITE TERRORS

So what do White people have to fear?

In traditionally White supremacist cultures, people of color, poor people, and others outside the norm of middle-class Whiteness have historically had the most to fear, from threats to their safety, to threats to their freedom, to threats to whatever prosperity they attained. But those aren't the kinds of fears that typically find their way into horror stories. Instead, horror stories tend to explore the dread of the privileged as they face the haunting proposition that their privilege cannot protect them from all dangers. The fears of the horror film are most often the fears of people with something to lose, not the fears of those struggling to get by.

The classic slasher film of the '80s, for example, almost always took up the perspective of middle-class Whites threatened by those without cultural or social power. As film scholars Aviva Briefel and Sianne Ngai point out in their analysis of the urban horror *Candyman* (1992), the traditional slasher formula in films such as *Friday the 13th* (1980) and *Nightmare on Elm Street* (1984) places its loyalties and perspective with privileged White teens stalked by working-class

figures who threaten the mundane rituals of White teenage life. Jason Voorhees—the son of Camp Crystal Lake's cook who drowned while the spoiled
camp counselors fooled around—should be a sympathetic figure, but instead
he becomes a horrific, supernatural killjoy who keeps privileged White teens
from having a good time. Freddy Krueger, a custodian at a day-care facility, was
burned alive by a gang of vigilante parents convinced that he had molested their
children. But, according to the film, the real horror lies with White middle-class
teens whose sex lives are terrorized by dreams stemming from their parents'
crimes. The fears of the powerless who might be victimized by the powerful at
any moment are relegated to the backstories of horrible villains, while the fears
of the White middle class dominate the narratives.[22]

As this suggests, the kinds of White terror reflected in popular horror stories
are often outward looking: What kinds of Others or abject monsters might
threaten the privileged life middle-class White folks have built for themselves?
What are the threats that White folks should be afraid of? Who are the outsiders who challenge their privileged place in the culture?

But this only tells part of the story of horror's inherent Whiteness. White
terror in the contemporary US is not simply about being afraid of the Other, but
rather about being terrified of the failures of your own Whiteness. Whiteness
in the era of multiculturalism means living in a culture (and therefore within a
narrative) that tells you that you are righteous and supreme, and yet the failures
of that narrative are apparent all around you, creating the creeping suspicion
that that narrative is false. The unwillingness to confront or come to terms
with that realization yields the horror of self-delusion, while the willingness to
accept the lies of White supremacy yields the horror of guilt.

These are the fears outlined by Robert Jensen in his book *The Heart of Whiteness*. For Jensen, being White in America carries with it a series of fears about
the state of Whiteness. Most obvious are those outward looking fears concerning your place in the culture—fears that you might lose whatever privileges and
prosperity you have or, even more terrifying for a predominately White culture,
fears that people of color might someday treat White folks as horrifically as
people of color have been treated across history. Coupled with these fears are
more introspective fears about White privilege—for example, the lingering
fear that White folks haven't really earned their privileges and prosperity in the
culture. What if the American dream that White folks think they have worked
hard for actually came through luck and the unearned benefits of Whiteness?
What if one's prosperity is rooted in the violent oppression of people of color?

There are additional questions for well-intentioned White folks in an
increasingly diverse culture: What if people of color actually see us for who we

are? What if they can see those unearned benefits, see the racist assumptions that always linger, see that we are the representatives of a White supremacist system that is a sham?[23]

But because US culture doesn't have an open dialogue about race, power, and history, these fears fester as White people come to believe that their place in the culture is precarious.[24] These anxieties remain unexamined and grow into both guilt and racial resentments.

The nightmares of the horror film reflect this festering. The contemporary horror film is not only about outsiders—grotesque monsters that threaten the sanctity of middle-class Whiteness—but also the introspective dread of White folks coming to grips with their own guilt and self-delusion as the culture changes. Across the Obama-era horror film, then, a similar set of often contradictory fears plague the almost-exclusively White characters who find themselves terrorized and haunted in the US:

- Fears that White folks in general and the middle-class White family in particular are losing their social standing and privileged place in the culture
- The simmering dread that maybe White folks actually deserve this loss of status
- Fears that the cultural authority of Whiteness—and the White patriarch in particular—is eroding in a multicultural society
- Fears that Whites—and especially White mothers—have allowed the White family to flounder as the share of Whites in the US population declines
- Fears that the history of Whiteness in the US might be forgotten
- Fears that the history of Whiteness in the US might be remembered for its atrocities

RACIAL POLITICS AND WHITENESS

Given the horror film's heavy focus on White racial anxieties, horror became a perfect vehicle for White terror in the wake of the election of Barack Obama. While the election of the nation's first Black president warranted a wave of celebratory discussions of a possible post-racial America, a steady stream of racist vitriol against Obama and the First Lady made clear that race and racism had not suddenly disappeared in the US. Throughout his campaign and presidency, Obama was accused of secretly being Muslim, an attempt to cast him as ethnically Other. And the vocal displeasure of activists on the far right, such as members of the emergent Tea Party movement, was often expressed in the form of racist stereotypes—for example, images of Obama in the style of nineteenth-century minstrelsy or represented as an African witch doctor. Racial discomfort with the president, of course, found its most public manifestation in the so-called birther movement, which insisted that Obama was actually born in Kenya but used faked documents to demonstrate that he was born in Hawaii. The birther conspiracy theory found its most vocal supporter in reality-TV-star Trump, who used the issue to insert himself via racially inflammatory language into US political discourse.

All the while, fueled by right-wing media, many Americans came to believe that Obama's policies and politics put minorities first over White folks, especially rural White folks. As documented in a series of studies on rural White America, such as Arlie Russell Hochschild's *Strangers in Their Own Land*, many rural White folks cultivated a deep sense of racial mistrust after the rise of Obama and media coverage extolling the virtues of diversity. Despite evidence to the contrary, the subjects in Hochschild's book, for example, came to believe that the government under Obama gave huge subsidies and benefits to immigrants and people of color to help minorities get a leg up on their chance at the American dream at the expense of White folks.[25] While these narratives of supposed White victimization in a multicultural and politically correct world had festered for decades, the election of Obama provided a high-profile affirmation of that worldview.

The economic recession following the housing crisis of 2006–2007 only exacerbated the fears of White folks in the US. Despite the fact that the so-called Great Recession impacted people of color with much more severity, the fate of middle-class Whites became a source of national concern in the media as the typical lifelines to middle-class life (homeownership, stable employment, a college education) became more inaccessible. Narratives about Whites who felt that the promises of the American dream would never be kept were much more dramatic than stories about the economic plight of people of color who never imagined that the American dream applied to them anyway.

Politically, then, the racial resentments of White folks began to reshape US politics. As Michael Tesler has meticulously documented with data from a range of public opinion surveys, the Obama era in the US was not the "post-racial" haven forecasted by pundits in the wake of Obama's election, but rather a "'most-racial' political era where racially liberal and racially conservative Americans were more divided over a whole host of political positions than they had been in modern times."[26] For Tesler, the data reveals that a growing number of Americans viewed politics through a racialized lens, seeing political issues and candidates as referendums on racial politics in America, all while polarization and racial resentments increased.

This racial resentment helps explain the rise and ultimate election of Trump as the president of the United States at the end of the Obama era. While initial political punditry pointed to the economic anxieties of the working class as the cause for Trump's Electoral College victory in 2016—barely delivering rust-belt states such as Michigan, Wisconsin, and Pennsylvania to Trump—a more detailed analysis of his victory pointed to the racial resentments of White folks as a primary factor driving voter behavior.[27] White folks delivered the election to Trump, not the economically insecure.

More troubling, it became apparent that many people voted for Trump not in spite of his racially inflammatory rhetoric, but precisely because of it, and were driven by a sense of racial resentment and victimization. Soon after Trump's election, these long-simmering racial resentments came bubbling to the surface, not only through Trump's racist statements and policies (his continued insistence that immigrants were criminals and rapists, his reference to the developing world as "shithole countries," his draconian border policies that imprisoned legal asylum seekers and separated families and their children), but also through the growing public presence of White supremacist organizations, most notably at high-profile rallies such as the one in Charlottesville, Virginia, in 2017, organized by the increasingly well-known White supremacist Richard Spencer—a rally that turned violent and left one counterprotester dead.

While these racial tensions came to a boil after 2016, they can be seen and felt in the popular horror films of the Obama era—films that centered on the same anxieties surrounding the supposedly declining fortunes of White folks in America that inspired the rise of Trump. This is not to say that the horror film paved the way for Trump's presidency, but rather that the horror film tapped into the same cultural fears that fueled the rise of Trump. While Trump was tweeting racist conspiracy theories that fed off racial resentments, horror storytellers were telling tales about the suffering White middle class.

However, it isn't only the conservative anxieties of Whiteness that find expression in contemporary horror. The genre's hand-wringing about the continuing place of Whiteness in the US also reflects a host of concerns from the left. In a media culture that increasingly valorized feel-good stories of diversity and inclusion, there was a growing pressure on Whiteness to adapt and reform itself, to demonstrate its magnanimity by embracing new forms of cultural diversity while still occupying a place of privilege and centrality. Could Whiteness in the US transform itself in an age of multiculturalism and a Black president? For diversity-minded White people, what kinds of guilt should be felt and expressed over past discrimination (without, of course, questioning the prosperity built on that discrimination)? Stories about diversity could be shared by White folks on social media to demonstrate their social awareness, but does this diversity rhetoric actually disrupt the dominance of Whiteness in US social and political institutions? In short, does the new multicultural society envisioned by the left actually mean diminishing social centrality for White folks?[28]

These questions also find themselves reflected in the Obama-era horror film, which explores the basis of White guilt and the historical terrors that underpin White prosperity. Especially in the haunted house film, the home invasion film, and the technological horror film, the horrific pasts of White dominance and the horrific present of inequality refuse to be sublimated by the middle-class White folks who try their best to ignore the basis of their privileges. But in horror, that which would be repressed always resurfaces to plague those who ignore history. The characters in such stories are forced to reckon with the consequences of these histories and inequalities, all while struggling to assert their own specialness and merit. Many of these narratives seek to acknowledge the past and the current horrors of Whiteness while still focusing on the deserving White family, mirroring the anxieties of the left about how to embrace and acknowledge a multicultural world without divesting from the privileges of Whiteness.

MAPPING CONTEMPORARY HORROR

These conclusions are based on an exhaustive analysis of every major US horror film produced between 2008 and 2016, although at times my analysis starts before 2008 and extends past 2016 to provide a fuller picture of the context of the horror trends of the Obama years. In order to analyze the scope of mainstream horror in this period, I created a list of all US horror films using data from the Internet Movie Database (IMDB) that met the following criteria:

- Films with a release date between January 1, 2008, and December 31, 2016
- Films tagged as "horror" in IMDB
- Films produced by a US company, including international coproductions in which at least one US company is involved
- Films that grossed at least one million dollars in a theatrical release (adjusted for inflation based on the value of the dollar in 2016)

The result is a list of 147 films across the nine-year period that reflect the core of mainstream US horror.

While this process provided a clear set of films to analyze, there are, of course, drawbacks and limitations to this approach. First, the genre coding of IMDB is not always consistent with popular understandings of horror. Films such as *Jaws* (1975), *The Silence of the Lambs* (1991), or *The Sixth Sense* (1999) are not categorized as "horror" on IMDB but as "thrillers," a distinction that leaves out films that may be popularly understood as horror films but aren't technically included on this list. Second, the benchmark of one million dollars in a theatrical release leaves out some of the innovative work in horror that goes straight to streaming services or appears on television. TV horror, in particular, represents a popular manifestation of the genre, thanks to shows such as *The Walking Dead* (2010–), *American Horror Story* (2011–), *Bates Motel* (2013–2017), *Scream Queens* (2015–2016), *The Haunting of Hill House* (2018), *Lovecraft Country* (2020), and others, but such work is not included in the core of this study in an effort to create a manageable set of horror stories to study. Certainly, more research is necessary to assess how well TV horror or nontheatrical cult horror fits into the conclusions I draw here.

Within these 147 films, I looked for the significant cycles and trends that characterized the genre between 2008 and 2016. Each film was categorized into a series of subgenres, hybrid genres, or themes (for example, *haunted house*, *action-horror*, or *horrific technology*), yielding a total of twenty-seven different subcategories of horror that indicate the variety and complexity of horror storytelling. Because horror narratives tend to be multifaceted and combine different generic elements, each film could be categorized in up to three areas (for example, the 2012 film *Sinister* is a haunted house narrative that also features horrific children and horrific technology). To make historical comparisons, this entire process was repeated for the horror genre between 1980 and 2007.

As a result of these historical comparisons, I have identified not only the most prevalent kinds of horror stories in the Obama years, but also the stories that are historically unique to it: cycles of films that didn't seem to resonate in the 1980s, 1990s, or early 2000s but became the staple narratives of horror from 2008 to 2016. Many of these cycles are very old horror tropes that have become resurgent lately, such as the haunted house film, which, as I note below, is perhaps the most prominent horror cycle of the Obama years. Other cycles are relatively new, such as the trend toward horror remakes that began in the mid-2000s.

The most significant cycles were:

- The haunted house film
- The home invasion film
- The possession and exorcism film
- The horrific child film
- The horrific technology film
- The nostalgic horror remake

These Obama-era cycles all highlight the horror film's focus on Whiteness, offering a variety of narratives often on the same theme: the supposed declining fortunes of White folks in an era of White guilt and perceived White victimization. In the chapters that follow, I explore how each of these cycles dramatizes the key cultural tensions surrounding Whiteness and social power in the US.[29]

Because of the large number of films examined in this project and my interest in subgenres and cycles, I'm primarily concerned here with narrative patterns: What kinds of stories and scenarios are repeated in this period, and what do these patterns tell us about the persistent anxieties of Whiteness in the US? What kinds of characters are used repeatedly in the films, and what kinds of plots are they dropped into? This leaves less room for really delving deeply into the style and nuances of individual films, but it keeps the bigger picture in focus: the trends and patterns across these films that bind them together and reflect our cultural preoccupations around race, gender, and social class.

Within those narrative structures, I also pay particular attention to the visual construction of space in these stories, especially the representation of domestic spaces, family homes, and residential neighborhoods. Even beyond the haunted house film and home invasion film, the spaces of the White family home take on an almost mythological importance in Obama-era horror filmmaking, from the family homes beset by possessed children in films such as *The Possession* (2012), to the domestic spaces infested with creepy children in films such as *Mama* (2013), to the suburban McMansions surveilled by disbelieving patriarchs in most of the *Paranormal Activity* series, to the reimagined suburban spaces of horror remakes such as Rob Zombie's *Halloween* (2007). Clearly, the Gothic-inspired Euro-American horror tradition has long been preoccupied with haunted, decaying, and uncanny homes. And the suburban neighborhood has been a constant presence in the horror film since the late 1970s. But in the Obama-era horror film, these spaces become laden with anxieties about White social standing and the perceived failures of White prosperity.

Appropriately, then, a major cycle of haunted house films would dominate the Obama-era horror. In the wake of the housing crisis in the mid-2000s, the home—particularly the White family home—became one of the most popular settings of the horror film. Between 1980 and 2007, Hollywood produced twenty-three films with a significant haunted house element, averaging less than one haunted house film per year in a nearly thirty-year period. But between 2008 and 2016, Hollywood produced a whopping thirty-two films with a significant haunted house element, around three and a half films every year of the Obama era. About 20 percent of all mainstream US horror films in that period featured haunted houses.

Contemporary haunted house narratives pay particular attention to issues of Whiteness and social class, an argument I develop in chapter 1. Across the Obama-era haunted house film, White families are haunted not only by ghosts, demons, aliens, and other supernatural entities, but also by the nagging fear that they have lost their privileged social standing in a changing economy. Homeownership, once a key lifeline in the quest for middle-class standing, in these films becomes instead an anchor dragging once-wholesome families into poverty and—even worse for White families in the US—a lower social class.

Similarly, in chapter 2, I explore the smaller but significant increase in home invasion films. The genre was ushered in by Wes Craven's seminal early film, *The Last House on the Left* (1972), but there were virtually no mainstream horror follow-ups to the subgenre until 2007, with Michael Haneke's *Funny Games*, a US remake of his 1997 Austrian film of the same name (although some home invasion films in that period may not have been gory enough to also be labeled as horror, such as 2002's *Panic Room*). Between 2008 and 2016, however, eight more home invasion films were released, a small but distinct cycle.

Instead of facing supernatural adversaries, White families in the home invasion film must confront packs of psychopaths who terrorize and torture until those seemingly wholesome families turn the tables and discover their own capacity for violence. While the haunted house film primarily explores White fears of social decline, the home invasion film takes a darker turn, asking whether the affluent and middle-class White families targeted by psychopaths may actually deserve their torment. What violence lies behind the accumulation of wealth by White folks, and what kinds of violence lurk beneath the surface of White respectability?

To illustrate the obsession with Whiteness and social mobility in the horror film, chapter 3 looks closely at two films exploring the aspirations of White folks in the neoliberal economy: *Dream House* (2011) and *Drag Me to Hell* (2009). *Dream House* follows a wealthy executive who quits his job to spend more time with his family in their suburban dream home, only to be terrorized by strange visions as he and his house seem to degrade. Meanwhile, *Drag Me to Hell* tells the story of a young, upwardly mobile mortgage broker who can't seem to escape her poor, rural roots after she forecloses on an old woman's property and becomes cursed. In each film, White folks are unsettled by bizarre and ghostly visions that only they can see, interrogating the realities of the American dream in the midst of the Great Recession.

Chapters 4 and 5 turn their attention to the intersection of gender and Whiteness through two prominent cycles in the Obama era. In chapter 4, I analyze the exorcism and possession film, which also saw a marked increase since 2008. From 1980 until 2007, Hollywood produced fifteen possession and exorcism narratives, around one every other year. By contrast, Hollywood produced sixteen possession and exorcism films from 2008 to 2016, roughly tripling the frequency of such films.

These Obama-era possession narratives foreground issues of White masculinity and authority, featuring downtrodden White men who have their traditional authority restored by performing or overseeing an exorcism. Mirroring cultural debates about the loss of traditional White male authority in the face of multicultural feminism, the contemporary exorcism film asserts the need for clear investments in White patriarchy in the face of supposed moral relativism.

Chapter 5 explores the flip side of these gendered crises: anxieties around White motherhood in the horrific child film, represented by twenty-one mainstream US horror films from 2008 to 2016. Only sixteen films featuring a horrific child narrative were produced from 1980 to 2007. In this cycle, horrific or demonic children plague White families, especially White mothers or White women experiencing maternal crises, such as mothers recovering from miscarriage or the death of children or else childless women who have turned their back on motherhood. By confronting the specter of creepy children in their lives, these mothers dramatize cultural tensions around White motherhood, especially in an era of demographic anxieties and the prospect of a possible future White minority in the US.

To provide another in-depth illustration of these racial and gendered anxieties, chapter 6 analyzes two horror films about young, economically precarious White women set against the backdrop of Detroit's postrecession decay: *It Follows* (2014) and *Don't Breathe* (2016). In each film, the ostensible source of horror—an anonymous and relentless force that constantly hunts you and a blind psychopathic patriarch who traps you in his crumbling neighborhood—reflects the sensations and effects of contemporary economic stagnation for millennials today. Of course, while such stagnation impacts young people of color with much more severity, each of these films focuses on the dramatic struggle of young Whites facing the realities of poverty that was supposed to be reserved for people of color in the US.

Issues of technology in horror also continued to resonate in the Obama era, although this cycle represents more of a mild resurgence than a stark increase. While issues of technology have long influenced horror in the US and elsewhere, there was a particularly strong horrific technology cycle from 1986 to 1993, with twenty technology-centered horror films in that period. After that, Hollywood produced around one horrific technology film each year, but starting in 2005 and continuing throughout 2016, twenty-one horror films addressed fears around technology running amok.

Focused primarily on White individuals and families dealing with technological change, these films most often address technologies of vision and communications: spirit photography, cell phones through which ghosts can travel, 8 mm film or old vinyl records infiltrated by demons, and so on. Interestingly, early in the period, most horrific technology films end with a reassuring assessment of technologies of vision. While those technologies may have shown the protagonists something they weren't ready to see, ultimately the characters come to a better understanding of their world thanks to their supernatural communication. But as the cycle progresses, the technology becomes more sinister and inescapable, showing the protagonists horrors from which there is no escape. In an era of pervasive cameras and microphones—from smartphones to police body cams—these horror films explore the anxieties of the White mainstream around the fallout of surveillance culture. While fears around pervasive surveillance might be allayed in the early years of the smartphone revolution, the culture becomes more terrified throughout the 2010s by the horrors that technology reveals, such as the realities of police brutality against people of color.

The Obama era also saw a bevy of remakes of 1970s and 1980s horror films, tapping into cultural nostalgia for that period. Really, the trend picks up steam in 2005 and 2006, with eight remakes of cult classics, such as *The Hills Have Eyes* (2006) and *Black Christmas* (2006). The trend would continue, with fifteen horror remakes produced between 2007 and 2016. By contrast, only fourteen were produced from 1980 through 2004.

The remake cycle sheds light on the nostalgia that has gripped US culture—particularly the White mainstream—as it reconciles with a perceived loss in privilege and yearns for an era of clear social centrality for Whites. Trump's call to "Make America Great Again" encapsulates this nostalgia for a period of clear-cut White patriarchal dominance. Horror remakes express these anxieties often by inserting narratives around social class and social decline into their visions of older stories. Stable White suburban families in the original films become White families struggling with economic precarity. Middle-class teens subjected to slasher monsters become affluent entitled monsters themselves before they are summarily slaughtered. The updating of older narratives often involves more drama around social class and the current state of the White middle class.

To conclude, the book looks briefly at the horror of the Trump era, examining how those films both affirm and challenge the dominant trends of the Obama-era horror. The success of *Get Out* and other politically engaged horror has suggested a new era of critical horror, but the realities of this new golden age are still contested.

NOTES

1. Alex Rayner, "Trapped in the Sunken Place: How *Get Out*'s Purgatory Engulfed Pop Culture," *The Guardian*, March 17, 2018, https://www.theguardian.com/film/2018/mar/17/trapped-in-the-sunken-place-how-get-outs-purgatory-engulfed-pop-culture.

2. Jeremy Fuster, "Horror Movies Have Grossed Over $1 Billion at the Box Office in 2017," *The Wrap*, October 31, 2017, https://www.thewrap.com/horror-movies-grossed-1-billion-box-office-2017/.

3. Justin Chang, "Has Horror Become the Movie Genre of the Trump Era?," *Los Angeles Times*, October 13, 2017, http://www.latimes.com/entertainment/movies/la-ca-mn-horror-movies-trump-20171013-story.html.

4. Anne T. Donahue, "In 2018, Horror Movies Are the Most Comforting Things I Watch," *Marie Claire*, November 19, 2018, https://www.marieclaire.com/culture/a25058660/horror-movies-2018-trump/?fbclid=IwAR2FJTSpdkHzcKfLPqiKkb_9N2jmidV2xXKjTnXw2O7z08sfPuS2PZw5P2Y.

5. Brandon Tensley, "Horror Films Emerge as Best Political Commentary of Our Times," *CNN*, September 1, 2019, https://www.cnn.com/2019/09/01/politics/ready-or-not-horror-movies-trump-politics/index.html?fbclid=IwAR1EC_kEc_ziGWElPDec35ZZoE5b-XmZ9H9-E9_HcAKH0PA5Eohj IruI3bs.

6. Robin Wood, *Hollywood from Vietnam to Reagan . . . And Beyond* (New York: Columbia University Press, 2003).

7. Christopher Sharrett, "The Horror Film as Social Allegory (And How It Comes Undone)," in *A Companion to the Horror Film*, ed. Harry Benshoff (Malden, MA: Wiley Blackwell, 2017), 56–72.

8. Chang, "Has Horror Become the Movie Genre of the Trump Era?"

9. For a more detailed reading of *I Am Legend* and its vision of Whiteness, see Gretchen Bakke, "Dead White Men: An Essay on the Changing Dynamics of Race in US Action Cinema," *Anthropological Quarterly* 83, no. 2 (2010): 400–428.

10. Stephen Prince, "Introduction: The Dark Genre and Its Paradoxes," in *The Horror Film*, ed. Prince (New Brunswick, NJ: Rutgers University Press, 2004), 1–14.

11. The most prominent horror books in this field are Carol Clover, *Men, Women, and Chainsaws: Gender in the Modern Horror Film* (Princeton, NJ: Princeton University Press, 1992); and Barbara Creed, *The Monstrous-Feminine: Film, Feminism, Psychoanalysis* (London: Routledge, 1993).

12. Joseph Maddrey, *Nightmares in Red, White, and Blue: The Evolution of the American Horror Film* (Jefferson, NC: McFarland, 2004), 1.

13. See, for example, Mathias Clasen, *Why Horror Seduces* (New York: Oxford University Press, 2017).

14. The most notable exception to this trend is Richard Dyer's reading of zombies as a critique of Whiteness in *White: Essays on Race and Culture* (New York: Routledge, 1997). But too often, even historicist approaches to US horror that see the genre as an expression of American history fail to acknowledge the racialized vision of that history. Maddrey's *Nightmares in Red, White, and Blue* and Kendall Phillips's *Projected Fears: Horror Films and American Culture* (Westport, CT: Praeger, 2005), for example, both make compelling arguments for horror as a reflection of cultural and historical tensions (arguments that inform my work here). But neither openly acknowledges the Whiteness of the horror they analyze and of US culture more broadly. Out of dozens of scholarly books outlining the history and theory of horror, in fact, only Peter Hutchings's *The Horror Film* (New York: Pearson, 2004) devotes significant discussion to the racial nature of horror narratives.

15. There are some important works beginning to explore horror and race in the US context with more detail, including an exploration of Whiteness. See Natalie Wilson, *Willful Monstrosity: Gender and Race in 21st Century Horror* (Jefferson, NC: McFarland, 2020); Elizabeth Erwin and Dawn Keetley, eds., *The Politics of Race, Gender and Sexuality in* The Walking Dead: *Essays on the Television Series and Comics* (Jefferson, NC: McFarland, 2018); Keetley, ed., *Jordan Peele's* Get Out: *Political Horror* (Columbus: Ohio State University Press, 2020); and the perhaps most foundational work on race in US horror, Robin Means Coleman, *Horror Noire: Blacks in American Horror Films from the 1980s to Present* (New York: Routledge, 2011).

16. Eugenia DeLamotte, "White Terror, Black Dreams: Gothic Constructions of Race in the Nineteenth Century," in *The Gothic Other: Racial and Social Constructions in the Literary Imagination*, ed. Ruth Bienstock Anolik and Douglas L. Howard (Jefferson, NC: McFarland, 2004).

17. Dixa Ramírez D'Oleo, "The Hills Are Alive: 'Pet Sematary' and the Horror of Indigenous Sovereignty and Black Freedom," *LA Review of Books*, May 17, 2019, https://lareviewofbooks.org/article/the-hills-are-alive-pet-sematary-and-the-horror-of-indigenous-sovereignty-and-black-freedom/.

18. Coleman, *Horror Noire*.

19. See Sophia Siddique and Raphael Raphael, *Transnational Horror Cinema: Bodies of Excess and the Global Grotesque* (London: Palgrave Macmillan, 2016).

20. Darnell Hunt, Ana-Christina Ramón, Michael Tran, Amberia Sargent, and Debanjan Roychoudhury, *UCLA Hollywood Diversity Report 2018*, February 27, 2018, http://documents.latimes.com/ucla-hollywood-diversity-report-2018/.

21. These numbers are also a reflection of producers' and distributors' assumptions about what will be popular, not simply the interests of screenwriters and directors. See screenwriter Tracy Oliver's discussion of horror and representation for some of the nuances of these issues in "Where Are All the POC in Horror Movies?," *Cosmopolitan*, October 29, 2018, https://www.cosmopolitan.com/entertainment/a24393125/tracy-oliver-survive-the-night-diversity-horror-movies/?fbclid=IwAR0a4LXmmIaiVPaADDiODcPZi9IIiEyOOtGQagwPmhLNE1rlAR_YSUlqVHA.

22. Aviva Briefel and Sianne Ngai, "'How Much Did You Pay for This Place?': Fear, Entitlement, and Urban Space in Bernard Rose's *Candyman*," in *The Horror Film Reader*, ed. Alain Silver and James Ursini (New York: Limelight, 2000), 71–91.

23. Robert Jensen, *The Heart of Whiteness: Confronting Race, Racism, and White Privilege* (San Francisco: City Lights, 2005).

24. A 2017 poll indicated that a majority of White people in the US (55%) feel that Whites are discriminated against. See Don Gonyea, "Majority of White Americans Say They Believe Whites Face Discrimination," *NPR*, October 24, 2017, https://www.npr.org/2017/10/24/559604836/majority-of-white-americans-think-theyre-discriminated-against.

25. Arlie Russell Hochschild, *Strangers in Their Own Land: Anger and Mourning on the American Right* (New York: New Press, 2016).

26. Michael Tesler, *Post-Racial or Most-Racial? Race and Politics in the Obama Era* (Chicago: Chicago University Press, 2016), 3.

27. Sociologists David Norman Smith and Eric Hanley found that voters who backed Trump in 2016 most often did so because he mirrored their existing racial and cultural prejudices, not because of frustrations about economic growth in the US. See Smith and Hanley, "The Anger Games: Who Voted for Donald Trump in the 2016 Election, and Why?," *Critical Sociology* 44, no. 2 (2018): 195–212.

28. For more discussion of these dynamics, see Russell Meeuf, *Rebellious Bodies: Stardom, Citizenship, and the New Body Politics* (Austin, TX: University of Texas Press, 2017).

29. That said, a number of the films analyzed here are remakes of international horror films whose core narratives are not rooted in US race and class politics. These films are especially represented early in this period, with five released in 2008 at the peak of the US film industry's interest in remaking international horror. But the trend declines dramatically after that, with only a single international remake each year in 2009, 2010, and 2011 and then no major international horror remakes from 2012 to 2016. When examining films whose core story concept is derived from outside a US cultural context, my analysis points to the differences between the international and US versions to illustrate how the film is adapted into a US context.

1

Haunted House Films

IN THE HOLLYWOOD HORROR FILM, the haunted house is almost always the White haunted house. In the movies, White families are tormented by some trauma in their house's history, haunted by disturbing legacies of abuse and violence that linger over the years in attics, basements, Ouija boards, unmarked graves, haunted mirrors, secret rooms, 8 mm home movies, or anything else that can be secreted in the dark corners of the house. Faced with the horrible realities of the past intruding into the present, White families in these films at first deny their victim status, then cower, eventually learning to fight back in the hopes of reclaiming their home, often with the help of some occult expert who reveals to them secrets that the mainstream refuses to acknowledge.

As Eddie Murphy joked back in 1983, the glaring plot hole in most haunted house narratives is the stubborn refusal of White people to simply leave. "Not only do they stay in the mother-fucking house in *Poltergeist*," Murphy quips, "they invited more White people over, sit around going, [in a nasally voice] 'Our daughter, Carol Ann, is in the television set.'"

"And in *Amityville Horror*," Murphy continues, "the ghost told them to get out of the house. White people stayed in there. Now that's a hint and half for your ass. A ghost say get the fuck out, I would just tip the fuck out the door."[1]

White families in haunted house films don't get up and leave, of course, because it would make for a very short film. But they also stick around because those families refuse (at first) to acknowledge that their home might not be a safe refuge. Haunted house films make a spectacle of White incredulity that middle-class homeowners might be victimized in their own homes or, even worse, that homeownership itself doesn't insulate them from the horrors of the world. Murphy jokes that Black people would never assume that proprietorship might protect them from violence and terror, so they would waste no time leaving behind their homes and their possessions to survive. If he were in *Poltergeist* (1982), Murphy says, he would just go down to his local priest and say, "Look, man, I went home and my fucking daughter's in the TV set and shit, and so I just fucking left. You can have all that shit. I ain't going back to the motherfucker."[2] But White folks in the haunted house film continue about their business until whatever malevolent force convinces them that they are not safe, in spite of their homeownership.[3]

The incredulity of White families in haunted house films is driven by the sacred status of the home in the popular imagination. After decades of government policy supporting a massive expansion of homeownership after World War II (for some Americans), the single-family home has taken on revered status in US culture, not only as a sign of financial stability for middle-class families, but as *the* symbol of capitalist prosperity in the postwar world. For Americans, the single-family home sits at the perfect nexus of wholesome family values and meritocratic fantasies of the Protestant work ethic, making it a particularly potent distillation of US national identity, especially for White Americans, who continue to represent the majority of homeowners.

It shouldn't be surprising, then, that the horror genre would see an increasing emphasis on the house in the Obama years (both in haunted house films and in their closely related cousin, home invasion films, the subject of the next chapter). A wholesome, well-educated Black family occupied the White House, while a massive economic crisis shook the public's faith in homeownership as a means toward financial stability. Suddenly, homeownership didn't seem to be such a secure path toward middle-class standing, a jolt to the financial stability of White Americans, who looked around and saw signs of upward Black mobility in the form of the Obama family.

The haunting feeling that White Americans' place on the social hierarchy was under siege coincided with a wave of haunted house films between 2008 and 2016. The US film industry produced thirty-two films that included haunted houses in that period, representing 21 percent of all the top-grossing US horror. By comparison, Hollywood produced only ten mainstream haunted house films in the 1980s and only two in the '90s. The pace increased starting around 2005, and the haunted house reigned supreme in Hollywood horror in the Obama years, spurred on by successful franchises like *The Conjuring* series, the *Paranormal Activity* films, and the *Insidious* films. The latter two were produced by horror mega-producer Jason Blum, whose company, appropriately, is called BlumHouse.

This wave of haunted house movies demonstrates the horror film's capacity for processing and mediating (White) cultural anxieties. As homeownership became a less stable means of securing middle-class standing, Hollywood studios capitalized on this fear, producing films in which the house becomes a site of terror and violence threatening to tear families apart. As a number of scholars have identified, the housing crisis of the mid-2000s produced a host of recessionary horror films that took on the terrors of neoliberal capitalism.[4] Fears of lost equity and low credit scores become grotesque visions of spectral visitors, insidious demons, and decaying bodies embedded in one's home.[5]

But Hollywood haunted house films in this period don't simply translate broad cultural fears about homeownership into ghosts and other unwanted visitors. Instead, the haunted house films of the Obama years tell specific stories about White families and the haunting feeling that they are losing their privileged place in society. These are not simply recessionary horror stories but rather White stories about precarity and guilt in the recession. What if the system that has propped up White privilege and White economic stability for so long was finally crumbling? What if White folks would have to face the same disadvantages that people of color have faced for so long? Over and over again in contemporary horror films, White families (almost always in a state of crisis concerning family relationships, their finances, or both) look to homeownership as salvation only to find that the home itself makes them vulnerable. And only in the dusty basements and shadowy attics of the haunted house can those families face the nagging dread that animates their ordeal—the horrifying realization that they might not be as privileged as they had imagined or, worse, that the horrific past of White violence in the US means that they should feel guilty about the privileges they do have.

FROM THE HAUNTED HOUSE TO THE HOUSING CRISIS

The house has been at the center of horror stories since the inception of modern horror, especially in the United States. Dale Bailey, in his book *American Nightmares*, outlines this history in horror fiction, tracing the transformation of the European Gothic's crumbling castles into the creepy, formerly aristocratic estates of the American haunted house tradition. For Bailey, the haunted house in American fiction became a way for the genre to explore the tensions of social class in America as the aspirations of middle-class families are bogged down in the sprawling former mansions of old-money elites. From Nathaniel

Hawthorne through Stephen King and beyond, the US horror story has relied on the trope of the haunted house to explore American anxieties about class and the family.[6]

The haunted house has figured so prominently in US popular culture thanks to the revered place of homeownership in the US and the important economic function of homeownership for the White middle class. Since the housing boom after World War II in the US, homeownership has been the primary means of accumulating wealth and economic stability for the middle class and a primary mechanism through which racial inequalities have been maintained. Widespread discrimination throughout US history, but particularly in the post-war housing boom, explicitly excluded African Americans and other people of color from sharing in economic prosperity. This discrimination has had long-term, multigenerational effects.[7] In fact, the ability of some ethnic groups, such as Irish Americans and Jewish Americans, to participate in government-subsidized homeownership after World War II and more fully enter the US middle class can be seen as one mechanism through which such groups became fully White in the US racial imagination.[8]

The important role of homeownership in the US, then, explains why the housing crisis of 2006–2007 was so troubling to not only the economy but also to US culture. The mythology of homeownership as a deeply secure financial investment but also a potent symbol of middle-class standing came under threat in the aftermath of the housing bubble and the ensuing Great Recession. Mainstream media obsessed over the idea of possible declining homeownership, especially as studies began to suggest that millennials aren't buying homes at the same rates as baby boomers, thanks to increasing student-loan debt, precarious employment opportunities, and memories of the housing market crash.[9]

But while the housing market crash was often framed in the media as a devastating blow to the US middle class in general, in reality, people of color bore the brunt of the crisis and the ensuing recession. As sociologists Jacob Rugh and Douglas Massey document, the long history of racial segregation and discriminatory housing practices in the US meant that racial and ethnic minorities were disproportionately targeted by unscrupulous lenders as the housing bubble grew in the mid-2000s. (In fact, Rugh and Massey argue that racial disparities were not simply by-products of the crisis but key, contributing factors to the foreclosure crisis itself.) And once the bubble burst, African Americans and especially Hispanic Americans were hit hardest by foreclosures and the following recession.[10]

In the wake of this crisis, mainstream horror intensified its attention on fears of the home as a site of terror, but not for the non-White homeowners who were most targeted by predatory lenders and most impacted by the economic downturn. Rather, the almost exclusive focus of this cycle of films were middle-class White families working through their own economic anxieties.

This cycle starts around 2005, at the peak of the housing market bubble in the US. That year, five haunted house films were produced (the remake of *The Amityville Horror*, the Southern plantation haunting in *The Skeleton Key*, *Boogeyman*, the international remake *Dark Water*, and *An American Haunting*). As US popular culture obsessed over the fantastical growth of the housing market with narratives about house flipping and home renovations, the horror film seemed to anticipate the impact that the housing bubble would have on the family home.

Building on this initial commercial success, the home-based horror cycle really picked up steam around 2009 in the wake of the housing market crash and subsequent financial crisis. Between three and eight mainstream horror films were produced each year with elements of the haunted house or home invasion narrative. The popularity of the cycle yielded seven haunted house films in 2016, suggesting its continuing resonance at least up through the contentious presidential election that year. Even the titles of horror films in this period became obsessed with property, prioritizing the house as the central figure of the film. These included *Last House on the Left* (2009), *Dream House* (2011), *Silent House* (2011), and *The House at the End of the Street* (2012).

The timing of this cycle indicates a clear relationship with the housing crisis: at a historical moment when the economic stability of homeownership plummets, Hollywood narratives tap into those anxieties with a cycle of films foregrounding homes that try to ruin the middle-class White families who occupy them. As a number of scholars and critics have noted, the housing market crash ushered in a wave of recessionary haunted house films and TV shows exploiting cultural fears around the economic instability of the family home. Bernice Murphy, for example, identifies the post-2009 haunted house cycle in US horror as a repository of cultural anxieties over homeownership and looks particularly at BlumHouse films as exemplars of suburban angst over the Great Recession.[11] Julia Leyda likewise explores the *Paranormal Activity* films and "the horror of debt that cannot be evaded or expunged" against the backdrop of neoliberal capitalism and the housing market crash.[12] And Dawn Keetley uses *American Horror Story: Murder House* (2011) to identify a pervasive sense of cultural entropy and torpor brought about by the trauma of economic collapse and perceived cultural decline.[13] As these scholars (and others) affirm, the haunted house film became a reflection of a culture grappling with the fallout of the Great Recession and the declining value (literal and cultural) of the family home.

HAUNTED FAMILIES AND SOCIAL PRECARITY

The structure of the haunted house film tends to be fairly regular. Many haunted house films begin on moving day, with a new family unpacking boxes and getting to know the quirks of their new spaces. The newness of the house for the family serves to explain the family's obliviousness to the dangers of their new abode; strange occurrences around the house are rationalized away as idiosyncrasies that they haven't adjusted to yet, so they push past all the warning signs that they are in spiritual, psychological, or physical danger and try their best to make the creepy house their home.

The *Sinister* films (2012, 2015), in fact, make the act of moving a prerequisite for the horrors that the family will face, centering the story on Bughuul, a demon who inspires children to murder their own families and record it as a snuff film on 8 mm home-movie equipment. When a new family moves into the site of the previous killings, new victims are selected, but it is only when the family eventually flees the haunting visions of Bughuul and his spectral children that they are finally tortured and killed. Moving into a new house seals their fate and perpetuates Bughuul's cycle, as the next people to occupy this new house become the subsequent target. This twist emphasizes the act of buying and selling property, making explicit the haunted house film's anxieties about moving, which are tied, in the real world, to either upward or downward social mobility.

The White family's willful disregard for the cryptic warning signs in their new home speaks to their desperation, either because they hope they are moving up in the world or because they are reeling from some kind of personal or economic trauma. And in the films where the house isn't new to the family, there is always some kind of new circumstance (a divorce, an illness, the loss of a child, a marital crisis) that forces the family to cling to their new home like a security blanket. Either way, the family in question is a White family in some kind of crisis that threatens their privileged place in the culture.

In the Obama-era haunted house film, this crisis is often economic and features White families teetering on the brink of financial ruin. In *The Haunting in Connecticut* (2009), the family is drowning in debt due to the high cost of their son's cancer treatments, and they move into a new home so they can be closer to the hospital where he is treated. In *The Conjuring* (2013), the family moves out into the country in the 1970s to make a better life for their five daughters, but the father, a working-class truck driver, is struggling to make ends meet and get enough routes to pay for their new home. In *Don't Be Afraid of the Dark* (2010), the father is remodeling a nineteenth-century estate and has all his money tied up in the project as he tries to reinvigorate his career as a high-end house flipper; he refuses to leave, despite his daughter's troubling behavior and nightmarish visions, because he needs to get his house on the cover of *Architectural Digest* to make a career comeback. Similarly, in *Sinister*, a true-crime writer whose career is on the rocks after a series of disappointing books clings to his new house (the site of an unsolved crime, unbeknownst to his family) as a way of redeeming himself professionally and financially. In the US/UK coproduction *The Woman in Black* (2012), the protagonist has to investigate a mysterious country estate to save his job after his poor work performance in the wake of the death of his wife.

For most of these families, the house in question is a lifeline. The house itself will be the means through which they will hold their family together and retain their place in the middle class, either as a rung in the social hierarchy they hope to climb or as the last foothold that will keep them from plummeting into poverty. In this way, the ghosts and demons of these films animate a more fundamental fear that homeownership can no longer save White families from pervasive economic anxiety.

The White families struggling economically are also beset by personal crises that prompt their move into a new home. These are typically gendered crises centered on parenthood and fidelity. Although the first *Paranormal Activity* (2007) film centers on a seemingly happy young couple, *Paranormal Activity 2* (2010) and *3* (2011) both focus on blended families dealing with divorces, new marriages, or new children. In *The Darkness* (2016), a family haunted by ancient Anasazi deities is also struggling to move past the father's infidelities, and he must reassert his commitment to the family. Likewise, in *Insidious* (2010), the husband becomes distant and absent from the family as his wife deals with their sick child and supernatural occurrences, only for the father to realize that he is the only person able to confront the demons and revitalize the family. In *Insidious, Chapter 3* (2015), a single dad and his teen daughter struggle to save their relationship in the wake of the wife and mother's death. And in *The Boy* (2016), the central character is a young woman fleeing an abusive relationship and the emotional turmoil of a miscarriage only to find herself haunted by a mysterious lifelike doll. These personal crises often provide camouflage for the haunting, with husbands, fathers, and various authority figures dismissing the claims of women and children as nothing more than their imagination.

I discuss the gendered dynamics of such narratives in future chapters, but at stake in the haunted house film is not only the economic standing of the White family, but their wholesomeness, as well; the families must face their demons both literally and figuratively by committing to the sanctity of the nuclear family as a way to survive the onslaught of supernatural entities.

The Conjuring 2 (2016), one of the more popular haunted house films in this period, combines personal and economic crises in its representation of the White family, often making explicit the anxiety that a middle-class White family might slip into poverty and lose social standing. Loosely based on the real-life haunting of the Hodgson family in the north London borough of Enfield in the 1970s, *The Conjuring 2*, like its predecessor, purports to chronicle the work of paranormal investigators Ed and Lorraine Warren (played by Patrick Wilson and Vera Farmiga). In the film, a single mother of four whose husband has recently abandoned the family must confront the terrifying supernatural events that are focused on her youngest daughter, Janet, as well as the fallout from her case becoming a media sensation. It is only through the intervention of the Warrens that her family can be saved.

As in other haunted house films, the threat of nefarious spirits in *The Conjuring 2* is a grotesque exaggeration of the family's possible loss of social standing. The house in question is government-subsidized public housing, and the frazzled single mom is desperately holding her family together despite major financial setbacks. Her husband isn't paying child support, and the mom complains that her work schedule means that she can't be present for her children the way she used to be. In one telling scene, her washing machine breaks, spewing water everywhere. She can't afford to fix it, so she simply allows the basement to slowly fill with water, setting the stage for a scary scene later in the film, where the malevolent spirit lurks in the water in the dark and dingy basement.

The family's poverty inspires the film's Gothic visual style, with their creaky, shoddily built home—on the verge of being dilapidated, with cracking plaster and peeling paint—providing a macabre backdrop to supernatural horrors while also signifying the family's precarious social position (see fig. 1.1).

Although set in England, this American film reflects US anxieties about the monstrousness of White poverty. Because of persistent racial inequalities in the US, poverty is often imagined (and represented in the media) as being specific to people of color, especially in the specter of crime-ridden, mostly Black inner cities often invoked as a sign of American moral decay. The idea of

Fig. 1.1. The young protagonist is haunted not only by malcontent spirits, but also by economic precarity, as seen in her dilapidated and crumbling home in *The Conjuring 2* (New Line Cinema, 2016).

poor White people disrupts the racialization of poverty. US culture stigmatizes poor Whites as *White trash*, people whose core Whiteness is often called into question by imagining them as messy, uncouth, and lazy.[14] In the film, as the mother struggles to pay the bills and keep her children from sliding into the excesses of youth countercultures (like the punk movement, seen in a montage of stock news footage meant to evoke the turmoil of the 1970s), the haunting the family experiences threatens to not only pull them into spiritual crisis, but also plunge them into full-fledged *trashy* status.

Trump's 2016 presidential campaign spoke directly to those who felt the sting of these stereotypes in the US by exploiting the same fears at work in the mainstream haunted house film: the notion that nice, White families might be subject to the same economic vulnerabilities as poor people of color is a horrifying proposition and necessitates the swift, unhesitating expulsion of evil outsiders.

The solution proffered by the Warrens in *The Conjuring 2* (and its predecessor) focuses just as much on a nostalgic reclamation of family values as it does on battling evil demons. Ed suggests that the single mother reconcile with her deadbeat ex-husband in order to restore the nuclear family, but that option is a dead end, so Ed instead starts filling a fatherly role for the family. He starts tackling odd jobs around the house that have been neglected (like that leaky plumbing in the basement), and when the family's record player fails, he leads them all in a cheesy sing-along of Elvis Presley's "Can't Help Falling in Love." With a keen sense of moral certainty (which I discuss more in chap. 3), the Warrens suggest that wholesome family values will stave off the evil—and implicitly the poverty—threatening to swallow the family.

HISTORY AND WHITE GUILT

The contemporary haunted house film also relies on another common Gothic theme: the presence of something physical inside the house, some place or object that makes the horrors of the past tangible in the present for those who possess the home. Mirroring the Gothic tradition in which houses are often a reflection of the psyche of the people who inhabit them, the contemporary haunted house film shows that evil is tucked away into the recesses of haunted houses like repressed memories that aren't supposed to be found, typically in attics and basements. These dark spaces in the home also suggest attempts to repress the traumas of the past, the dark histories that can never fully be buried.[15]

For example, although the haunting in *Paranormal Activity* isn't focused on the house (but on the protagonist, Katie), the demon leaves behind a partially burned photograph of Katie as a child inexplicably tucked into the insulation of her new attic. An ancient furnace in the basement is actually the gateway for evil fairy-like creatures in *Don't Be Afraid of the Dark*. The true-crime writer in *Sinister* discovers an old box of 8 mm home movies containing the demon Bughuul in the dark attic of his new home. In *Ouija* (2014), although the evil seems to be the product of the old Ouija board, the board is merely a means of communication and possession for the spirit of a dead girl hidden away in a secret room in the basement (and in the sequel, we learn that even more horrors were committed in that secret room). In *The Boy*, the wealthy estate hides a series of hidden passageways and rooms, while in *Oculus* (2013), the source of evil hides in plain sight in the form of an antique mirror with the power to manipulate and possess. When these sources of evil are disturbed, specters of the past torment the people in the present who are struggling to redeem or reclaim their families.

As this suggests, the horrors of the past are often built into the physical structures of the house itself. At the climax of *The Haunting in Connecticut*, for instance, we learn that former owners had literally lined the walls of the dining room with dead bodies that were preserved and marked with occult writings intended to amplify the psychic powers of a prior inhabitant. The protagonist has to bash open the walls with a sledgehammer (and then burn the house to the ground) to free their souls and end his own torment.[16]

The physical remnants of the past in the haunted house reflect the central obsession of the cycle (and of most horror films in general): the inescapable persistence of the past as it intrudes into the present. Horrible violent acts, sadistic psychological torture, and gruesome abuse can never really be left behind and will continue to haunt the White families just trying to claim their share of the American dream. And even when this past seems unrelated to the families who occupy the haunted house—connecting them through the seeming coincidence of ownership as the property changes hands over time—it troubles the new owners and calls into question whether, by virtue of ownership and occupation, they are indebted to the same systems of privilege and brutality that caused the trauma in the first place.[17]

One persistent theme in the contemporary haunted house film, for example, centers on the horrific actions of wealthy families trying to maintain appearances by hiding away the corruption and abuse that has occurred in their homes. In *The Boy*, a wealthy couple fakes the death of their young son after he brutally murdered a playmate, locking the boy into a series of passageways hidden in the house and only allowing him to live vicariously through a lifelike doll. In *The Woman in Black*, a decrepit mansion and the local village are haunted by the spirit of a deranged young woman born into a wealthy family but hidden from the community. When that young woman's son (raised by the sister who had imprisoned her) dies in a tragic accident, the woman hangs herself, and her ghost torments the children in the village, forcing them to commit suicide whenever a visitor comes to the mansion. While not technically a haunted house film, *The House at the End of the Street* depicts a family in a well-off rural community who spent years forcing their young son to pretend that he is their daughter who had died when the siblings were young. Eventually, the young man murders his parents and then serially kidnaps young women in the community, locking them in a hidden room in the house and forcing them to pretend to be his sister, much as his parents did to him.

That so many haunted house films in this period expose the hidden violence of White wealth shouldn't be surprising; the very existence of the White family home in the US is predicated on a host of racial injustices and systemic violence, from practices such as redlining to the use of racial violence to maintain residential segregation. For researchers such as Juan Valencia, then, the post-2009 haunted house cycle isn't simply a reflection of recessionary anxieties but of White racial anxieties around housing practices. For Valencia, the Great Recession rattled the institution of White wealth though homeownership, allowing the repressed history of systemic racism to bubble to the surface in horror stories. In such stories, White families like those in *Insidious* and *Sinister* are tormented by dark figures making fleeting appearances in their homes and threatening their home's value and economic stability, much in the way that the desegregation of neighborhoods has been seen as a threat to White wealth. These dark figures evoke White fears of the Other, but they also call attention to past racial violence and discrimination that such families would rather not face up to.[18]

These anxieties are also foregrounded in films that juxtapose a White family in the present with a financially struggling family in the past who committed atrocities to improve their situation. In *The Haunting in Connecticut*, the haunting is traced back to a family who engaged in bizarre occult rituals to enhance their young son's psychic powers, which they exploited in an at-home séance business. An almost identical backstory is used in *Ouija*: an at-home psychic reading business delves too deep into the occult to stay afloat, and a family is ruined (although the sequel offers a backstory to this backstory).

As the White families in the present teeter on the edge of personal or economic ruin, they are forced to face the horrible violence White families in the past have used to secure their own social standing. Some families confront and transcend these visions from the past, while others are dragged down by them. White poverty remains an abject and horrific threat in the haunted house film, but the family's struggle to escape also involves a sense of guilt, as homeownership makes them complicit in past violence that cannot be repressed.

For example, the embarrassment and corruption of the wealthy is at the core of the horror in *The Disappointments Room* (2016), in which an affluent urban family of three moves into a rural estate, hoping to remodel the house and heal their family. Back in the city, the mother accidentally suffocated their infant daughter while sleeping with her in the same bed. Guilt-ridden, she turned to antidepressants and attempted suicide before deciding to move to the country with her husband and young son. She plans on using her skills as an architect to remodel the long-neglected estate.

Her sanity is threatened when she discovers a small room off the attic that was hidden behind a heavy armoire and locked shut. The room, which isn't on any of the blueprints, prompts a series of haunting visions of a young girl, a stern patriarch, and an aggressive German shepherd. As the visions plunge her into madness, she reaches out to a local librarian, who tells her that she has a "disappointments room," a secret room where wealthy families can hide away children born with disabilities and deformities.

Fig. 1.2. A secret room hides the spirit of a violent and corrupt White patriarch who felt humiliated by his young daughter's deformity in *The Disappointments Room* (Demarest Films, 2016).

The visions then reveal to the mother the events that linger in her new house: disgusted with the idea that he could have fathered a little girl with a deformity, the original owner of the house (who used a German shepherd to intimidate his imprisoned daughter) bludgeoned his sweet and innocent daughter with a hammer one night in the secret room (see fig. 1.2).

In the film, the restoration of the White family in the present hinges on the mother's discovery of the corruption of the rich in the past. In one scene, the mother reads a book about "disappointments rooms" called *The Horror of Nobility*, which appears to document a range of cruel practices surrounding wealthy White people's treatment of their disabled offspring and uses images of disfigured bodies as a grotesque metaphor for the corruption and violence that bolstered White affluence. By confronting this cruel past, the mother is finally able to assuage her guilt about her daughter's death. She is not a monster like the patriarch in the past, and she deserves a happy family.

In *The Disappointments Room* and other haunted house films, then, the guilt-inducing discovery that homeownership links the White family to a horrific past rarely results in any thoughtful reflections on White privilege and the violence upon which White prosperity was built in the US. The films raise the specter of White guilt only to absolve the current homeowners of that guilt;

the homeowners recognize past horrors without truly reckoning with them, allowing further repression to be the narrative resolution. By confronting the horrors of the past, the White family in the present is able to transcend the violence of the past. The haunted house film assures them that they aren't as bad as the oppressors of the past and, in fact, are victims too.

This is perhaps why, despite the genre's obsession with the horrific violence of the past, the significant history of White violence against people of color in the US is remarkably absent from the contemporary haunted house film. In several haunted house films of the Obama years—especially in nostalgic horror films set in the '60s and '70s—the source of evil is not necessarily rooted in the past corruption of wealthy White families but in past historical traumas that cannot be repressed by history. In *The Conjuring*, for example, the investigations of Ed and Lorraine Warren reveal that a rural Pennsylvania farmhouse was haunted by a spirit of a wealthy landowner who practiced witchcraft and had ties to the Salem witch trials (the Salem witch trials are also a source of lingering evil in *The Lords of Salem* [2012], and they inspire the backstory of season 3 of the popular horror-themed television program *American Horror Story: Coven* [2013–2014]). Similarly, in the film *Annabelle* (2014), a spin-off from *The Conjuring* films, the evil nature of a seemingly possessed porcelain doll is partially attributed to the murder of a middle-aged couple by their daughter and her cult-member friends in the 1960s or 1970s, a reference to the Manson family murders and fears of cult violence in the wake of the Jonestown massacre. And in *Ouija: Origins of Evil* (2016), the tormented spirits are the result of an escaped Nazi doctor known for his Mengele-style medical experiments and interest in the occult. After changing his identity, he relocated to Los Angles and continued to perform his bizarre experiments in a secret room in his basement, removing the tongues and vocal cords of his prisoners so that no one would hear their screams while he pretended to be a normal middle-class doctor.

For these films, White families (themselves struggling with the cultural turmoil of the '60s and '70s) must confront the atrocities of the not-too-distant past, even if they are not directly linked to those atrocities. This is often the core work of horror storytelling—insisting that no matter how distant history may seem, the past (and past traumas in particular) have shaped our present. The day-to-day lives of seemingly normal middle-class families are always intertwined with the horrible violence of the past that they wish they could forget.

But the horrific violence that has most significantly shaped modern life for the White middle class is unarguably White violence against people of color, from the displacement and genocide of Native Americans to the atrocities of slavery, Jim Crow laws, and the structural discrimination that continues to fuel racial inequality. And yet these forms of violence often remain unimaginable in the horror film, especially the contemporary horror film. While the old trope of the ancient Indian burial ground is rife in scary stories, it is actually infrequently used in the mainstream horror film. And while a few films, such as *Candyman* (1992), address issues of slavery, lynching, and segregation in their haunting narratives, White violence against Black bodies is rare in popular horror films from this period.

So while haunted house films remain dedicated to the idea that we will never escape the horrors of the past and even explore the horrors of White corruption that still torment White families today, they also provide easy scapegoats (Nazis, cultists, demons) that obscure the violent foundations of White economic privilege today. It seems there are still evils from the past that will remain repressed, even in the horror film.

DARK SKIES

No haunted house film in this period better reflects the anxieties around White social standing in the wake of the housing crisis than the 2013 film *Dark Skies*. The film tells the story of the Barretts, a seemingly normal White suburban family who begin to experience supernatural events in their house. Bizarre and elaborate structures built out of cans of food materialize in the middle of the night. Mysterious figures stand over their beds while they sleep. Birds keep inexplicably crashing into their house. And it all seems to have something to do with the recent sleepwalking habit of their younger son, Sammy. As the family slowly accepts that they are being targeted by paranormal forces, they discover the nature of their tormentor: mysterious alien invaders who have singled out the family and intend to abduct one of their children.

Although the source of the haunting in *Dark Skies* is extraterrestrial instead of a more typical ghost or demon, the film follows the usual plot of the haunted house film, especially in its depiction of a family in economic and personal crisis. Directly referencing the Great Recession, the film links the family's crisis with the housing crisis. The father, Daniel, is an architect who lost his job in the wake of the housing market crash and subsequent slowdown in new home construction. The mother, Lacy, is desperately trying to keep the family afloat with her job as a realtor, but because of the recession, her sales (and her commissions) are way down, and she is struggling ethically with selling lackluster properties to reluctant buyers in a turbulent market. As a result, the family is struggling to sustain their upper-middle-class lifestyle. They are behind on their mortgage payments and are having to make hard decisions about day-to-day expenses in the wake of the strange occurrences. Thinking that perhaps Sammy is simply acting out because of the stress on the family, they want to send him to therapy but can't afford it. The Barretts then have to cancel their cable in order to afford a security system that they hope will protect their home from the mysterious happenings. Their economic crisis means that they are losing a grip on not only homeownership, but on the idea that their home is a safe haven for their family.

The threat of supernatural intruders in *Dark Skies* cannot be separated from the threat of downward social mobility for the White family. In the film, Daniel is particularly sensitive to the family's standing in their affluent community and how their financial setbacks *and* supernatural setbacks will humiliate them in front of their neighbors. When the bruises left by the alien visitors on Sammy are made visible at the local pool, for example, a series of shots shows the concerned and judgmental stares of the neighbors (including many people of color), who are thinking that perhaps the family is abusive. Embarrassed, Daniel hurries the family back home as he tries to keep all of their crises hidden from view in order to maintain a facade of normalcy. The alien tormentors in the film only exaggerate his anxieties about losing his privileged place in the community.

These financial crises are, of course, accompanied by a series of marital and parental crises. The Barretts' marriage is strained because of Daniel's unemployment, and the children are struggling, as evidenced by Sammy's odd behavior and his older brother Jesse's tumultuous transition into his teen years. Jesse starts watching porn with his obnoxious neighbor, smokes pot, and becomes distant with his parents. The family doesn't have the resources to protect the teenager and ease his transition from childhood to manhood without losing him to moral depravations. And just when the family is on the brink of more financial stability when Daniel finally lands a new job, the aliens ramp up their campaign against the family, literally interrupting a romantic evening at home that was a chance for the parents to rekindle the romance in their relationship. It is hard to keep your marriage together when aliens disrupt your sex life.

The family's financial and personal crises converge in the form of a lower-middle-class house that the mother is struggling to sell. In contrast to the Barretts' suburban McMansion and Pottery Barn decor, this small house has dated wallpaper, a drab little kitchen, and tacky wood paneling (see fig. 1.3). Jesse, knowing that the house is unoccupied, indulges in "unwholesome" behavior there as an escape from the stress of his home life; he hangs out with friends, dabbles in pot smoking, and makes out with his neighborhood crush, signaling

Fig. 1.3. A tacky lower-middle-class home contrasts with the affluent McMansion the family calls home, teasing their possible social decline in *Dark Skies* (Alliance Films, 2013).

the breakdown in his parents' authority. The house even becomes the setting for one of Jesse's hallucinatory visions—brought on by the aliens—in which his father murders his mother and commits suicide.

The drab lower-class space of this other house is like a mirror that reflects the Barretts' fears of losing social standing; it signals the mother's workplace failures and is a place where stressed-out parents lose control of their pot-smoking teenagers, where a strained marriage may descend into violence, or, perhaps worst of all, where the Barretts may have to actually live if they cannot keep their home in an affluent neighborhood. Underscoring the whole narrative is the Barretts' fear that a tacky, run-down house (or one much like it) might be in their future. The lower-class house encapsulates the family's worst fears, all of which center on the horror of moving down a rung on the ladder of social hierarchies.

These fears seem founded when they have to trek to the wrong side of town to a dark and cluttered apartment to speak to a conspiracy theorist they found on the internet, Edwin Pollard, who claims to have answers for them. He tells the Barretts that they have been singled out by nefarious alien invaders that he calls "the greys" (based on a real-life alien mythology), who experiment on and torment human families before abducting one of the children. Claiming to have documented a string of similar cases, the expert tells the family that the strange encounters will only escalate until, inevitably, the aliens will come for one of their children.

In other words, an online conspiracy theorist convinces a middle-class White family that their privileged position in the culture is under threat from non-White entities who have already installed themselves here and are slowly taking over. The racial undertones are almost overt in the film. The name *the greys*, after all, evokes racialized language from US history (most notably *Blacks*, *reds* or *redskins*, *yellow* to refer to Asian people, etc.), setting up a binary between the grey aliens and the White family. And in this bleak vision of outsiders tormenting middle-class White families, the real horror is that the greys strip away the special privileges of Whiteness. When the Barretts ask Pollard why they were being singled out by the greys, he tells them that it was probably random. They look despondent as they discover that they aren't special, that they are just like everyone else in the world who might be victimized by the aliens. Neither homeownership nor their Whiteness can protect them from becoming victims in their world of economic instability.

The Barretts take a stand against the aliens-of-color on the Fourth of July, weaving the fate of the White family with a sense of national identity. Nothing is more American than White families inflicting violence on those who would make them feel insecure about their place of privilege in the culture. Armed with the knowledge provided by Pollard, the Barretts then literally arm themselves—they buy a shotgun and adopt a hyperaggressive dog from the pound—and prepare for their conflict with the greys. After a quiet evening reminiscing about better times, they bring the fight to the aliens, but they lose; thinking that the greys are after Sammy, they leave Jesse vulnerable, and he is abducted instead.

The Barretts' worst fears come to pass. In a brief epilogue, we see them settling into their new home, a bland, cheap, white-walled apartment, without Jesse. A cutaway to Pollard pinning a news clipping about the Barretts on his wall tells us that the parents are suspects in Jesse's disappearance. Back in the apartment, the Barretts look through old pictures drawn by the boys and realize that Jesse had drawn pictures of the greys as a small child; he had been the target all along. From seemingly nowhere, Jesse's voice flickers through the radio, letting them know that he is alive but has been lost to the greys.

Just as other haunted house films do, *Dark Skies* dramatizes the core fears of the White middle class: a future of economic vulnerability, a dramatic fall from a position of privilege, and the subsequent disintegration of the family.

CONCLUSION

As the housing market slowly improved throughout the Obama years, the culture may have become more optimistic about the prospects for White families to purge themselves of their demons. In 2019, a new mobile streaming service announced the forthcoming arrival of *Murder House Flip*, a home renovation series in which contractors work alongside historians and occult experts to remodel and cleanse homes that had been the site of horrific violence. After researching the violent history of the homes in question, the team will work to rid the house of its figurative (maybe literal) demons for the new owners while also providing a high-end renovation.[19]

In many ways, the show sounds like a new entry in *The Conjuring* series, only this time Ed and Lorraine Warren bring Bob Vila onto their team. *The Conjuring* movies are perhaps the most overt of all the haunted house films in their quest to make haunted homes safe for wholesome families. Throwing up a new color scheme or adding a cutesy mudroom seems like the logical extension of the *Conjuring*'s quest to protect the White middle classes from ghosts and the specter of poverty.

Murder House Flip, then, makes explicit the connections between hauntings and the financial security of homeownership seen across the haunted house cycle. Purging the home of evil entities cannot be separated from making investments in the home as a financial asset for middle-class families. The truly evil forces at work are diminishing value and bad taste, both of which the White middle classes must overcome to retain their privileges.

NOTES

1. *Eddie Murphy Delirious*, directed by Bruce Gowers, aired August 17, 1983, on HBO.

2. Ibid.

3. Dale Bailey also discusses Eddie Murphy's haunted house routine in relation to the genre in his book *American Nightmares: The Haunted House Formula in American Popular Fiction* (Madison: University of Wisconsin Press, 1999).

4. See, for example, Tim Snelson, "The (Re)possession of the American Home: Negative Equity, Gender Inequality, and the Housing Crisis Horror Story," in *Gendering the Recession: Media and Culture in an Age of Austerity,* ed. Diane Negra and Yvonne Tasker (Durham, NC: Duke University Press, 2014), 161–180; or April Miller, "Reel-to-Reel Recessionary Horrors in *Drag Me to Hell* and *Contagion*," in *The Great Recession in Fiction, Film, and Television:*

Twenty-First Century Bust Culture, ed. Kirk Boyle and Daniel Mrozowski (Plymouth, UK: Lexington Books, 2013), 29–50.

5. These anxieties were not just confined to cinematic horror. As Lindsey Michael Banco argues in "Recession Horror: The Haunted House Crisis in Contemporary Fiction," these same post-recessionary terrors were expressed in contemporary horror literature. For Banco, these texts disrupt the standard Gothic fixation on past and present, instead questioning the stability of the future in a neoliberal world on the verge of collapse. Banco, "Recession Horror," in *Dark Forces at Work: Essays on Social Dynamics and Cinematic Horrors*, ed. Cynthia Miller and A. Bowdoin Van Riper (Lanham, MD: Lexington Books, 2020), 79–98.

6. Bailey, *American Nightmares*.

7. See Dalton Conley, *Being Black, Living in the Red: Race, Wealth, and Social Policy in America* (Berkeley: University of California Press, 2009); and Matthew Desmond, "How Homeownership Became the Engine of American Inequality," *New York Times*, May 9, 2017, https://www.nytimes.com/2017/05/09/magazine/how-homeownership-became-the-engine-of-american-inequality.html.

8. Karen Brodkin, *How Jews Became White Folks and What That Says About Race in America* (New Brunswick, NJ: Rutgers University Press, 1998).

9. Jordan Weissman, "Student Debt Is Indeed Hurting Homeownership, Federal Reserve Study Finds," *Slate*, January 17, 2019, https://slate.com/business/2019/01/fed-estimates-college-loans-millenials-home-ownership.html.

10. For more on the impact of the foreclosure crisis on Latinx Americans and media coverage of ethnicity during the crisis, see Jillian Báez and Mari Castañeda, "Two Sides of the Same Story: Media Narratives of Latinos and the Subprime Mortgage Crisis," *Critical Studies in Media Communication* 31, no. 1 (2014): 27–41.

11. Bernice Murphy, "'It's Not the House That's Haunted': Demons, Debt, and the Family in Peril in Recent Horror Cinema," in *Cinematic Ghosts: Haunting Spectrality from Silent Cinema to the Digital Era*, ed. Murray Leeder (New York: Bloomsbury, 2015), 235–252.

12. Julia Leyda, "Demon Debt: *Paranormal Activity* as Recessionary Post-Cinematic Allegory," *Jump Cut* 56 (Winter 2014–2015), https://www.ejumpcut.org/archive/jc56.2014-2015/LeydaParanormalActivity/index.html. Leyda argues that the first two *Paranormal Activity* films allegorize postrecession, neoliberal anxieties around domesticity, gender, and homeownership, affirming that the haunted house film responded to the shifting cultural conditions of the Great Recession.

13. Dawn Keetley, "Stillborn: The Entropic Gothic of American Horror Story," *Gothic Studies* 15, no. 2 (November 2013): 89–107. Focusing on imagery of twins, reproduction, and motherhood, Keetley argues that *American Horror*

Story: Murder House explores social collapse and cultural death in the wake of the Great Recession in the US.

14. Annalee Newit and Matt Wray, eds., *White Trash: Race and Class in America* (New York: Routledge, 1997).

15. Keetley explores the psychological dynamics of the Gothic haunted house against the backdrop of the Great Recession in "Stillborn."

16. The link between the physical structures of the house and the lingering evils of the past are even joked about in *Ouija: Origins of Evil*. After a character admires the haunted house and says that it has "good bones," a possessed little girl later tells him that he is right by showing off the literal bones in the basement (before she forces the young man to hang himself).

17. For a discussion of the haunted house and issues of time and pastness, see Barry Curtis, *Dark Places: The Haunted House in Film* (London: Reaktion Books, 2008). On page 10, Curtis writes, "'Ghosts' and the dark places where they dwell have served as powerful metaphors for persistent themes of loss, memory, retribution and confrontation with unacknowledged and unresolved histories."

18. Juan Valencia, "The House Settling: Race, Housing, and Wealth in the Post-Recession Horror Film," *Emergence*, November 25, 2017, http://emergence journal.english.ucsb.edu/index.php/2017/11/25/the-house-settling-race-housing -and-wealth-in-the-post-recession-horror-film. Valencia offers a thorough explanation of racial segregation in the US and the ways in which history that is supposed to be repressed in the US culture bubbled to the surface in the post-recession horror film.

19. Jessica Wang, "The New Show 'Murder House Flip' Sounds Like 'Fixer Upper' for True Crime Fans," *Bustle*, August 27, 2019, https://www.bustle.com /p/the-new-show-murder-house-flip-sounds-like-fixer-upper-for-true-crime -fans-18704878.

2

WHITENESS UNDER SIEGE, PART 2
Home Invasions

NEAR THE CLIMAX OF THE home invasion film *The Strangers* (2008), the young White couple who has been tormented and tortured all night by three masked assailants asks why they in particular have been singled out. The character dubbed Dollface replies, "Because you were home." The line is meant to evoke the randomness of the attack and the film's nihilistic worldview. There is nothing special about the young couple, nor is there any inherent motive in the attack other than sheer psychopathy. The couple just happened to be home.

But the line also suggests the uncanniness of the home invasion genre; "because you were *home*" suggests that the couple was targeted precisely because they were in a space that was supposed to shelter and protect them, a space that for most people in the US (especially White people) has been emblematic of their class standing and chance at upward mobility. They were attacked because they felt at home, because they took their own privileges for granted in a tumultuous and hypercompetitive world.

The attack in *The Strangers* highlights the supposed vulnerability of the White nuclear family in a changing culture. The couple was spending the night at the boyfriend's family home in the woods after a friend's wedding. The boyfriend had hoped that they would be celebrating after he proposed to his girlfriend. But she declined his proposal, and now they must spend an awkward night together, surrounded by reminders of the boyfriend's idyllic childhood—a wholesome domestic world that is now eluding him because his girlfriend isn't ready to commit.

The nuclear family has functioned for decades as the centerpiece of White economic and cultural stability. But as young people transform the norms around domesticity by marrying later (if at all), avoiding parenthood at higher

46

rates, and putting off homeownership (thanks in part to the economic precarity of neoliberal capitalism), the future stability of the White nuclear family seems in jeopardy. In the film, at this exact moment when the privileges of the White middle-class family seem to be breaking apart for a younger generation of White folks, a trio of masked psychopaths transform a moment of personal crisis into a matter of survival for the young couple. The psychological and physical torture in the film exhibits in exaggerated form US anxieties about the White family.

This chapter examines the close cousin of the haunted house story: the home invasion film, which offers a less supernatural and often more cynical take on the home-under-siege storyline of the haunted house. Instead of ghosts, evil fairies, demons, or aliens intruding on the day-to-day life of a struggling White family, the terror in the home invasion film stems from the psychopathic actions of violent people who push ordinary families to the brink of sanity. This usually comes in two major forms. In the classic home invasion structure, psychopaths force their way into a typically White family home and terrorize its inhabitants until those inhabitants fight back (despite the fact that middle-class White folks remain one of the least likely demographics to be targeted for violent crime), exemplified by films such as *The Strangers* or *The Purge* (2013). In the inverted home invasion structure, by contrast, somewhat sympathetic invaders find that the seemingly normal family homes they have entered are actually occupied by psychopathic murderers, seen in films such as *Don't Breathe* (2016), *The Collector* (2009), and, to some extent, *Ready or Not* (2019). Sometimes home invasion films blur these boundaries; for example, in *You're Next* (2011), a classic narrative structure reveals itself to be partially an inverted structure, with the seemingly random attacks having been orchestrated—we later find out—by members of the family being attacked.

These different visions of victimhood, however, tend to reinforce the same preoccupation: the White family home as a site of horrific acts of sadism and violence, often committed by the people you least suspect. In the classical structure, seemingly wholesome families are harassed into brutal retaliation, while in the inverted structure, the seemingly innocent family home is actually a haven of degradation and cruelty.

For both kinds of invasions, then, the horror is rooted in the uncanny vision of the family home as a site of brutal and bloody violence, as scholar Michael Fiddler argues. For Fiddler, home invasion storylines contrast seeming opposites by transforming a wholesome domestic space into a space of danger and violence, with horrifying results. The violent psychopaths in such stories threaten the boundaries established by bourgeois culture between domesticity and danger, respectability and barbarity. In the classic structure, the outsider draws out the repressed brutality that was always already present in the ostensibly wholesome home as the story slips into graphic violence. The family's confrontation with the outsider only blurs the boundaries underpinning the ideal of the safe, White, domestic space.[1] Similarly, in the inverted structure, disempowered and sympathetic outsiders discover the same thing: the White family home is corrupt and dangerous.

In this way, the home invasion film is often propelled by the kinds of White guilt that are typically assuaged in the haunted house film. As I discuss in chapter 1, the corruption of White prosperity is a nagging presence in the haunted house story, insinuating White homeowners in the sins of past brutality. But in many haunted house films, those sins can be washed away by the middle-class White families who purge their tainted legacies and start anew. In the home invasion film, by contrast, White guilt is not so easily contained. Much more so than their supernatural cousins, home invasion films provide a cynical commentary on White corruption and the violence lurking just beneath the surface of seemingly decent families.

THE WHITE FAMILY AND THE HISTORY OF THE HOME INVASION FILM

While exploring themes of White guilt in the home invasion film, one shouldn't downplay the persistent emphasis on White victimization in this cycle of films. The racial dynamics of the contemporary home invasion film are certainly still invested in White privilege and fragility. After all, the idea of the nuclear family home as a respite from the chaos of the public sphere has always been implicitly racialized in the US, framing the White middle-class family home as the symbolic opposite of the gritty, crime-ridden, and violent city inhabited by people of color. Since the massive expansion of suburbs in the US starting after WWII, the idealized vision of the nuclear family home has been symbolically white and supported by racially discriminatory practices that sought to preserve those spaces for White families. The resulting racial segregation of neighborhoods in the US has led to a powerful symbolic binary shaping how the culture imagines the idea of home, with images of predominately White single-family homes serving as a cultural shorthand for wholesomeness and safety, all while images of run-down city streets associated with people of color function as the symbolic opposite, signifying crime and social breakdown.[2]

The uncanny horror of the home invasion film upends this symbolic division, questioning the safety and wholesomeness of the single-family home. The films are intended to be terrifying precisely because the White home is supposed to be insulated from violent crime. Uncannily (at least for White folks), the kinds of viciousness and terror that are supposed to be reserved for poor, urban people of color in the US have somehow found their way into White domestic spaces in these films.

Not surprisingly, then, with the exception of *No Good Deed* in 2014, starring Taraji P. Henson and Idris Elba, the Obama-era home invasion film is entirely White, focusing on White families feeling insecure in their homes or sadistic White families who punish would-be invaders. A much smaller cycle than the haunted house film, the home invasion horror cycle is comprised of nine films between 2008 and 2016, although many home invasion films of this period were too low budget to register on my official count of mainstream theatrical horror (films such as 2014's *Mischief Night*, for example). Additionally, non-horror thrillers, such as the 2011 remake of *Straw Dogs*, aren't included in this discussion but show a renewed interest in the narrative structure of the home invasion. Between 1980 and 2005, by contrast, there were no horror-based mainstream home invasion films in the US, according to my parameters, although several non-horror home invasion films were released, such as the dark comedy *The Ref* (1994) or the Jodie Foster thriller *Panic Room* (2002), among others. Starting in 2006, with the remake of *When a Stranger Calls*, and then continuing in 2007, with Michael Haneke's English-language remake of his own 1997 film *Funny Games*, a steady stream of horror home invasion films was released, peaking in the box office with the 2013 film *The Purge*, which launched its own horror franchise. Across all but one of these Obama-era home invasion films, the families in questions are White, centering the White nuclear family in the cycle's depiction of psychopathic violence.

The prototype for all these films is Wes Craven's 1972 exploitation film *The Last House on the Left*. In Craven's foundational entry to the subgenre, the viewer is presented with two White families—the Stillos, a troop of sadistic criminals on the run from the law, and the Collingwoods, a respectable middle-class family. Fate brings the two families together when, after raping and murdering the Collingwoods' teenage daughter, the Stillos seek shelter in a nearby home, not realizing that it is the home of the parents of the girl they just murdered.

As the Collingwood parents discover the true nature of their guests, they engage in a frenzy of violent revenge against the Stillos. In one scene, Mrs. Collingwood graphically bites off the penis of one of the Stillos after seducing him and giving him a blow job. Later, Mr. Collingwood minces up Krug, the leader of the Stillo clan, with a chain saw.[3]

In this way, *The Last House on the Left* establishes a common generic theme for the home invasion film: there is a hidden brutality underpinning the White family, a brutality that can and will come out in the right circumstances. At first, the two White families are presented as polar opposites. The Colling-woods are a typical middle-class family whose only concern is protecting the wholesomeness of their teenage daughter, Mari, who is dabbling with drugs and counterculture bands. The Stillos, on the other hand, are vicious lower-class rapists and murderers who take psychotic pleasure in inflecting pain on others. Krug's girlfriend, Sadie, is described in news reports as feral after she kicks a police dog to death to help Krug and his sidekick, Weasel, escape from jail. These differences are highlighted when the film intercuts between scenes of the Collingwoods preparing a birthday party for Mari and scenes of the Stillos tormenting Mari and raping her friend Phyllis after the girls visited the city for a concert.

But when the Collingwood parents confront the Stillos, they too find that they are capable of the kinds of violence the audience would associate with the Stillos, efficiently setting up a series of trip wires and lethal traps for the intruders, including an electrified front doorknob. While news coverage of the Vietnam War showcased the atrocities committed by US soldiers—seemingly normal American boys and men—Craven's film highlights not just the brutal-ity of the Stillos, but also the conditions under which the normal middle-class family can be pushed to horrific violence.[4] In a carnivalesque twist, the respect-able middle-class parents perform acts of brutality that only psychopaths and sadists like the Stillos are supposed to be capable of, turning the binaries under-pinning bourgeois culture on their head.[5]

This narrative structure is often reproduced in the home invasion films, which tend to start with a typical middle-class family or woman pitted against one or more sadistic psychopaths who want to harm and terrorize them. The *us* versus *them* structure, however, invariably blurs as the protagonists give in to their base survival instincts and commit appalling and bloody acts of brutality to survive the night. This structure tends to be highly gendered as well, with contemporary home invasion films often focusing on young women who are forced to harden themselves and engage in brutal action (for example, in the Netflix home invasion film *Hush* [2016] or the horror-action film *You're Next*).

Throughout this process, the symbolism of the White family home is stripped away, leaving behind only its most crude functions: What is useful to my survival and what is not? The home invasion film sees everyday objects transformed into lethal weapons and spaces of the home transformed into tactical arenas. In *The Strangers*, the couple tries to find weapons wherever they can while navigating the home like a war zone, wondering what horrors might be lurking in a kitchen or a spare bedroom. In *You're Next*, the protago-nist utilizes a series of makeshift weapons, including a kitchen blender that

Fig. 2.1. An unlucky victim falls into a foyer full of bear traps after a family home is rigged with gory traps in *The Collector* (LD Entertainment, 2009).

she impales—blade side down—on the attacker's head with so as to puree his brains. Once the veneer of bourgeois respectability is put aside, the characters can recognize the utility of a blender as a lethal weapon.

This transformation of domestic objects and spaces into gory death traps is gleefully on display in the 2009 inverted home invasion film *The Collector*. In the film, a well-intentioned former criminal breaks into the house of his affluent employers in an attempt to pay off the debts of his ex-wife and mother to his child. But once in the house, he finds that the home has already been invaded by a sadistic serial killer dubbed The Collector, who has rigged the house with a series of bloody booby traps that make escape impossible—kind of like a *Saw*-inspired version of *Home Alone*. The once warm and inviting home has become tainted, offering only horrible ways to hurt and dismember yourself. The windows are boarded and rigged with razor blades that slice your knuckles when you try to open them. The phones have needles protruding from the receivers that puncture your face when you try to make a call. The foyer is littered with open bear traps (see fig. 2.1). The family home that is supposed to offer stability and security to White families has become a space of hyperviolent competition for survival.

The uncanny representation of the domestic sphere in this cycle of films reflects larger social concerns around the home and the White middle class, just as earlier films such as *Last House on the Left* (1972), *Straw Dogs* (1971), and

Funny Games (1997) explored the anxieties of their historical moments.[6] For this recent cycle of films, the brutality of the domestic space reflects the intense competition of neoliberal capitalism in the contemporary US. The extreme competition of capitalism has increasingly seeped from the public sphere into people's domestic lives in the social-media era, especially as the constant pressures toward self-improvement and self-documentation have progressively made what was once private the fodder for social-media analytics. As every aspect of one's domestic life is mediated, evaluated, and commodified via social media, the tactical and violent representations of the domestic sphere in films such as *The Collector* offer a grotesque exaggeration of the private sphere as a site of intense competition.

These violent domestic realms also indicate that the prosperity of affluent Whites is built on repressed viciousness. While the symbolism of the White family home signals the supposed wholesomeness and civility of the White middle classes, home invasion narratives draw out the repressed violence that has underpinned White affluence. In the US, after all, the success of White folks is built directly on historical racial violence against people of color (especially African Americans and Native Americans), as well as by continuing systems of racial discrimination that are sometimes explicitly violent, such as systems of policing and incarceration. By demonstrating how affluent and middle-class Whites might slide into acts of violence to protect their homes, the home invasion film reveals that behind the seemingly polite veneer of White economic prosperity lie violence and moral degradation.

This moral degradation is perhaps most explicit in the ending of the 2009 remake of *Last House on the Left*. In the updated version, the Collingwood parents find Mari wounded on the shores of the lake near their home, but this time the father treats her injuries and keeps her alive (in the original, she is already dead when the parents find her). After taking the fight to the Stillos, the Collingwoods eventually escape in the family boat to get more medical treatment for Mari, this time with the help of young Justin Stillo, who betrays his family to help the Collingwoods (in the original, Junior tries to intervene, but Krug berates him into shooting himself in the head). In a twist, though, the film cuts back to the family's home to find that Krug has survived and is being held prisoner by Mr. Collingwood in the family garage, paralyzed from the waist down. Intercutting between idyllic images of the exterior of the home and its immaculate landscape are images of Mr. Collingwood calmly and clinically torturing Krug, exploding his head in a microwave oven.

This twist is especially dark given that Mari lives, so the father isn't seeking retribution for her murder, as he was in the original. After the violent events of the evening, Mr. Collingwood escalates very quickly to elaborate vigilante torture, hinting that the Stillos have awakened something dark in the father that demands excessive violence. As the film cuts between this violence and the images of the Collingwood home, it points to a cynical possibility: this darkness has always been part of the seemingly wholesome family, just waiting to spill out.

THE HORRORS OF AFFLUENT WHITENESS

The economic foundations of this moral decay are often on display in the contemporary home invasion story, as the films are typically set in affluent or formerly affluent homes, interrogating the prosperity of White families in the US. This exploration of wealth and violence often signals that perhaps there is something morally corrupt about White families and their wealth, something that precipitates the invasion or facilitates a violent response to it. In these films, the violence that erupts in affluent White households lays bare the repressed violence supporting White wealth in the US.

In *The Strangers*, for example, while the decor of the home is middle class, the house itself is a sprawling ranch deep in the woods. In 2009's *The Last House on the Left*, the action takes place at a wealthy family's lakeside vacation home. The family home in *The Collector* is a country mansion currently being remodeled by its wealthy owner. In *You're Next*, masked invaders attack a beautiful country estate used as a vacation home by a wealthy but dysfunctional White family. And the McMansion in *The Purge* is the envy of the White family's suburban neighbors, to name a few examples. Alternately, home invasion films without an affluent family home may instead explore formerly affluent or middle-class homes that have fallen into disrepair, as in the dilapidated vacation home in *Silent House* (2011) or the decaying home in an economically blighted Detroit in *Don't Breathe* (discussed in more detail in chap. 6).

Certainly, part of this trend stems from narrative structure: affluent homes are targeted for home invasions because their inhabitants have something to lose, namely wealth that can be lost from robbery. But the only home invasion horror films in this period that actually involve robbery are *The Collector* and *Don't Breathe*, and in both the would-be robbers themselves become victims to the monsters that lie in wait inside the home. There is something else driving this fascination with wealthy White households under siege from sadistic forces, something that goes beyond robbing the rich: White guilt around the horrors of affluence.

In several films, the corruption of White affluence is made explicit. *You're Next*, for instance, demonstrates the moral degradation of White wealth. The film follows Erin, a young woman traveling with her boyfriend, Crispian, to his family's vacation home to meet his parents, his siblings, and their partners. As everyone arrives and dinner commences, however, a crossbow bolt crashes through the window, killing Crispian's sister's boyfriend and sending the family into a panic as a group of attackers wearing animal masks surround the house and begin to pick off its inhabitants one by one (see fig. 2.2). But the attackers are not prepared for Erin, who spent her childhood on a survivalist compound in Australia and is well versed in self-defense, first aid, and ass-kicking. As the masked invaders continue their assault, Erin constructs some makeshift weapons and begins setting her own traps for the killers. After fighting them off and getting injured in the process, she discovers that Crispian and his brother Felix have orchestrated the attack, hoping to hasten their inheritance from their wealthy family. Crispian offers to share the inheritance with Erin, but she kills him instead.

Even before the killing starts, the family in the film shows their dysfunction. Crispian is mocked by his siblings and is a disappointment to his father, who wishes he were more successful. But the emotional dysfunction has clearly sparked a desire for murderous revenge and a quest for the family's wealth, indicating the corrupting influence of wealth on the family. Moreover, the family's wealth in the film stems from the father's position as an executive in a defense contracting firm, a fact that Erin shows her discomfort with as she and Crispian drive to the house: the family has grown rich by literally profiting off of the horrors of war.

The bloody body count in the family's massive vacation home that night resulted from the horrors of White affluence. White privileged brothers who enjoyed a comfortable lifestyle, thanks to war profiteering, used their petty grievances to fuel a violent rampage against their own family, all to avoid splitting an inheritance among the siblings. Linking the family's wealth to the historical violence of White people against others, the film emphasizes the corruption on which all White prosperity is founded. Instead of signaling wholesomeness and security, the family home in *You're Next* demonstrates the depravity of White prosperity, both in its sources and in its corrupting effects on those who benefit from it.

Similarly, *Silent House*, also from 2011, exposes the moral decay of the affluent White family. In the film—a remake of a 2010 Uruguayan film presented as a ninety-minute-long single take—a young woman named Sarah is helping her father and uncle remodel the dilapidated lakeside mansion that had been used as the family's vacation home for decades but is now falling apart. All the windows are boarded up, the doors are locked to keep out squatters, and the electricity in the home is unreliable. When Sarah explores the house to

Fig. 2.2. An affluent family dinner is interrupted by an arrow in the forehead, a prelude to a violent assault in *You're Next* (Snoot Entertainment, 2011).

investigate the sound of her father taking a fall, she finds herself trapped inside, unable to escape through a window or find the keys to open the locks on the door. As she looks for her injured father, she finds that she is being stalked by a mysterious figure tromping through the house and is forced to hide in the various bedrooms, all overflowing with decades' worth of junk. When she finds her uncle, they continue the search for her father, but the power goes out, and she can only light her way with the flashes of an old Polaroid camera.

After a series of bizarre visions revealing disturbing scenes of men abusing a small child, the audience and Sarah come to a startling realization: Sarah is, in fact, the mysterious figure stomping through the house in a fugue state and attacking her father because he had sexually abused her in the vacation home when she was young. Her visions were repressed memories that had come flooding back, and the dark specter was her, exacting revenge. Ultimately, Sarah bludgeons her father to death with a sledgehammer and threatens to do the same to her uncle, who knew about the abuse but did nothing. But she lets the uncle walk freely out the doors, which weren't actually locked all along.

The US version makes several significant revisions that shift the focus to the dynamics of prosperous White families. In the Uruguayan film *La Casa Muda* (2010), the home where the film is set belongs to a wealthy neighbor and family friend, who hires the protagonist, Laura, and her father to help clean up the rural estate. Like her US counterpart, Laura recovers repressed memories of sexual abuse in the home, perpetuated by the homeowner, Nestor, and known by her father, who forced Laura to have an abortion when she became pregnant with Nestor's baby. But the house of the film's title has no connection to Laura's family, other than it being the site of her abuse. It is not connected to her family, and there is no history of incest in that space.

The US film adds a Gothic twist by migrating the setting to a White family's vacation home, one that has long hidden a past of incest and abuse. In the US version, the formerly prosperous but now crumbling vacation mansion is a physical manifestation of Sarah's traumatized psyche and the moral degradation of the family. The labyrinth of junk-filled bedrooms, like the recesses of Sarah's mind, hold dusty memories and clues from the past, revealing horrific secrets that refuse to be lost to time. The dilapidated structure signals the decrepit morality of the White family, who tries to bury their own horrific actions and maintain a facade of normalcy, but the peeling wallpaper and rotted foundation indicate the moral rot behind this particular family.

While the White families in *You're Next* and *Silent House* might seem to be under threat from sadistic outsiders, evoking fears of White victimization, both films truly show the horrors behind such families, evoking instead the anxieties of White guilt and fragility, the fear that White privilege is not only unearned but based on violence and depravity. These fears are made even more prominent in 2019's *Ready or Not*, which is not technically a home invasion film but still envisions the affluent family home as a site of intra-family graphic violence. In this film, the wealthy family must hunt down and ritualistically sacrifice the son's new bride because the family's ancestors made a deal with the devil to ensure their prosperity. Here, White wealth is literally unearned and evil and perpetuates violence against others.

THE PURGE AND WHITE GUILT

No home invasion film makes the corruption of affluent Whiteness clearer than *The Purge*, which takes place in a semi-futuristic society in which a hyperconservative political party has instituted a once-a-year purge night, during which all crime is legal for twelve hours. Supposedly as a result of the yearly purge, unemployment and crime rates are at all-time lows. According to the ideology of the ruling party, The New Founding Fathers of America, the economic and cultural stability that comes in the wake of the purge night stems from the annual release of the country's frustrations, anger, and violence in a contained, legally condoned outburst that allows people to follow social and legal rules the rest of the year.

The first *Purge* film's narrative tells the story of the Sandins, an affluent suburban White family living in an immaculate and sprawling McMansion built from the father's income selling home security systems to other affluent families, systems particularly designed to protect those homes on purge night. The family—father James (Ethan Hawke), mother Mary (Lena Headey), teenage daughter Zoey (Adelaide Kane), and preteen Charlie (Max Burkholder)—expects this year's purge night to be like any other as they settle in for a night watching television, safe thanks to their state-of-the-art security system. But their safety and moral outlook are challenged when their son lets a Black homeless man into their house to protect him from a band of aggressive purgers, all while the teenage daughter's older boyfriend has stowed away in the house in an attempt to murder Mr. Sandin, who disapproves of their relationship. As the aggressive purgers systematically attempt to break through the security system, the Sandins must decide if they will risk their lives to protect the unnamed homeless Black man (Edwin Hodge) or give him up to the purgers in an attempt to save their own lives.

The conceit of the film speaks to the idea of violence lurking just beneath the surface of the outwardly typical White family. As everyone prepares for purge night, the Sandins see their neighbor sharpening his machete, apparently preparing to sate his bloodlust (see fig. 2.3). Moreover, some of the Sandins are eventually saved when their affluent suburban neighbors surprise and murder the remaining purgers laying siege to the Sandin home—not to save the Sandins, but because they want to murder the family themselves after harboring years of jealously over the Sandins' wealth. But time runs out on purge night, and the neighbors are foiled. Throughout the film, ordinary prosperous Americans are shown to be capable of horrific violence, if only it were legally allowed. This capacity for brutality in the film crosses racial and ethnic boundaries; people from all walks of life are sitting on untapped rage and sadism, just waiting to let it out. In the *Purge* sequels, in fact, much of the visual terror stems from over-the-top images of murderous and intimidating purgers, from affluent suburban Whites to poor people of color in the cities.[7]

The *Purge* franchise, however, also explores the systemic violence of Whiteness and affluence in the US, at times suggesting that the violence of purge night is not a universal human desire, but rather a result of systemic discrimination

Fig. 2.3. An average White suburban man sharpens his machete just before purge night starts, hoping to sate his bloodlust in *The Purge* (Universal Pictures, 2013).

against the poor and people of color. As a TV news commentator argues in the background as Mr. Sandin prepares to lock up his house, the low unemployment and crime rates are probably due to the murder of the most vulnerable on purge night, not the psychological effects of releasing pent-up violence.

The Sandins embody these structures of inequality: they have built a lavish, affluent lifestyle for themselves by selling wealthy people security systems that poor people cannot afford. Their wealth literally flows from an unequal system that preys on the bodies of the vulnerable. But the Sandins are gleefully ignorant of the moral consequences of the system they inhabit. Mr. Sandin in particular is only concerned with earning enough commissions to buy a boat, along with protecting the wholesomeness of his teenage daughter. Neither he nor his family—save perhaps his conscientious son—seems capable of critically understanding the racial and economic inequalities they profit from.

These inequalities are made much more apparent in the *Purge* sequels, which eschew the narrative structure of the White home invasion film, instead following a diverse ensemble of characters struggling to survive the nightmare of purge night out on the streets without an expensive home security system. To make matters worse, it turns out that the government authorizes secret teams of military personnel to liquidate poor people of color on purge night in a kind of violent eugenics operation.

The system of purge night in the films, then, is only a mild exaggeration of the realities of race and violence in the US, where, thanks to the unequal distribution of wealth, racial housing segregation, and policing practices, middle-class and affluent White folks are insulated from the kinds of crime and violence that are far more likely to affect people of color.[8]

In the first *Purge* film, however, it takes a violent confrontation with an exaggerated vision of White class privilege for the Sandins to come to terms with their moral responsibilities. The aggressive purgers seeking the Black homeless man in the film all don elite prep school uniforms and speak of purging the poor and vulnerable from society as their inalienable right. They offer a terrifying but cartoonish image of sadistic White privilege and are hell-bent on killing the Black homeless man because he had the audacity to fight back when they attacked him on the streets, killing one of the purgers. The Sandins see in these privileged psychopaths a reflection of their privileges—the violence against poor folks and people of color is now literally surrounding the Sandins' idyllic suburban home.

The *us* versus *them* logic of the home invasion genre, however, takes a few twists and turns as the family is caught between their fear of the wealthy psychopathic purgers and their growing sympathy for the Black homeless man, coded as a veteran with his military jacket. As the family violently hunts down the homeless man, who had been hiding in the house, they begin to recognize their similarities to the sadistic preppy purgers, ultimately deciding that they should fight the purgers instead of sacrificing the homeless man. Of course, once they decide to take the moral high ground and repudiate the violent logic of the purgers, the family goes into action-film mode and engages in a crescendo of violent antics in an effort to protect the house, with the homeless man joining in the fight against the purgers as they force their way into the house. Mr. Sandin is killed along the way, but Mrs. Sandin and the children survive, holding their last attackers (the jealous neighbors) at gunpoint until purge night ends, rather than killing them, insisting that there has been enough killing that night.

While the film exposes the violence underpinning White affluence in the US, *The Purge* and other home invasion films still center on the experience of White families, exploring the horrors of having the safe White home transformed into a space of violent crime. As much as *The Purge* critiques systems of racial violence and injustice in the US, the film still asks us to root for a wealthy White family to reclaim their home, pitting the family against a caricature of White corruption in order to make their middle-class Whiteness more palatable; the token Black character helps them acknowledge their own guilt and privilege. That said, like other home invasion films that center on Whiteness but wallow in White guilt, *The Purge* explores the nagging dread that the violence erupting in the tainted White family home signals that affluent Whites are somewhat culpable for the brutality on which our system is based.

CONCLUSION: *US* AND THE HOME INVASION CYCLE

I discuss the horror of the early Trump era in the book's conclusion, but one film from 2019 especially takes up the racial dynamics of the contemporary home invasion film: Jordan Peele's *Us*.

The film tells the story of a Black woman named Adelaide who, after a bizarre encounter with her doppelgänger in a beachside carnival funhouse as a child, spent years in therapy, convinced that her double was out there, coming for her. Those premonitions would prove true when Adelaide, now upper middle class, married, and a mother of two children, finds her family terrorized one night at their lakeside vacation home by doubles of each family member donning red jumpsuits, each figure armed with a large pair of brass scissors.

Captured by their shadow selves, the family learns that the doubles have lived deep underground for their entire lives, tethered to their aboveground counterparts but living out a grotesque mirror image of their doubles, unable to assert their own autonomy. As Adelaide's double, dubbed Red, tells the family, the shadow selves have had only cold, sharp toys and raw rabbit meat while the family has enjoyed the warmth and comfort of the aboveground world. The doubles then attempt to murder each member of the family, prompting the family to fight back, often gruesomely.

The first act of Peele's film, then, inserts an affluent Black family into the *us* versus *them* structure of the typical home invasion film, working as a commentary on Black double consciousness and the guilt of the Black middle class. The family's grunting, primal avatars can be seen as stand-ins for the kinds of brutal lives of poverty and violence that this Black family has escaped but that many other Black families in the US have not. And since the avatars—the tethered—are linked to their counterparts, the aboveground family's successes are literally built on the horrific echo of their lives experienced by the tethered. The film, after all, contrasts Adelaide's working-class childhood with a distant, alcoholic father against the prosperous and stable family life she has created with her upwardly mobile, college-educated husband (whose attempts at an affluent lifestyle are themselves a scaled-down echo of their more prosperous White friends: the Black family has a cozy but not fancy lake house, while the White friends have a swanky lakefront mansion; the Black dad buys a used, sputtering motorboat, while the White friends have a large yacht). The tethered are a guilt-laden reminder that the family's upward mobility is not possible for many poor people of color, even if it still lags behind the privileges of White folks.

However, Peele's film, unlike the standard White-centric home invasion film, looks beyond the isolated family, connecting their individual struggles to a larger network of social structures. As Adelaide and her family fight off and flee from their shadow selves, they find that their White friends and neighbors have also been gruesomely killed by their own shadow selves. In fact, thousands of people across Southern California (and maybe the entire country) are being attacked by thousands of the tethered, and once the tethered have killed their doubles, they are joining hands in their red jumpsuits to recreate the 1986 Hands Across America event in which millions of people attempted to form a human chain across the entire country to raise money and awareness for poverty, hunger, and homelessness. Mass killings and chaos mean that the family is on its own as it continues to flee from the tethered.

By scaling the action beyond the family to the scope of the nation, the film loses logical consistency (are there really enough secret, underground facilities to house thousands, maybe millions, of the tethered and enough rabbits to sustain them?). But the scale of the story opens up the film's exploration of prosperity and suffering in the US to the national level, making far more explicit the guilt of the White home invasion film. In the standard narrative, the White family's corruption or descent into sadistic violence hints at the historical and continuing violence used to shore up White prosperity. In Peele's film, these relationships are laid bare. It isn't just Adelaide's family's prosperity that has precipitated the suffering of their shadow selves—the entire facade of US prosperity dictates the oppression of the tethered.

The true focus of the film, then, is not the family but *us*—the US. As Red insists to the family when asked who they are early in the film, "We are Americans!" So when Adelaide seeks out Red in the underground facility that has held the tethered for decades, she is probing the depths of the national subconscious. She descends an uncanny number of staircases and underground passageways in pursuit of Red—imagery that is typically used in horror filmmaking to explore the individual psyche. Basements and tunnels usually hold all that has been repressed, and here those tunnels hold the realities that the nation would rather forget, the realities of those we oppress.

Peele's film also pries into the us/them binary and muddles any distinctions between the wholesome family and the others who threaten it. As Adelaide finally fights and kills Red, we learn that the aboveground Adelaide was actually born and raised among the tethered. When the two girls came face-to-face in that house of mirrors years before, the tethered girl forced her aboveground counterpart into the tunnels and took her place among the privileged population. Red—the only one of the tethered to speak English because she was raised aboveground—used her memories of Hands Across America as a young girl in the '80s to organize the tethered to rebel against their doubles, complicating our sympathies and troubling the idea that the tethered are grotesque monsters; when given a chance, one of them leads a perfectly normal and successful life among the privileged.

As critic Aja Romano explains it, these plot twists open up the film's exploration of guilt beyond any one family to our national guilt:

> Once we start thinking about the Underground as an allegorical space that represents dehumanized and marginalized bodies, then suddenly "we" are forced to contend with the troubling idea that perhaps the only things separating "us" from various "thems"—society's countless marginalized communities—are chance and privilege. And even this isn't enough to ever fully sever us. We are all, as the movie repeats, tethered not only to each other, but also to the sins of our country's past and present, to the people and cultures we have tried to erase and diminish. And that connection leaves its traces, even when we try to deny it.[9]

In this way, *Us* transforms the highly individualized terror of the White home invasion film into a national terror. Instead of focusing on the anxieties of White families worried about their place in society or reckoning with their guilt over their privileges, *Us* points us toward a community terror: Who is left behind as others prosper? And will there be a reckoning?

NOTES

1. Michael Fiddler, "Playing *Funny Games* in *The Last House on the Left*: The Uncanny and the Home Invasion Genre," *Crime Media Culture* 9, no. 3 (2013): 281–299.

2. Robin Means Coleman offers a more detailed exploration of the racial dynamics of suburbs and cities in horror films in her book *Horror Noire: Blacks in American Horror Films from the 1980s to Present* (New York: Routledge, 2011).

3. For a detailed overview of *The Last House on the Left*, its production, and its critical reception, see David A. Szulkin, *Wes Craven's* Last House on the Left: *The Making of a Cult Classic* (Guildford, UK: FAB Press, 2000).

4. For more on the depiction of violence in *Last House on the Left* and its relationship to the media culture around the Vietnam War and the social upheavals of the 1960s, see Adam Lowenstein, *Shocking Representation: Historical Trauma,*

National Cinema, and the Modern Horror Film (New York: Columbia University Press, 2005). Lowenstein explores how the unsettling violence of the film negotiates the cultural turmoil around the counterculture and the Vietnam War, with the Stillos functioning as a kind of Manson family who expose the dark excesses of the counterculture, all while mainstream culture becomes steeped in the violent images of war and protest.

5. Fiddler also explores the concept of the carnivalesque in his analysis of the home invasion genre, "Playing *Funny Games* in *The Last House on the Left*," 289–290.

6. See Fiddler, "Playing *Funny Games* in *The Last House on the Left*," for a discussion contextualizing *Last House on the Left*, *Straw Dogs*, and *Funny Games* against their social and cultural contexts.

7. For more discussion of *The Purge* and its dystopic vision of neoliberal capitalism, see Wheeler Winston Dixon, *Hollywood in Crisis or: The Collapse of the Real* (New York: Palgrave, 2018). Dixon commends the film's "assuredly bleak presentation of suburban life as a living hell" and its ability to sketch "an all too realistic vision of the stop-at-nothing consumerism that drives American culture," 20–21.

8. The class dynamics of the violence at the heart of the *Purge* movies is explored by A. Bowdoin Van Riper in "All Against All: Dystopia, Dark Forces, and Hobbesian Anarchy in the *Purge* Films," in *Dark Forces at Work: Essays on Social Dynamics and Cinematic Horrors*, ed. Cynthia Miller and Van Riper (Lanham, MD: Lexington Books, 2020), 127. Van Riper argues that the racialized violence seen in the films (especially in the *Purge* sequels) is simply an extension of historical violence against the vulnerable, the new form of a violence that has always underpinned American history.

9. Aja Romano, "*Us*'s Big Plot Twist, Explained," *Vox*, March 22, 2019, https://www.vox.com/2019/3/22/18277163/us-movie-ending-what-happened-adelaide-red-explained.

3

—ɯ̄—

AMERICAN DREAMS

Fantasies and Social Mobility in *Dream House* and *Drag Me to Hell*

AS THE PREVIOUS CHAPTERS ATTEST, the housing market crash tarnished the collective cultural fantasy of the American dream, especially for White folks grappling with the realities of the neoliberal economy. Even if prosperity in the US was shared unequally, the American dream of good wages and economic stability became a reality for many people who worked their way into the middle class in the several decades following World War II. And for those who didn't, the idea that it might still be possible for them or their children remained a powerful fantasy. But as globalization and automation chipped away at industrial jobs in the US and the erosion of labor unions chipped away at stable wages, the fantasy of the American dream seemed more and more out of reach for many Americans. Meanwhile, the nagging dread of precarity even descended on people poised to benefit from an economy that now privileged college-educated knowledge workers. The ascendance of the gig economy, rising student loan debt, and skyrocketing housing prices in urban centers meant that the American dream didn't look as stable as it once had for previous generations. The collapse of the housing market in 2007 and lingering recession that followed only made the crumbling veneer of the American dream look that much worse, as one of the last remaining stable forms of wealth generation—homeownership—now seemed perilous.

These fears were especially potent among White folks, who had the most to lose in the new economy, since they had benefited most from the inequalities of the past. It took a psychological toll on the White middle classes to find themselves subjected to the cutthroat competition of the neoliberal economy after generations of privilege had insulated them from the extremes of capitalism.

Even as the economy slowly recovered throughout the Obama years and into the Trump years, the act of dreaming was far more fraught after the Great Recession. Was it reasonable to still fantasize about upward mobility for yourself or your children? Do we still dream that most American of dreams that our world will be better for everyone in the years to come?

Of course, these are not new fears for the White middle class, nor is this the first time those fears have found expression in the horror genre. In the late '70s and early '80s, films such as *The Amityville Horror* and *The Shining* (among others) told tales of dream houses that should have buoyed financially precarious White families but instead tormented their aspirations for upward mobility. At the dawn of the neoliberal economy, those films also explored the tormented fears of White folks who felt they were promised something better than a working-class existence.

As the Great Recession brought those fears back to the surface in the mid-2000s, the horror genre responded accordingly. This chapter examines two horror films from the Obama years that explore the fantasies and aspirations of White people in the neoliberal economy: the Daniel Craig thriller *Dream House* from 2011 and Sam Raimi's *Drag Me to Hell* from 2009. Both films tell stories of White people whose aspirations for a better life run aground because of unsettling visions that they cannot seem to escape from. Both films consider the acts of fantasy and aspiration, interweaving the character's personal dreams and goals with at times dark and disturbing visions of violence. As the characters aspire for something better in the neoliberal economy, their fantasies undercut the very notion of aspiration in today's world.

That said, the two films offer radically different outlooks on the act of aspiration, reflecting the gendered perspectives of their White characters. In *Dream House*, the middle-aged male corporate executive's fantasies, while at times horrific, help guide and reassure him through a period of economic precarity, leading to the rejuvenation of White male stability and prosperity. But in *Drag Me to Hell*, the millennial woman's violent visions only accentuate how brutal and immoral upward social mobility has become in the neoliberal economy.

DREAM HOUSE

If you removed the murders, ghosts, and fantasy worlds from the 2001 film *Dream House*, you'd be left with a story that should still terrify all the Gen Xers who find themselves at the midpoint in their careers. In the film, a successful executive in the corporate world quits his job in order to retire early, spend time with his family, and write the novel that he's been dreaming about for years. But as he settles into life with his wife and two young daughters, his relationship with his seemingly idyllic family unravels, he becomes visibly poorer and unhinged, and his wholesome dream house seems to inexplicably need more and more repairs until it resembles an abandoned, derelict shack.

The film, however, *does* involve murders and ghostly fantasies, using the tropes of horror to explore the terrors of a seemingly stable White man who spirals down the social ladder. In the film, Daniel Craig plays Will Atenton, who leaves behind his corner office in a Manhattan publishing house to devote his time to his family and fulfill his dream of writing a novel. He comes home after quitting his job to find his wife, Libby (Rachel Weisz), and two little girls painting elaborate vines and flowers in their entryway and up the stairs in their newly purchased suburban home, a scene of domestic tranquility and new beginnings. But this is a horror film, so just as he commits himself to a new life and home in the suburbs, a series of unusual disturbances disrupts their peaceful family life. His daughters and wife begin seeing a strange figure lurking in the woods just beyond their backyard. He wakes one night to find a gaggle of Gothic teens performing bizarre rituals by candlelight in his basement. And a cryptic neighbor, Ann (Naomi Watts), always avoids his questions about the neighborhood and the previous owners.

In a standard home-under-siege plot development, Will discovers that his idyllic suburban home was the scene of several grisly murders five years ago. A mother and her two young daughters (about the age of Will's daughters) were shot in the house, and the husband, Peter Ward, was the prime suspect, despite receiving a gunshot wound himself that night. Absent any hard evidence of Ward's guilt, he wasn't charged with a crime, but in the wake of the tragedy, he has spent years in a local mental hospital. Anxious over the security of his new home, Will investigates Peter Ward, only to find that Ward was recently released from the hospital to a halfway house nearby. While surreptitiously searching Ward's room at the halfway house, Will discovers a picture of his own wife and children, presumably stolen from their home, leading him to believe that Ward is the mysterious figure in the woods and that he has been stalking his family because they took possession of his former home.

Dream House mirrors other home-based horror films in its use of the suburban family home to stage a melodrama around White economic stability and male authority. Across this cycle of films, the abnormal events that befall White families echo or exaggerate tensions around their class standing. The ghosts or aliens or demons cause normally stable families to become more precarious or, alternately, exacerbate their already-precarious class standing.

Building on this trend, *Dream House* explores the class anxieties of a privileged White man who tries to leave the corporate world behind, translating his apprehension about his new life into the visual construction of his world. Early in the film, Will looks the part of a Manhattan executive, in a sharp grey suit and wool trench coat, his blond hair looking soft and clean. But as Will explores the mystery around Peter Ward, he inexplicably begins to look shabbier and more working class. He begins wearing jeans that seem to gradually get dirtier and dirtier and a canvas work jacket over a grey hoodie. Later, he is wearing a crisp white button-down but puts a dingy black leather jacket over the top as he confronts Peter Ward's doctors at the hospital about Ward's release.

These visual transitions also impact his house, a cozy two-story home on a cul-de-sac abutting the woods. At first, the home looks picturesque and well maintained. But as his family's turmoil begins, the house shows more severe wear and tear. A canvas awning on the back of the home is now tattered and torn, its metal structure barely clinging to the house. The basement is filled with a significant amount of garbage and debris, with graffiti all over its stone walls.

Will's home, in fact, signals a looming fear around the loss of his patriarchal authority as his cozy domestic space is threatened. Idealized scenes of domestic life inside the house depict traditional gender roles: a beautiful and supportive stay-at-home wife who never seems to leave the house and two adorable children who are helping their mother paint a lovely flowering vine mural up the walls of their staircase. But these warm scenes of familial tranquility are threatened by the shadowy figures lurking at the edge of the lawn and the local teens who invade and vandalize the basement. As Will's family becomes more scared and his house becomes more run-down, we are asked to wonder whether this vision of traditional nuclear families can weather the threats of financial precarity and disrepair that are also looming in their lives.

Will had hoped that his years of work in the corporate world would prepare him for an early retirement fulfilling his dreams of becoming a novelist. Instead, in the Great Recession era, his new suburban home seems to be pulling Will into a world of class anxiety and gritty murders, a world where he is losing his grip on middle-class security.

In a plot twist, however, we find that Will is actually just losing his grip on his own sanity. When Will sits down with Peter Ward's psychiatrist, he is shown a video of Ward in the hospital, wild-haired and violent, frantic to escape. A close-up on Ward, however, reveals Will's face in the video. Will is Peter Ward, recently released from the hospital. Ward adopted a new identity as Will that he uses to try to forget the horrible trauma of his family's murders, but Will's

investigation is leading him back to the truth. His family back at home is a fig-
ment of his imagination.

When the scene cuts back to the shot of Will watching the video after this
revelation, we now see Will as he actually is. His crisp white shirt is dingy and
yellowed. His face is haggard and stubbly. His clothes are wrinkled and ill-
fitting. He isn't an affluent executive trying for an early retirement but rather a
formerly middle-class man who has been institutionalized for five years and is
now poor and destitute. And his home is equally derelict, its windows boarded,
its exterior vandalized, the gutters drooping listlessly from the roof. He has
only imagined it as the wholesome family home that it once was, filled with his
imaginary family, as he squats in his former residence (see fig. 3.1).

This plot twist doubles down on the film's exploration of White class anxieties. *Dream House* invites the audience to identify with an affluent protagonist
who might be losing his class standing a bit only to pull the rug out and reveal
him to be a destitute murder suspect, blighting his former neighborhood with
his ramshackle home and wild antics. The narrative and imagery of an impoverished Daniel Craig evoke fears about the horrors of White poverty. What if
this image of abject poverty is what's in store for the formerly secure middle
classes in the US?

But the film also explores the dynamics of aspiration and dreams in the
new economy. As the plot unfolds in the second half of the film, Will/Peter
has to navigate his new reality. He knows that his wife and children waiting
back home are fantasies that he uses to distract himself from his current state
(and from considering his own role in their murders: Did he kill them?). But
the fantasies are reassuring and appealing, an apparition of middle-class family
domesticity for an essentially homeless man who has lost everything. How can
he adjust to the despairing realities of his actual life when those realities must
compete with such a compelling fantasy of affluence and success?

In this way, his fantasy world exemplifies the American dream for the White
middle classes: a beautiful, comfortable home that a normal family can still
afford, even though the wife doesn't work and the husband retired early to
pursue his passions. As a viewer, we should have recognized that Will's world
was make-believe, not only because of the foreshadowing clues that dot the first
half of the narrative but because of how unattainable his fantasy life would be
for even upper-middle-class folks in the US.

Of course, this would hardly be the first film or television program to offer
a highly unrealistic vision of affluence for White families, but *Dream House*
makes explicit how alluring and deceptive the American dream is. This fantasy
is deeply comforting but also a trap for someone like Will/Peter, who needs to

Fig. 3.1. The seemingly affluent executive is revealed to be a disheveled squatter in an abandoned and boarded-up home in *Dream House* (Cliffjack Motion Pictures, 2011).

accept his gritty reality and past traumas in order to move on with his life. As he slides in and out of his elaborate fantasy world, his life is literally crumbling all around him, and his dream house is now a nightmare. Will/Peter's story is echoed all across the US—in less elaborate and horrific terms—by families who tirelessly work for an American dream that will never become a reality for them.

Luckily for Peter, he's a heterosexual middle-aged White man. Despite being a homeless murder suspect with a long history of mental illness, Peter aspires to reclaim his affluence, which isn't too unrealistic for him. In the film, as Peter begins to confront the realities of his situation, his memories of the night of the murder come back to him, allowing him to identify the mysterious man in the bushes as the real killer all along. His neighbor and friend, Ann, had been going through a messy divorce with her asshole husband, Jack, so Jack hired a local criminal to kill his wife. But the criminal got the wrong house and attacked Peter's family instead, killing Peter's wife and daughters after Peter's wife accidentally shoots Peter while aiming for the assailant. Now, five years later and with Peter back at the crime scene, Jack and the criminal try again, especially since Jack is having financial woes and has lost custody of his daughter with Ann. They ambush Peter and Ann, hoping to kill them both and make it look like a murder-suicide perpetrated by the unhinged Peter. But Peter manages to fight back (with the help of his imaginary Libby, who might actually be a ghost and not just a fantasy, as she is inexplicably able to touch and move objects in the home, distracting Jack as Peter tries to save himself and Ann).

In the end, Jack and the hit man die in the fire they started in Peter's house. Peter saves Ann from the flames and gets to say goodbye to his imaginary family before the house goes up in smoke. He wanders off into the night.

The film closes with an image of Peter now looking like his fantasy identity, Will. He is walking the streets of New York, dressed sharply in another grey suit and tie, when he stops in a bookstore window and sees his own face. This time, instead of seeing himself in the throes of madness, as he did when shown the video of himself in the hospital, Peter sees his face in an advertisement hovering over rows and rows of his best-selling novel, also called *Dream House*. He has become Peter Ward again, now vindicated in the murders, and has turned his story into a novel that has brought him back into affluence and economic stability. His fantasies of success and prosperity, as far-fetched as they may have seemed when he was at his lowest point, still became a reality for him in the end.

DRAG ME TO HELL

The twenty-something protagonist of *Drag Me to Hell* also dares to dream of upward mobility, but in Sam Raimi's film about the dreams and nightmares of the US recession, desiring more for yourself in the neoliberal economy only leads to damnation, as the title suggests.

The film tells the story of Christine Brown (Alison Lohman), a loan officer at a small bank branch in Los Angeles. Christine was raised on a farm somewhere in the country but left home to make her life in a big city, like so many other young people who leave behind the economic stagnation of rural life. She's dating a young assistant professor of psychology who comes from a wealthy family (Justin Long), and she's desperately hoping for a promotion to assistant manager at her bank. But her hopes for upward mobility are challenged when she denies a mortgage extension to an old Eastern European woman (labeled as a gypsy in the film) in an attempt to impress her boss, who wants to know if she can make hard decisions that will help the bank's bottom line. Later that night, the old woman attacks Christine in a parking garage and curses her with a powerful demon who will come to harvest Christine's soul in three days. In the meantime, the demon torments Christine, as does the spirit of the old woman (who died just after her encounter with Christine). The young woman's life spins out of control as she tries to impress her boyfriend's parents, vies for a promotion with a sleazy coworker, and dabbles in the occult to try to reverse her curse.

Released in 2009 in the early years of the Great Recession, *Drag Me to Hell* explicitly connects its storyline to the recent housing market crash and the behavior of mortgage lenders.[1] Christine's ambitions, the film asserts, lead her to make an immoral decision: booting an old, sickly woman out of her home so the bank can make a tidy profit on the fees from this kind of foreclosure. Even if the old woman in question is not exactly a nice person—she physically assaults Christine, curses her with a horrible demon, and steals all the candy off Christine's desk in the bank—Christine's attempts to impress her boss nevertheless leave an old woman homeless. This callous act in the name of profit sets in motion the supernatural torment that befalls Christine. The film's story condemns the callous, profit-driven banking practices that helped bring down the whole US economy along with millions of people who lost their homes when the housing bubble burst. For scholars such as Cynthia Miller and April Miller, *Drag Me to Hell* depicts the brutal logics of neoliberal capitalism in the wake of the housing market crash; it is a perfectly timed horror story about the kinds of monstrous sacrifices people are asked to make in the name of profit and economic growth.[2]

As both Millers argue, *Drag Me to Hell* critiques the entire neoliberal economy for the pressures it puts on those hoping for upward mobility. In the film, Christine embarks on a strict regime of personal transformation and self-discipline designed to ferret out any signs of low social standing. Christine uses daily elocution lessons to erase her country accent and make her diction as innocuous as possible. These efforts seem a vital necessity, as she overhears her boyfriend's mother suggesting that a farm girl is not a suitable match for their family's social standing. Christine has also radically transformed her body, thinning down since she moved to the city with a strict diet. Even as she is tormented by the shadows of demons and the ghosts of decrepit old women, she is still visibly tormented by the baked goods that will ruin her figure. To achieve success in today's economy, Christine knows that every aspect of her personal appearance is subject to intense scrutiny; she can't be seen as a chubby farm girl if she wants that promotion to middle management.

She also must navigate intense competition in the workplace, especially as a woman. Her brownnosing coworker Stu takes every opportunity to try to make her look bad, from making small digs, like lying to make it seem like Christine messed up his lunch order, to committing massive breaches of professional ethics like sabotaging a huge deal Christine had brokered with a local business. Stu also seems to have some wealth or resources to draw on in his quest to become assistant bank manager; in one scene, he gifts the boss tickets for good seats at a Lakers game. It is hard to imagine Christine having the kind of money to buy those tickets. Of course, once the demon starts toying with Christine, her wild antics in the workplace make Stu's efforts unnecessary, but in the meantime, the film highlights the kinds of pressure and competition facing young people in a cutthroat neoliberal economy.[3]

Much like Peter in *Dream House*, Christine experiences a series of visions that are only visible to her—the shadows of the demon closing in on her or the old woman violently confronting her. But the visions in *Drag Me to Hell* are the inverse of Peter's fantasies in *Dream House*. In *Dream House*, Peter uses a fantasy of upper-middle-class stability and domesticity to delude himself over his own failures, obscuring the nightmare of his own destitution as a White man. In *Drag Me to Hell*, Christine's visions are nightmares that her gender and lack of cultural capital will haunt her as she tries to move up in the world. Her visions are an extension of the neoliberal economy, blocking her opportunities for success.

This obstruction of her opportunities is quite literal in the film, as the demon rears its head just when things are looking up for Christine. After her boss praises her for her decision with the old woman, Christine imagines the old woman's long, disgusting fingernails on the hands of her coworker Stu, causing her to lash out at him before getting a wildly bloody nose that sprays all over her boss. Later, after she thinks she has satiated the demon by ritualistically sacrificing her adorable kitten, she heads off to a fancy dinner at her boyfriend's parents' mansion. She wins over the father with her financial knowledge (she reads the *Wall Street Journal*!), and she bonds with the mother by discussing her struggles with her alcoholic mother. But then the old woman's eye appears in Christine's slice of cake, spewing blood and pus when Christine skewers it with her fork. She then throws a glass at a door and screams in response to the noises of the demon, irreparably ruining her chances of impressing the wealthy parents. Just as it is in her workplace, her comportment is subject to intense scrutiny in her personal life if she hopes to move up the social ladder, and the demon helps ensure that she won't.

Christine's struggles with social mobility also reflect cultural anxieties that White folks don't have the same opportunities to advance as they once did. Her encounters with the supernatural are all racialized in one way or another, suggesting that the intense competition of neoliberalism is dragging young folks—and young White folks in particular—into a world where the privileges of Whiteness are fading.

For example, all of her supernatural support comes from non-White characters (who act out very old clichés around race and the occult). First, she seeks the help of Rham Jas, an East Asian Indian psychic who runs a dinky fortune-telling business and charges sixty dollars for a reading. Jas eventually leads Christine to Shaun San Dena, a Latina medium with a history dealing with this particular demon. San Dena lives and works in a crumbling Pasadena mansion built by her long-dead husband to channel the spirits of the dead and charges a hefty ten thousand dollars for her assistance. Christine's supernatural affliction pulls her into the world of well-intentioned but disreputable people of color who her affluent boyfriend thinks are scamming her. She wants to be spending her time with well-to-do White folks but instead is forced to consort with tawdry ethnic Others who the wealthy elite look down on.

The real horror for Christine is that she might never escape from her roots as so-called poor White trash; she will always be tainted somehow in the eyes of affluent White society. These fears manifest in the abject Whiteness of the old woman and her Eastern European clan, who are identified as gypsies in the film. Invoking old cultural stereotypes of gypsies as sneaky and mystical, the film relies on their status as ethnic Others within Euro-American culture to taunt Christine that she, like them, will always be on the outskirts of elite White culture. Their status as White-adjacent is made clear when Christine goes to visit the old woman in her home, hoping to make amends and have the curse lifted. The old woman's house—once a middle-class craftsman home—now bears the markers of poverty: fading and chipping paint, an overgrown yard, dingy children's toys everywhere, and the old woman's decrepit 1970s sedan parked in the driveway. Let into the house by the old woman's cold and hostile granddaughter (who still sports an Eastern European accent—there is no cultural assimilation for these immigrants), Christine finds that the old woman has died, and her family is throwing her a raucous wake. The basement is filled with dishes from the old world, gambling, and a host of family members costumed to suggest their status as poor Eastern European migrants, the men in dated leather jackets with long stringy hair, the old women with dingy earth-toned sweaters and scarves over their heads, and the young women with dark makeup and slightly too-revealing clothing for a wake. The old woman's family evokes the kind of poor, ethnic, White-but-not-quite status that Christine worries she will embody if she can't shake her poor and rural roots.

Following the typical stereotypes of White trash in US culture, the film evokes these anxieties around poor Whiteness through its depictions of other characters. The old woman, for example, is distinguished by her long, gnarled, yellowed fingernails, which she taps impatiently on Christine's desk. She also has a discolored eye—the result of a recent illness, she suggests—and persistently coughs up phlegm into a dingy handkerchief, massaging the phlegm into the cloth with her fingers as she talks about her loan with Christine. If Christine devotes her time and energy into physically maintaining a tidy, trim, respectable body to meet the norms of middle-class Whiteness, the old woman flouts almost every single one of those norms, suggesting that in the absence of self-discipline, this is what becomes of poor Whites who don't try to fit the mold.[4]

Not surprisingly, then, when Christine begins to be tormented by the demon and the spirit of the old woman, her haunting takes the form of disgusting bodily abjection and penetration. In her visions, the old woman vomits insects and maggots into her face or punches Christine in the mouth, shoving her entire arm down Christine's gullet, to name a few examples (see fig. 3.2). These scenes clearly reflect director Sam Raimi's quirky visual style—his previous horror films included manic, borderline comedic scenes of the grotesque. But in the context of this narrative, the persistent challenges to the sanctity of Christine's disciplined White body highlight her paranoia around embodying middle-class Whiteness. What if her regimes of discipline break down and she reverts back to her past self?[5]

These fears prove well-founded in the scenes where Christine's haunting hinders her social advancement. Her sterile office space is sullied by Christine's comedically exaggerated bloody nose when she sprays bodily fluids all over a respectable middle-class space, where the body and its functions are supposed to be controlled and obscured. Her boss frantically asks if any blood got in his mouth as Christine's body transgresses the norms governing the workplace. And when Christine meets her boyfriend's parents, in one scene she belches up a fly that had wormed its way into her mouth while she slept. Flies are associated with dirt, feces, and contagion—all things that are supposed to be controlled and eradicated when meeting potential in-laws in their immaculate mansion. The White middle-class body that she has worked so hard to maintain and control is literally bursting at the seams with all the fluids and decay that young White women are supposed to hide from the world.

After all of Christine's failed attempts to rid herself of the curse (Shaun San Dena's expensive intervention fails to break the curse), Rham Jas offers Christine one last solution: embrace the hypercompetitive and immoral nature of the world. She can pass along the demon to someone else by simply gifting them the coat button that has been the host for the curse. This would rid Christine of the demon, but it would also mean that the new owner of the button would have their soul tortured for all of eternity. If a decision based on self-interest in the neoliberal economy got Christine into this mess, another selfish act can

Fig. 3.2. The abject old woman appears even more horrific in Christine's nightmares in *Drag Me to Hell* (Universal Pictures, 2009).

save her. In essence, she can beat the demon by playing by the cutthroat rules of the new economy, but at a tremendous moral cost. After scanning a late-night diner for possible new victims of the curse, she contemplates passing along the button to her slimy coworker Stu before feeling sorry for him and backing out.

But then she discovers a loophole: she can gift the button to a dead person, whose soul would then be reaped. Grabbing her shovel, she heads to the local cemetery to dig up the old woman's body in the rain, forcing the button (safely enclosed in an envelope) into the old woman's mouth, a seemingly just decision, since the old woman unleashed the demon in the first place.

The next morning, Christine's tidy life seems to have come back together. Her boss leaves her a message on the phone detailing his discovery of Stu's treachery and promising her the promotion. Christine then flits off to the train station to meet her boyfriend, so they can head to Santa Barbara for a weekend at his parents' cabin (and, unbeknownst to her, he plans to propose). The world of affluent Whiteness is opening up to her. To celebrate, she buys an expensive jacket on the way to catching the train, probably not a smart financial move after having pawned everything of value to try to raise money to pay Shaun San Dena and only earning $3800. But she feels great in the new coat, certain of her financial and social future.

Of course, things never work out in the new economy. To her horror, Christine discovers that her cursed button had been accidentally swapped with a rare quarter she was saving as a gift for her boyfriend, a coin collector. As both had been stashed in white envelopes, she mixed them up, meaning that she actually shoved the rare quarter into the dead woman's mouth the night before. She is still the owner of the cursed button. Before her horrified boyfriend's eyes, she falls onto the train tracks and is swallowed up into a flaming pit by a swarm of demon arms. Today's world is harsh, and one small slipup can ruin your chances at upward mobility, dragging you down to a horrifying world of White poverty.

CONCLUSION

Drag Me to Hell and *Dream House* offer competing visions of aspiration and social mobility for White folks in the Great Recession. While *Dream House* wallows in the horror of an affluent White man who finds himself destitute and literally squatting in the decrepit ruins of his former life, the film assures him and us that dreams and fantasies of reclaiming economic stability can help him recover his lost success and sanity. In a time of economic and personal crisis, he literally loses himself in the American dream, only to have his financial stability, social class, and humanity restored to him. By contrast, *Drag Me to Hell* offers a more cynical take for the young woman at its core, who finds that the exhausting processes of self-transformation necessary for social mobility in the neoliberal economy only lead to immorality and damnation. Her aspirations turn into nightmares that challenge her place in the White middle class.

NOTES

1. Scholars often mention *Drag Me to Hell* as an example of the recessionary horror film, given its subject matter and release at the start of the Great Recession. See, for example, Tim Snelson, "The (Re)possession of the American Home: Negative Equity, Gender Inequality, and the Housing Crisis Horror Story," in *Gendering the Recession: Media and Culture in an Age of Austerity*, ed. Diane Negra and Yvonne Tasker (Durham, NC: Duke University Press, 2014), 161–180.

2. Cynthia Miller, "Making the Hard Choices: The Economics of Damnation in *Drag Me to Hell*," in *Elder Horror: Essays on Film's Frightening Images of Aging*, ed. Cynthia Miller and A. Bowdoin Van Riper (Jefferson, NC: McFarland, 2019), 108–118; and April Miller, "Reel-to-Reel Recessionary Horrors in *Drag Me to Hell* and *Contagion*," in *The Great Recession in Fiction, Film, and Television: Twenty-First Century Bust Culture*, ed. Kirk Boyle and Daniel Mrozowski (Plymouth, UK: Lexington Books, 2013), 29–50.

3. April Miller's analysis in "Reel-to-Reel Recessionary Horrors" explores the gendered pressures that Christine faces in the workplace in more detail, as well as how Christine is asked to participate in a highly masculinized vision of capitalist power at the expense of her morality.

4. Cynthia Miller's analysis of *Drag Me to Hell* in "Making the Hard Choices" explores the Othering of Mrs. Ganush in terms of race and class but also around aging and abject imagery of older women. For Miller, Ganush disrupts the neat and tidy middle-class spaces of neoliberal capitalism, exposing all the messy realities that Christine tries to repress about herself and her background.

5. Her past self is also associated with pigs: she finds an old picture of herself back on the farm where she is overweight standing next to her prize pig. Her old self is unruly and associated with animals and dirt. See Kathleen Karlyn's chapter on pigs and unruly women in *The Unruly Woman: Gender and the Genres of Laughter* (Austin: University of Texas Press, 1995).

4

—ᴍᴍ—

SAD WHITE MEN AND THEIR DEMONS

Possession Films

IN THE FINAL MOMENTS OF the 2010 film *The Last Exorcism*, Reverend Cotton Marcus, a longtime practitioner of exorcisms that he admits are shams, finally comes face-to-face with evil. Throughout the film, Marcus insists that Nell Sweetzer—a young woman exhibiting signs of demonic possession—is really just a psychologically scarred victim of an abusive father. But when Marcus returns to the Sweetzer farm at dusk, he sees Nell strapped to a wooden table in a field. She is writhing in pain as she gives birth at the center of a Satanic ritual put on by her small-town community. A hooded figure, revealed to be the local pastor, helps deliver a bloody demon-child. He then tosses the child into a giant bonfire, sending the flames rippling into the sky. Clutching a crucifix that had up until now only been a prop in his farces, Marcus recognizes his duty as a man of God. He boldly steps forward to face off with the demonic ball of fire. His fate and that of Nell are unknown at the film's end.

Marcus's redemption provides the emotional payoff of the story; the cynical huckster embraces his faith and transforms himself into a man of virtue. Nell's tragic story literally acts as the background, the fiery stage upon which Marcus can redeem his faith and manhood.

Most other possession films include a similar story; the exorcisms provide salvation for the (almost always male) exorcist more than for the possessed (typically, but not always, women and children). As scholar Carol Clover wrote about occult possession films from the 1970s and '80s, behind the story of a possessed female is "always the story of a man in crisis."[1] In these stories, the possession of an innocent victim by an evil entity is simply an opportunity for the exorcist to overcome some kind of personal crisis and find the strength and moral certitude to conduct the exorcism. Demonic possession stories create unruly women and children who must be reined in by a male who was formerly dogged by doubt but comes to accept the righteousness of his moral authority.

Such narratives proliferated in mainstream US horror in the Obama era. Possession and exorcism films were scant in the 1990s and early 2000s, with only three produced between 1992 and 1999 (around 3% of all mainstream horror films in that period) and then another three between 2000 and 2008 (around 2% of all mainstream horror). But starting in 2009, Hollywood produced sixteen films with a significant possession and exorcism storyline, representing 10 percent of all mainstream horror films from 2008 through 2016. The films included standard Catholic exorcism narratives (*The Rite* [2010], *The Devil Inside* [2012], *The Vatican Tapes* [2015]), the Evangelical exorcism depicted in *The Last Exorcism*, and also several Jewish exorcism stories (*The Unborn* [2009], *The Possession* [2012]). This period also saw several generic mash-ups, like the police-procedural/exorcism film *Deliver Us From Evil* (2014), the *Inception*-inspired dreamworld exorcisms of *Incarnate* (2016), and the highly successful blending of haunted houses and possessions in the popular *Insidious* franchise, which also disrupted the usual focus on male occult experts with the charming character of Elise Rainer.

Possession stories explore a host of cultural anxieties around bodily control, rationality, and gender. Offering tales of ordinary people who find themselves engaging in bizarre and demented behavior, possession films negotiate our fears around identity and cultural norms. What would drive someone to commit horrific acts? Why might someone break foundational cultural taboos? And why can't rational science explain the sometimes-brutal mysteries of human behavior? Possession narratives allow for the vicarious pleasures of watching someone completely disregard social norms and let their base impulses take over, even when those behaviors are abject and horrifying. They also suggest that one must forsake the rigid structures of bureaucratic rationality to navigate the evils of the world.

These debates around rationality and cultural norms often yield an examination of gender roles in the possession film. Writing about 1970s and 1980s horror, Clover argues that possession stories in that period negotiated the changing meanings of manhood during the second wave of the feminist movement. For Clover, these possession films dramatized the tensions between cold, rational, masculine science and feminized, emotional spirituality. As the female body in the possession film becomes abject and horrific, the overly rigid and masculine male protagonist must reject the dictates of traditional manhood and become more open to emotionality, intuition, and (implicitly) homoeroticism. Reflecting the *new man* discourses of the post-Vietnam era, the male crisis storylines of the possession film transformed tough and terse men into more sensitive and emotional people who began opening up to the possibilities of the supernatural—but not too much, as the extreme "openness" of women and femininity made them ripe for demonic possession in the first place.[2]

The resurgence of possession stories in the Obama era also espouses the need for men to open up and embrace the supernatural. However, rather than yielding an introspective look at the horrors of hardened manhood, these more recent possession stories suggest that embracing faith and the supernatural will help downtrodden White men reclaim the cultural authority they have supposedly lost. In the possession films at the core of Clover's research, embracing a feminine "Black Magic" over a rational "White Science" meant rethinking the tough manhood celebrated in the early Cold War era. But in the Obama-era possession film, the gendered negotiation is inverted: ineffectual White men, supposedly stripped of their cultural and economic power by bureaucracy and multiculturalism, must reject official knowledge and institutions in order to reclaim patriarchal authority. Mirroring the backlash against science, education, and rationality by the far right in the US, the men of these possession films come to embrace a rigid spirituality based in moral polarity in order to reject the supposed chaos of the uncertainty, purposelessness, and emasculation of the modern world.

In this way, spirituality and faith are vehicles for reclaiming White manhood in a world in which the privileges of White patriarchy are challenged, even if only modestly. Obama-era possession stories largely explore the struggles of White manhood in the face of economic stagnation and the perceived devaluing of White patriarchy. Opening up, for these men, means finding their anger and righteous indignation now that their privileged place in the culture seems (to them) to be under siege.

Eventually, these fears would erupt in the form of Trump's 2016 presidential campaign. Trump combined misogynistic dismissals of his female opponent with overt calls to rejuvenate White manhood in America. He made populist appeals to the "Forgotten Man," the implicitly White, working-class man who was supposedly left behind in an era that values diversity. And he made persistent (and persistently false) claims that Obama had cut military spending so drastically that the armed services were left impotent. Trump ran a campaign exploiting White fears that traditional manhood was on the decline. So when recordings emerged during the campaign in which Trump boasted about sexually assaulting women, they were so easily dismissed as manly locker-room talk and sometimes even embraced by his supporters as evidence of his robust manhood.

Throughout the Obama era, the possession and exorcism film dramatized these uncertainties about American manhood. Telling stories of White men who have lost social standing or are facing debilitating personal crises, the possession film assumes that traditional male authority is in decline and focuses on angst-ridden White dudes struggling against a world in which they have lost their purpose. The demons that mock these men, however, set the stage for male rejuvenation, as the exorcisms conducted in the films assure the men that adherence to a strict moral order will restore their authority and give them a sense of meaning.

Of course, not all possession films see these struggles with male authority from the same perspective. Several innovative horror films in this period challenge the narrative of White male decline, examining instead the struggles of women who must choose between the temptations of evil and the brutal control of male authority—and can't decide which is worse.

THE EXORCIST AND BEYOND

While the belief in demonic possession and the practice of exorcism have a long (and continuing) history across a variety of religions, the contemporary possession film owes its existence to the phenomenal success of the 1973 film *The Exorcist*. William Friedkin's classic film, based on the novel by William Peter Blatty, spawned a host of imitators and parodies and explored the tensions between faith and science in the 1970s. In the film, Regan, the daughter of an American movie star living in London, begins exhibiting strange and decidedly unladylike behavior (cursing, urinating on the floor, breaking things with her superhuman strength). When the local doctors are at a loss, Regan's mother brings in Father Karras, a priest who has trained as a psychiatrist and whose faith in God has been shaken by the recent death of his mother. At first skeptical of demonic possession, Karras eventually becomes convinced and brings in the imposing Father Merrin—an expert on demonic possession—to perform the exorcism. Merrin dies in the midst of the exorcism, so Karras takes matters into his own hands. He tempts the demon to leave Regan and enter his own body, then sacrifices himself, throwing himself and the demon out of Regan's window to his death.

The Exorcist established the key themes and narrative devices of the possession film, from the priest nagged by self-doubt to the implication that women and children are particularly susceptible to demonic possession, especially in times of personal crisis. Regan, after all, is the child of a single working mother, the product of divorce being raised by a powerful woman. Karras renews his faith, then, by finally understanding that the unruly and rebellious behavior of a young woman is pure evil. While doctors and scientists dither with invasive tests and jargon, it takes Karras's faith in his own authority to save Regan.[3]

The Exorcist's concern with authority, faith, and generational conflict resonated with the cultural context of the 1970s. Such concerns were also reflected in other books and films in that historical moment. Historian Sean Quinlan analyzes The Exorcist novel alongside popular books-turned-movies, such as Rosemary's Baby (1967 book, 1968 film) and The Omen (book and novelization developed together in 1976), identifying a cycle of demonic and Satanic stories in popular culture. For Quinlan, these stories expressed a deep sense of generational mistrust stemming from the youth counterculture of the 1960s, as middle-aged and older Americans tried to come to terms with a generation that seemed to reject traditional values so vehemently.[4]

These generational conflicts, moreover, signaled a larger loss of faith in scientific and religious institutions. For Quinlan, these stories explored a world in which the authority of science and medicine, coupled with declining faith in the US, generated an acute ennui concerning traditional forms of authority. Stories of young people who struggled to be controlled by doctors, priests, or other authority figures resonated in the midst of these cultural struggles.[5]

Many of these historical tensions are mirrored in post–Great Recession America. Newer generations, such as millennials and Gen Z, have become a source of anxiety for older Americans as they enter into adulthood and positions of power with vastly different assumptions about labor, social media, and government.[6] At the same time, science and medicine have been politicized, with Americans now debating everything from climate change, to the dangers of vaccines, to the quality of health care. Thanks in part to a concerted effort by conservative politicians and groups, the perceived value of science and education in general is now closely tied to political affiliation.[7] More and more conservative Americans see appeals to science and intellectualism as, at best, out-of-touch elitism or, at worst, part of a globalist conspiracy to undermine American values.[8] And while Evangelical Americans have used this distrust in secular science to advocate for theological authorities, religious institutions overall have had their authority greatly diminished following the child sexual abuse scandals in the Catholic Church, other sex scandals involving pastors,[9] and the rise of a politically provocative Evangelical community obsessed with anti-LGBTQ messages.[10]

In the Obama years, these crises surrounding traditional authorities were often grafted onto a perceived crisis in White masculinity. Failures of traditional institutions such as education or science, from this perspective, stemmed from the dictates of "political correctness" within those institutions or even from the simple fact that academia has more women working in it than in the past.[11] Critics claimed that today's US universities privilege identity politics over unbiased inquiry, supposedly leading researchers to fabricate findings on climate change or destabilize White manhood by teaching feminism and multiculturalism. As secular institutions became more diverse, those institutions became suspect. Meanwhile, institutions that still largely centered on White manhood—churches—saw their faith in male authority repaid by sex scandals and other abuses of power.

The declining economic status of White working-class men was perhaps the most visible icon of the Obama-era masculinity crisis. Especially in the wake of the so-called "Man-cession"—the idea that the Great Recession impacted male workers more severely than female workers—the struggles of the White working class became a stand-in for a general sense of male victimization.[12] The economic anxieties of the White working-class male bolstered a larger and pervasive narrative of White decline—especially the idea that White men are victims in a more diverse and politically correct age.[13]

This yielded a lot of angry White men in the culture. A sluggish, neoliberal economy no longer rewarded non-college-educated White men with stable middle-class employment. Racial and gender equality became highly coveted values for many institutions, especially in higher education. And demographic shifts raised the specter of a majority-minority population in the near future. In response, many White men across social classes turned to anger and what one sociologist calls "aggrieved entitlement"—the fear that the privileges of White men in the past have been unfairly stolen from them.[14]

Possession films in the Obama-era mirror this anger and entitlement. Using the mythology of demonic possession to explore the supposed decline in male authority, these films argue that in order to contain the unruly women and children threatening the social order, the privileges of White patriarchy have to be restored to the sad and pathetic White men of the Obama years.

MEN IN CRISIS

The men at the center of this new wave of possession films seem to face two kinds of crisis when a demon enters their life: an economic crisis centered on their social standing and possible downward mobility or a personal crisis around their faith or their family. Most often, however, these crises are inextricable. Familial crises are tinged with the threat of losing social standing, economic crises around stable employment threaten to tear families apart, and crises of faith are set against the backdrop of economic and moral decay in the US. But at their core, these crises all center on besieged and despondent White men who have lost their sense of purpose.

The 2012 film *The Possession*, for example, centers on a recently divorced father struggling with the separation and his new social standing. In the film, Clyde—a dedicated and inspiring college basketball coach—has moved out of the warm, expansive family home that he made with his now ex-wife and two daughters. He now lives in a cheaply made suburban tract home in a partially completed subdivision. Presumably, the other homes were never built in the aftermath of the housing crisis, linking Clyde's somewhat pathetic new life with the new realities of the US during the slow economic recovery. Clyde's home is surrounded by empty dirt fields and only a few other completed homes. No neighbors are seen, and the film's cinematography draws out the eerie blandness and isolation of Clyde's new digs, where his youngest daughter starts showing signs of demonic possession (see fig. 4.1).

Meanwhile, back at Clyde's old home, his ex-wife has turned his old office into the headquarters of her new jewelry business, literally transforming his old space in the home into an economic opportunity for herself. Not only has he been displaced, he has been displaced by his wife's newfound entrepreneurship, and in a stereotypically feminine venture no less. To make matters worse, his ex-wife's new boyfriend has moved in, and he is an opera-loving intellectual, unlike Clyde, who has a more traditionally masculine job in sports. Clyde's isolated suburban home, then, illustrates not only his emasculation and expulsion from the family unit, but also his plummeting economic standing in the wake of the divorce as he tries to support both homes.

The 2008 film *Mirrors*, while not strictly an exorcism film, explores a similar crisis of manhood in the flailing economy. The protagonist, Ben, is a former NYPD detective who has been suspended from the force after he accidentally killed a fellow cop while working undercover. Ben's life has been in a guilt-induced tailspin ever since. He's popping pills and crashing at his sister's apartment after being kicked out by his wife. Thanks to his angry outbursts, he's not supposed to visit his children unannounced in the family home. The only work he can get in the rough economy is as a night watchman in an abandoned department store, an embarrassing step down in the law enforcement hierarchy. Naturally, the festering department store is a source of evil—a former psychiatric hospital with mirrors that contain the trapped spirits of its former patients, waiting to possess people when they gaze into the mirrors.

The Gothic ruins of the abandoned department store help tie Ben's failures as an authority figure to the struggling economy, especially since the closing

Fig. 4.1. An empty and largely abandoned suburban development becomes a site of demonic possession in *The Possession* (Ghost House Pictures, 2012).

of department store chains has long been a prominent indicator of sluggish retail sales and the decay of once-vibrant downtown commercial districts. The beautiful ruins of the art deco store in the film reveal the economic collapse of the US in the midst of the recession as old institutions crumble, just like Ben's authority.

The contemporary US possession film is populated with sad White men like Clyde and Ben, men who attained their version of the American dream and held respected positions of authority (coaches, cops) but find both their authority and their social standing slowly crumbling around them. In a world marked by divorce, intractable children, unemployment, and the fallout of a sluggish economy, men like Clyde and Ben find themselves adrift and purposeless, surrounded by cheap tract homes and decaying department stores, signs of their failures as breadwinners. The demons that plague their lives are a symptom of a world in which White men have supposedly lost their moral authority.

This trajectory also informs the 2016 exorcism film *Incarnate*, which focuses on another sad White dude who has lost his family. The protagonist, Dr. Seth Ember (we never quite find out what he is a doctor of), was born with a special gift for entering into the minds of possession victims. Refusing to use his talents, however, he builds a typical life for himself, with a wife and an eleven-year-old son. However, sensing his gifts, an archdemon dubbed Maggie possesses a woman, who then crashes her car into Ember's SUV, killing his family and leaving Ember paralyzed from the waist down. In the wake of the accident, Ember cultivates his paranormal skills, learning from other so-called incarnates and using his gift to help possession victims evict the parasitic entities that have taken over their minds. He ultimately hopes to find and kill the demon Maggie, so when a representative from the Vatican calls hoping he will help a young boy they suspect Maggie has possessed, he gears up for the eviction he has been waiting for.

The film makes sure we appreciate Ember's loss by using the imagery of social class. Before his accident, he is clean-cut, wearing a stylish suit as he drives his family around in his luxury SUV. But after the accident, he lets his hair grow long and stringy. His stubbly face never smiles, and he wears a dingy military jacket as he wheels around the city in his wheelchair, giving him the appearance of a struggling, disabled veteran (see fig. 4.2). His tech-support sidekicks are punk twenty-somethings that accentuate his new life on the fringes of society. He has lost not only his family, but his grasp on middle-class standing.

Of course, when men in possession films aren't facing economic crises, they still struggle with a sense of purpose or meaning in their lives. In *The Last Exorcism*, for example, Marcus is struggling with his own guilt and lack of faith as a purveyor of sham exorcisms. Having been trained in the art of the exorcism by his father, Marcus has spent most of his life performing exorcisms on those who think they need them. He thinks that the ceremonies are mostly harmless and may even offer a psychosomatic benefit, so he doesn't mind embellishing his performances with trick candles or other theatrical devices. But after hearing of the death of a young child in an exorcism ceremony, Marcus has a change of heart and sets off on one last exorcism with a documentary film crew in tow, determined to help reveal exorcism ceremonies as charades.

Likewise, in the 2011 film *The Rite*, the protagonist, Michael Kovak, is a young, disillusioned priest who only entered the seminary to get a free education. In an effort to keep him in the priesthood, his mentors in the US send Michael off to the Vatican to take a course on exorcisms and demonology, noting that there has been a sharp rise in claims of demonic possession. The church needs a new generation of exorcists. Skeptical of the course content, he is further advised to assist Father Lucas, a Welsh priest in Rome who routinely performs exorcisms around the city. (Apparently, if you are a young White priest with a crisis of faith, the church *really* thinks that you should be an exorcist.) Exposed to the unexplained and horrific cases that Lucas sees on a daily basis, Michael slowly discovers his faith.

Crises of faith in the contemporary exorcism film, however, are inseparable from anxieties about social class and Whiteness in the US. Narratives like *The*

Fig. 4.2.   A formerly affluent doctor is now a shabby possession specialist after his encounters with demons in *Incarnate* (IM Global, 2016).

Possession and *Mirrors* explore fears about White men losing authority and social standing, but for Michael in *The Rite* and Marcus in *The Last Exorcism*, their spiritual crises reveal anxieties about men who have lost touch with the working class. In *The Last Exorcism*, for example, Marcus has built an affluent suburban life for his family, thanks to his charismatic preaching and reputation as an exorcist. When he leaves his suburban bubble for the nether regions of rural Louisiana, he shows his condescension for what he thinks is the super-stitious zeal of poor rural folks. Nell Sweetzer's father bears the brunt of this condescension, as Marcus becomes convinced that the father is a stereotype of White-trash masculinity—an abusive, incestuous rural patriarch. But in the film, Marcus is forced by circumstances to realize a horrible truth: the father was right, and the world *is* filled with demons and Satanists around every corner. His affluent suburban condescension has failed him. This realization prompts him to toss aside his cynical worldview and face evil with a sense of earnestness.

Similarly, in *The Rite*, Michael comes from an anonymous working-class rust-belt town in the US. His father, a mortician, wants him to skip college and enter into the profession with him, but Michael is desperate to escape life in the downtrodden town. That ambition to leave takes him away to seminary and eventually to Rome, but after finding his faith renewed, Michael returns home, now dedicated to saving his economically depressed town from the demonic evil that fills the world. His revitalized faith and restored authority lead him back home to the heart of economic despair.

All exorcism films, then, envision a world of pervasive evil and chaos that threaten the social standing of White folks—fathers on the verge of financial and familial ruin or people living in downtrodden White communities, like the rural towns in *The Last Exorcism* or the rust-belt towns imagined in *The Rite*—who need heroic White men to save them.

This vision of chaotic evil and White male saviors finds a particularly muscular expression in 2014's *Deliver Us From Evil*, an odd genre mash-up that is equal parts police drama and exorcism film. In the film, Eric Bana plays Ralph Sarchie, a NYPD detective who works the night shift in Brooklyn with his knife-wielding adrenaline-junkie partner. Apparently, Sarchie has a sixth sense for people in crisis, which means that he has seen the worst that humanity has to offer. When we first meet him, he is hovering over the dead body of an infant who had been tossed into a dumpster, desperately trying to resuscitate the child. His constant contact with evil is turning him into a bad husband and father, and he is tormented by an incident in the past in which he beat a child molester to death with his bare hands in a secluded alley.

Things only get worse for Sarchie when he realizes that a series of seemingly unrelated incidents are all tied to a trio of Iraq war vets, now dishonorably discharged, who became possessed by an evil entity in an underground temple in Iraq. As he investigates the different incidents, he teams up with a heavy-drinking, chain-smoking former drug addict who is now an undercover priest, and Sarchie discovers his calling for battling evil. Eventually, Sarchie helps perform an exorcism on the leader of the former Marines and, in the process, saves his own family, who had been targeted by the possessed soldiers.

In this way, *Deliver Us From Evil* explores the horrors of White men who become depressed by a chaotic world that they cannot control. The possessed Marines are men struggling with the violence of war, men who became tainted by a foreign evil. Sarchie, likewise, is a sad but heroic man who is slowly becoming tainted by the moral degradation of the contemporary world and must find his own moral compass.

This moral degradation, of course, is expressed visually through the signifiers of poverty: the film's vision of a surprisingly White Brooklyn at night is filled with dilapidated apartments, dirty streets, and abandoned industrial buildings. Relying on the oft-used notion that the city is a cesspool of poverty and vice, the film links its vision of evil with economic decay. As in *The Last Exorcism* and *The Rite*, a landscape of poverty—especially White poverty—is clearly fraught with demonic activity. Rather than systemic economic investment, of course, what that landscape really needs is a confident male patriarch who can restore order (and, in *Deliver Us From Evil*, bust some heads in the process).

MORAL CLARITY AND THE RESTORATION OF MALE AUTHORITY

In the end of *Deliver Us From Evil*, Sarchie—who is based on the real-life occult expert Ralph Sarchie—rediscovers his lost faith, becomes a more committed family man, and devotes himself to ferreting out demonic activity in the city. The end credits reveal that the real Ralph Sarchie eventually left the NYPD to work full-time assisting those afflicted by demons, becoming prominent enough to work with Ed and Lorraine Warren on some cases. His transformation from cynical cop to spiritual demon-buster to acclaimed occult expert reflects a common trajectory across the contemporary exorcism film: the clear restoration of male authority and family values and the triumph of moral clarity. In the possession films of the '70s and '80s that Clover discusses, a transformation such as Sarchie's would hinge on his ability to accept feminization and spirituality. But in the 2010s, Sarchie's embrace of spirituality goes hand in hand with a process of remasculinization and restoration of unambiguous patriarchal authority.

As this suggests, these films also articulate a much more rigid vision of moral clarity than the older possession films studied by Clover. In past possession narratives, overly rational and rigid men must open themselves to new possibilities and greater knowledge than the masculinized world of science allows. These films emphasize flexibility and openness in the face of unbending manhood. But for the White men in the Obama-era possession film, embracing their faith means accepting an intractable vision of moral clarity. The films present a world of uncertainty and immorality (implicitly caused by the absence of White patriarchal authority), and the only way to find stability for unmoored White men is to accept an inflexible view of good and evil. Rather than opening up to a myriad of possibilities, these men must accept a rigid moral clarity organized around traditional families and White authority.

For example, in *The Rite*, Michael is only able to battle the demons all around him when he accepts that the world is black and white. Michael discovers that Lucas, prone to depression, given all the evil he has witnessed, is possessed. Although unprepared, Michael performs the exorcism and is sorely tested: the demon tries to exploit Michael's poor relationship with his father, who died while Michael was away in Rome. But just as the exorcism is about to go astray, with images of all the horrors that he has seen flashing before his eyes, Michael acknowledges that the demon is real and, thus, so must be God:

Demon/Father Lucas: Do you believe in me now, Michael? Do you believe in me now?

Michael: Yes. Yes, I believe in you. I believe in the Devil. I believe in you. So I believe in God. I accept him in this moment. I accept God. I believe in God, the father, and maker of heaven and earth and all that is seen and unseen. I believe. I exorcise you, most unclean spirit.

And then Michael uses his newfound faith and clarity to expel the demon. This insistence that seeing evil firsthand can restore a White man's faith is also noted in the film *Devil* by a sad cop whose family has been killed in a hit and run. The cop is given an opportunity to unlawfully take revenge on the culprit but decides not to after witnessing a series of horrors when a group of people are trapped with Satan in an elevator.

Incarnate requires a similar leap of faith. Ember realizes that in order to kill the demon and save the possessed young man, he has to commit to his own death, another noble self-sacrifice in the genre that celebrates men for doing whatever it takes in the face of true evil. For the troubled men in the exorcism film, salvation comes not simply through faith, but through a simple vision of moral clarity. While the world may be complicated in these films, evil is real and can only be defeated by those brave enough to acknowledge the reality of a spiritual world.[15]

Central to this worldview is its moral simplicity and clarity: evil is very real and requires constant vigilance, often in the form of traditional family values and patriarchal authority. This message is also conveyed by the most popular of the cinematic occult experts, Ed and Lorraine Warren (played by Patrick Wilson and Vera Farmiga and based on the real-life occult investigators). In the *Conjuring* films, the Warrens are actually the main characters as they sweep in to save families facing hauntings and possessions. But their prescription is always the same: strong families (i.e., White, heterosexual, Christian, nuclear families) will survive their paranormal trials, and the Warrens themselves are held up as exemplars of such values. In each film, the Warrens inspire the families to use their love for one another to triumph over the evil spirits, even as those spirits test the Warrens themselves and the sanctity of their own family.

Exorcism and possession films, then, posit the need for everyone to practice constant vigilance in the face of pervasive evil. In the opening of *The Vatican Tapes*, for example, two high-ranking Vatican officials are seen in news interviews describing the constant threat of Satan in the world. As one of them puts it, "From the day you are conceived, the devil seeks your destruction." This vision of constant, inescapable evil is both horrifying and reassuring. It imagines a dark world that requires discipline and a willingness to see the signifiers of evil that the mainstream ignores, but it also imagines a world where everyday people can be significant actors in an epic struggle with clear boundaries between good and evil. The world may be dark, but if you are willing to see the signs, the solutions are clear.[16]

This unflinching worldview in possession and exorcism films mirrors the logic of right-wing media commentary—both mainstream and on the fringes—that flourished in the Obama years and edged toward mainstream acceptance in the Trump years. From the rise of Breitbart to the surging popularity of Alex Jones, a wave of voices from conservative websites (often amplified by more mainstream conservative-leaning sources, such as Fox News), sold themselves as self-trained experts who would dramatically reveal what the mainstream media sought to repress. Seeking to undermine typical bastions of expertise like teachers and scientists, these voices were often directed at White men and claimed to reveal secret knowledge about masculinity and race relations that has been forbidden by political correctness.

This logic would find a particularly insidious outlet in the QAnon network of conspiracy theories, which played no small part in stoking the anger of a crowd of Trump supporters who stormed and vandalized the Capitol building on January 6, 2021, hoping to disrupt the official transfer of power to president-elect Joe Biden after Trump's election loss in 2020. For QAnon supporters and many Trump enthusiasts, the world looked a lot like a possession film: an inherently dark and evil world where scientists, educators, and commentators refused to acknowledge the nefarious demons that have taken control of our institutions. Only the dire actions of true believers could exorcise these demons. And so, like the exorcists and occult experts in horror films, this right-wing movement appealed to the entitlement of White manhood, arguing that only White male patriarchal authority—not scientists, academics, or other experts—could restore the greatness of America.

SAVING MANHOOD IN *INSIDIOUS*

Although the *Insidious* franchise tends to blend the haunted house film with the possession film—and it offers a dynamic and powerful female occult expert—the first film in the *Insidious* series demonstrates the genre's obsession with resuscitating White manhood and its power.

The first *Insidious* film introduces us to the Lambert family as they move into a beautiful new home with their two young sons and infant daughter. The father, Josh, is a dedicated schoolteacher, and the mother, Renai, hopes to revive her skills as a pianist after taking a break and having children. But after one of their sons, Dalton, takes a fall in the home's attic, he slips into a mysterious coma. Strange events then plague the stay-at-home mom: bizarre sounds come through the baby monitors, strange, dark figures appear in the bedrooms, and songs play on the piano when no one is around. Frustrated by the bleakness of the situation, the father retreats from the family, staying late at work when he doesn't have to. Unlike other families in a haunted house scenario, however, the Lamberts simply move when they are finally fed up, selling their home and moving across town. But when the strange events continue to afflict them, Josh's mother comes clean about a family secret.

When he was a boy, Josh was also subjected to strange supernatural events. Whenever he was photographed, a faint image of an old woman dressed in an antique black wedding gown always appeared behind him. At first, the woman materialized at a great distance from Josh in the photos, but as time passed, her image moved closer to his. When the woman appeared in one photo directly behind Josh, her hand resting on Josh's shoulder, Josh's mom brought in an expert, Elise Rainer, a clairvoyant with a knack for solving bizarre paranormal problems. Elise revealed that Josh was an accomplished astral projector. While sleeping, Josh could explore a spirit world called The Further, a mirror image of our world where the spirits of the dead and other entities roam. While exploring in his sleep, Josh had been noticed by a malevolent spirit, dubbed the Bride in Black, who sought to take possession of the young man. The easiest solution was simply to hypnotize Josh to repress his powers, essentially making him forget that he can astrally project, thus making him off-limits to the Bride in Black.

Now, years later, his son has inherited his abilities and has been taken hostage in The Further by a different insidious demon who wants to possess him. While Dalton's body remains unoccupied, other spirits are drawn to it, causing the strange events in the home. The only solution is for Josh to revive his powers, venture into the strange landscape of The Further, and free his son from the insidious demon, all while avoiding the Bride in Black, who surely has been waiting for Josh's return to the spirit world.

While Elise Rainer and her comic-relief tech support provide the secret knowledge that can save Dalton, ultimately men must literally reclaim their lost powers in order to revive the struggling nuclear family. Because of the emasculating threat of the Bride in Black, Josh was forced to repress his natural gifts, and while that allowed him to lead a seemingly normal life, his powers must be restored to face off with the evils that haunt his family. That his mother, helped by a female occult expert, hypnotized Josh in the past into forgetting his powers only accentuates his emasculation. Although well-meaning, the hypnotism he underwent as a child is hindering the adult Josh from fulfilling his promise as a man. He is still living under the protective spell of his mother and Elise Rainer,

Fig. 4.3. Josh encounters unsettling scenes of grotesque nuclear family domesticity in The Further in *Insidious* (Film District, 2010).

and only his escape from that protection will provide the opportunity for him to man up, as it were. Reflecting the common refrain of so-called men-rights activists that the contemporary world asks men to unfairly repress their natural manhood, male power must be restored to the patriarch in *Insidious* before he can undertake his quest.[17]

When Josh reassumes these powers, he must navigate the uncanny mirror image of his family home in The Further. Now dark and filled with a sickly mist, the home is the site of unsettling scenes of grotesque nuclear family domesticity. Most notably, Josh finds a traditional nuclear family frozen in time in his inverted living room, the mother at the ironing table, the father reading the newspaper, and a daughter sitting happily in a pretty white dress next to her father. They are perfectly still and unmoving, except for the occasional blink, with dark makeup around their eyes, giving them the appearance of corpses. Josh finds their other daughter, also clad in a girlish dress, in the kitchen preparing her rifle. Hearing gunshots, Josh returns to the living room to find the family slaughtered, their eldest daughter standing over the bodies with a maniacal grin plastered on her face. The Further, it seems, is horrific not only because it is filled with the spirits of the unsettled dead, but also because the nuclear family is a gruesome reflection of its wholesome ideal—static, oppressive, and violent (see fig. 4.3). Gendered norms and ideals are tossed aside as the pretty young daughter pelts her family with bullets.

Josh must rescue his son from this space where the gendered norms of the White nuclear family are degraded, where the White patriarch quietly reading his newspaper has no authority to protect his family from the violent whims of his deranged daughter. Appropriately, Josh effects this rescue through masculine antics—a fistfight with a tough spirit in a leather jacket with long, greasy hair—before confronting the cloven-footed demon holding his son hostage. Josh must reassert his masculine authority in the inverted world of The Further in order to protect his family. He faces off with the emasculating force of the Bride in Black, whom he is unable to defeat until the sequel.

CONCLUSION: CAUGHT BETWEEN DEMONS AND PATRIARCHY

Not all of the possession films from this period follow this general trajectory of men under siege who find solace in the moral certitude of a world of demons. Several take up alternative narratives, although they often revolve around the question of male power and authority.

The nonlinear narrative of *Oculus* (2013), for example, centers on a highly motivated and resourceful young woman whose father had become possessed via an antique mirror when she was young and murdered his wife. Now an adult, she and her brother bring the mirror back to their childhood home with the hopes of proving its occult powers. Ultimately, the woman hopes to vindicate her father's memory, but the mirror has other plans for her. Similarly, *The Devil Inside* follows a young woman hoping to investigate a possessed parent—in this case her mother, who killed several people while possessed by a demon. The woman, now an adult, brings a documentary film crew to investigate her mother, who is housed in a Vatican-run mental hospital, and eventually convinces several priests to attempt another, unauthorized, exorcism. But the narrative eventually switches from the young woman to the two priests, who are struggling with the Vatican's rules limiting the exorcisms they can perform and who become susceptible to possession themselves.

But the most prominent alternatives to the male-centric possession film are a series of films exploring possession and the stifling structures of patriarchy: *Jennifer's Body* (2009), *The Last Exorcism 2* (2013), and *The Witch* (2015).

Jennifer's Body, written by Diablo Cody and directed by Karen Kusama, tells the story of a popular high school girl, Jennifer, who becomes possessed by a demon after a sleazy band tries to sacrifice her in an occult ritual. As Jennifer seduces and feasts on her classmates (mostly male), her insecure and codependent best friend has to decide if she can still be friends with a demonic succubus. The film humorously skewers the genre conventions of the slasher genre as it explores issues of friendship between women.

By contrast, *The Last Exorcism 2* and *The Witch* provide narratives exploring patriarchy and its obsession with controlling young women. These films expose the reactionary gender politics of the Obama-era possession film, demonstrating the unequal negotiations between masculinity and femininity in the narrative formula. In the possession films of the '70s and '80s, according to Clover, the exaggerated abjection of the possessed female body is necessary to renegotiate the closed and hardened manhood of the protagonist; in order for them to "meet in the middle," the female body must be pushed to the extreme to facilitate the softened, more open masculinity of the protagonist.[18] The female body is still pushed into extreme and taboo behavior in the Obama-era possession film, but rather than making room for a more nuanced manhood, the abject female body simply provides the pretext for male control and authority. So in films that privilege the point of view of women tempted by demons into evil and possession, it's no wonder the women think that possession looks like a better alternative than patriarchy.

The Last Exorcism 2 abandons the found-footage style of the first film and opens with Nell—having inexplicably survived the Satanic ritual, perhaps because of Marcus's intervention—wandering out of the woods. She enters a nearby house in a trancelike state. The police take custody of her and eventually send her to a halfway house in New Orleans for troubled young women. Freed from the constraints of her religious father's house, Nell begins to explore the world and even develop a fledgling romance, but strange figures haunt her from a distance, and she is troubled by intense sexual dreams. People around her start dying. She eventually seeks help from a secret society that has been stalking her in the hopes of keeping demonic activity at bay. They tell her that the demon has fallen in love with her and if she accepts the demon, it will be a sign of the end of times. She reluctantly agrees to a ritual to expel the demon but realizes that the people helping her are more than willing to sacrifice her life to deny the demon her body.

The Witch also tells the story of a teenager beset by both evil forces and those who claim to want to help her. When Thomasin's family is banished by the Puritans in New England in the 1630s for being too conservative in their view of the Bible, the family makes a new homestead deep in the wilderness. But when Thomasin's newborn sibling is kidnapped by a witch in the woods, her deeply religious parents begin to suspect that Thomasin is involved. Soon after, Thomasin's younger brother, who had been harboring incestuous feelings toward Thomasin, becomes possessed by the witch, and the parents place the blame on Thomasin (despite the fact that the family's young twins have been talking to the family goat, Black Phillip). Eventually, the goat gores the father to death, and the mother tries to strangle Thomasin, believing her to be the source of the evil. Thomasin is forced to murder her own mother.

In the end of both films, the women choose evil over patriarchy. In *The Last Exorcism 2*, after the secret society injects Nell with poison to keep her from accepting the demon, Nell chooses instead to embrace demonic possession. She suddenly has the strength to survive the poison, kill the would-be exorcists, and go on a spree of destruction. She returns to the halfway house and burns it to the ground, killing her new friends. In the final shots, Nell drives the streets of New Orleans and uses her powers to set fire to anything she passes, taking pleasure in the destruction of the world.

Similarly, in *The Witch*, Thomasin speaks to Black Phillip, who speaks back to her and takes a human form, asking her to sign his book in exchange for earthly pleasures. She does so and wanders into the woods, finding a coven of nude witches. She joins their circle, undresses, and gleefully levitates with them, reveling in her new powers.

The young women at the center of these films reject the stifling structures of patriarchy, deciding to take their chances with demons and the pleasures of evil. Nell, fed up with the purity-focused control of her father, decides to give in to the pleasures that society keeps telling her are bad. For Thomasin, after being isolated by her family's oppressive religious beliefs and denied any kind of joy in life, the promises of Black Phillip sound like freedom. Ogled by her sexually repressed brother and subjected to her parent's violence, Thomasin decides to take pleasure and power where she can. Unlike the sad White men who dominate the possession cycle in the Obama era, these young women aren't interested in rejuvenating the authority of imperiled patriarchs.

The final scene in each film reveals a different kind of opening up for women than is typical in the possession film. As Clover details, the female body in such narratives is seen as too open—too easily penetrated by evil—and this is conveyed through grotesque and taboo behavior. The female body becomes ugly, distorted, hypersexual, and violent—in short, quite unladylike. The female anatomy becomes a monstrous portal for demons, who encourage a rash of behavior that disrupts traditional gender norms. The monstrosity of such behavior then necessitates male intervention.

But *The Last Exorcism 2* and *The Witch* both end with scenes of women's power and pleasure and highlight the freedoms and ecstasy of young women who suddenly find themselves extricated from patriarchal control. From Nell's manic laughter as she sets New Orleans ablaze to the look of wild joy on Thomasin's face as she levitates naked with the coven, it becomes clear that these two women are opening themselves up to alternatives to patriarchy and finding elation and emancipation, not the grotesque nightmares of the men who want to control their bodies and sexuality. Given the rigid moral vision across most of the Obama-era possession films, these endings provide a rather powerful challenge to the dominant narrative trends, suggesting that maybe it would be better (and certainly more fun) to just let the world of White patriarchy burn to the ground in a frenzy of female laughter and pleasure.

Of course, neither film performed well at the box office. The moral clarity of *The Conjuring* films, with their insistence on White patriarchal authority, seemed to resonate more in the Obama years.

NOTES

1. Carol Clover, *Men, Women, and Chainsaws: Gender in the Modern Horror Film* (Princeton, NJ: Princeton University Press, 1992), 65.

2. Ibid. For Clover, the negotiations between the monstrous openness of the female body and the rigid, closed-off nature of masculinity allow for a complex exploration of gender identity and performance in the possession narrative of the '70s and '80s.

3. Ibid., 65–113. Clover offers a detailed reading of the gender negotiations of *The Exorcist*, demonstrating that Regan's hyperbolic and taboo behavior makes room for the overly rational Karras to open himself to faith and more nuanced masculinities.

4. Sean Quinlan, "Demonizing the Sixties: Possession Stories and the Crisis of Religious and Medical Authority in Post-Sixties American Popular Culture," *Journal of American Culture* 37, no. 3 (2014): 314–330.

5. Ibid.

6. For an example of this generational tension in popular discourse, see Jean M. Twenge, *Generation Me—Revised and Updated: Why Today's Young Americans Are More Confident, Assertive, Entitled—and More Miserable Than Ever Before* (New York: Atria, 2014), in which Twenge outlines the many anxieties that older generations feel about the rise of millennials in the US.

7. See, for example, Lawrence C. Hamilton, "Education, Politics and Opinions about Climate Change Evidence for Interaction Effects," *Climatic Change* 104 (2011): 231–242. Additionally, researchers have found that individual decisions around vaccinations are often driven by political ideology, not by a deficit of knowledge on the issue. See Bert Baumgaertner, Juliet E. Carlisle, and Florian Justwan, "The Influence of Political Ideology and Trust on Willingness to

Vaccinate," *PLoS ONE* 13, no. 1 (2018), https://doi.org/10.1371/journal.pone
.0191728.

8. For more on the social psychology behind science denial, see Kristin Haltinner and Dilshani Sarathchandra, "Climate Change Skepticism as a Psychological Coping Strategy," *Sociology Compass* 12, no. 6 (2018).

9. For a discussion of Evangelical church sex scandals, see Elizabeth Dias, "Her Evangelical Megachurch Was Her World. Then Her Daughter Said She Was Molested by a Minister," *New York Times*, June 10, 2019, https://www.nytimes .com/2019/06/10/us/southern-baptist-convention-sex-abuse.html.

10. For example, see the widely covered activities of the Westboro Baptist Church, which organized protests of the funerals of fallen soldiers as part of their anti-abortion, anti-LGBTQ ideology, or of the Evangelical shock-jock pastors such as Doug Wilson, who proactively suggested that executing LGBTQ people today would be condoned by the Bible.

11. Nancy S. Niemi, "Why Does the Public Distrust Higher Ed? Too Many Women," *Chronicle of Higher Education*, April 13, 2018, https://www.chronicle .com/article/Why-Does-the-Public-Distrust/243114?key=2K4N4HYtD2a A1V-c_T84p2lvrzcVrcnmYJrvzIw3tfUs3n48voHArlQJP7P-ah1PekkxTVRPcm81SzU1MmlTLUlQaWRUSFFsYVBWU3ZJWkUyOUNMMGxtWUhtVQ.

12. For a discussion of the male workforce that engages in this narrative of White working-class despair, see Binyamin Appelbaum, "The Vanishing Male Worker: How America Fell Behind," *New York Times*, December 11, 2014, https:// www.nytimes.com/2014/12/12/upshot/unemployment-the-vanishing-male -worker-how-america-fell-behind.html.

13. Michelle Rodino-Colocino analyzes the gendered dynamics of the "Mancession" moral panic, arguing that the media discourses around White manhood in the Great Recession stifled larger discussions of inequality within neoliberalism capitalism that could have led to broader challenges to the existing system, in "The Great He-Cession: Why Feminists Should Rally for the End of White Supremacist Capitalist Patriarchy," *Feminist Media Studies* 14, no. 2 (2014): 343–347.

14. Michael Kimmel, *Angry White Men: American Masculinity at the End of an Era* (New York: Nation Books, 2013). Also, see Annie Kelly's analysis of alt-right masculinity in this context of perceived victimization in "The Alt-Right: Reactionary Rehabilitation for White Masculinity," *Soundings* 66 (Summer 2017): 68–78.

15. This worldview is often shared in haunted house films, in which tormented families are advised by an occult expert who offers a kind of secret knowledge outside the mainstream. Like exorcism figures, these characters usually play a prescribed role in the narrative: to assure tormented families that there is a logic to their predicament, but one that exists outside Western rationality and science.

They initiate the family into an alternative worldview that is horrifying—a world of spirits, demons, and astral fields—but also deeply reassuring because it can explain the unexplainable incidents plaguing the family.

16. For a lengthier discussion of how horror cinema navigates religious and spiritual debates, see Douglas Cowan, *Sacred Terror: Religion and Horror on the Silver Screen* (Waco, TX: Baylor University Press, 2008).

17. The themes of emasculation and male rejuvenation are also evident in *Insidious, Chapter 2*. After the events of the first film, the audience discovers that Josh's body is now possessed by the Bride in Black, while Josh's spirit remains in The Further. Josh's spirit then haunts his wife to get her attention, leading to the revelation that the Bride in Black is actually the spirit of a male serial killer who was systematically abused by his mother. Josh has been possessed by the spirit of a gender-deviant serial killer, and the only way to survive is to face off with the bad mother who set this cycle of emasculation into motion.

18. Clover, *Men, Women, and Chainsaws*, 105.

5

SUFFERING AND RELUCTANT MOTHERS
MEET THEIR MATCH

Horrific Children

MARIA HARWOOD, THE PROTAGONIST OF the 2016 horror film *The Other Side of the Door*, drops to her knees early on in the film, hands pressed to her face, sobbing. Maria is centered in the frame, and the camera lingers on the shot for a few seconds so we can wallow in the sight of her collapsing onto the tile floor. Maria and her eldest daughter, Lucy, survived a traumatic car accident while living in Mumbai, but her younger son, Oliver, died. When their car crashed into a river and was submerged, Maria was able to help Lucy to the surface. Young Oliver's leg, however, was pinned, and Maria couldn't pull him out of the sinking car. Plagued by guilt, Maria sobs on the tile floor of their home after her husband leaves for work, and eventually she attempts suicide but lives. So when her live-in maid and nanny, an Indian woman named Piki, tells of an abandoned temple where an ancient ritual can allow Maria a few more brief moments with Oliver, a desperately sad Maria attempts the ritual, with disastrous results, naturally. Soon, horrific visions of Oliver and other ghastly figures haunt her family.

While the possession and exorcism films of the Obama years make a spectacle of sad White men who believe their authority is deteriorating, a cycle of films about horrific and demonic children offers the other side of the coin: a spectacle of suffering White mothers (or would-be mothers) whose maternalism has been called into question. Contemporary US horror films with ghastly or evil children tormenting those around them—whether sociopathic child killers or children from beyond the grave—almost always tell stories of suffering White mothers. This includes mothers who have lost children and must cope with the pain and guilt, women who have miscarried and have yet to cope with their loss, and women whose tortured relationships with their own mothers have left them fleeing motherhood but who then find themselves struggling to be caretakers to traumatized children.

Maria's situation in *The Other Side of the Door* illustrates the particular Whiteness of this maternal suffering in the horror film. While these kinds of tragedies impact all women (in fact, women of color, especially African American women, experience higher rates of reproductive trauma than White women in the US[1]), the horror film privileges the spectacle of White tragedy. Maria's grief in *The Other Side of the Door,* for instance, is set against the backdrop of poverty in India. The sprawling inequality of Mumbai—which the film exploits for its exotic appeal—certainly contains a multitude of personal tragedies and unspeakable grief. But the suffering of poor Indians is simply the colorful backdrop to Maria's all-encompassing anguish. As she is a White mother who has lost a child, her grief is a black hole in the narrative, inescapable and all-consuming. Maria didn't even know that her longtime nanny, Piki, had also lost a young child (despite the painfully obvious shrine to the daughter in Piki's room). Though Piki tells Maria her own story of loss, it nevertheless remains a minor subplot in the film. White tragedy is the film's central fixation.

This fixation on the suffering of White women is the primary feature in a set of horror films deploying the imagery of horrific children. While not a discrete subgenre like the possession and exorcism film, these films share a central visual occupation with creepy children who terrorize the adult world. Sometimes this occurs in the context of other subgenres, like the haunted house film (as is the case in *Sinister* [2012], *The Woman in Black* [2012], *The Other Side of the Door,* and others). Sometimes the imagery of horrific children is integrated into hybrid genre films, such as the horror/sci-fi film *Splice* (2009). Or sometimes it functions as its own small cycle in which mysterious children are integrated into a family home and horror ensues (*Orphan* [2009], *Case 39* [2009], and *Mama* [2013]). All these films, however, share similar narrative concerns with White motherhood: the creepy and monstrous children plaguing the White family are signs that something is amiss with White motherhood today.

Such narratives proliferated in the Obama-era horror film. While the use of horrific child imagery in horror has historically been a small but persistent visual trope, starting around 2009, that trope was more frequently deployed by horror filmmakers and more often in narratives around White motherhood. Between 1980 and 1991, Hollywood produced nine horrific child films, representing around 5 percent of mainstream horror output. Another three were produced between 1992 and 1999, and another four in the early 2000s, representing around 3 percent of mainstream horror in each of those periods.

Between 2008 and 2016, however, Hollywood produced twenty-two horrific child films, around 15 percent of all mainstream horror in the Obama era.

Individually, some of these horrific child films seem genuinely invested in exploring reproductive traumas that used to be taboo but are now discussed more openly in US culture. *The Disappointments Room* (2016) addresses the traumas and grief surrounding infant mortality, *Annabelle* (2014) seems to be a loose allegory for postpartum depression, and *The Boy* (2016) centers on a woman who grieves over a miscarriage, for example. Indeed, compared to the domineering, evil, and murderous mothers traditionally depicted in US horror—from "Mrs. Bates" in *Psycho* (1960), to Mrs. White in *Carrie* (1976), to Mrs. Voorhees in the first *Friday the 13th* (1980)—the mothers in recent horror films feel almost progressive, thanks to filmmakers' willingness to imagine moms and would-be moms as actual human beings with complex emotions who may justifiably struggle with the impossible demands of motherhood.[2]

But as a group, this cycle exhibits a tendency to punish White women who have turned their backs on motherhood or who have failed as mothers in some way, subjecting them to the bizarre torments of demonic, psychopathic, or haunted children (or sometimes haunted dolls that resemble evil children). These moms may not be monsters like their horror foremothers, but the hordes of creepy children across the films enact a cultural desire to see White women punished for their transgressions, especially transgressions of their supposed maternal instincts. On film at least, White mothers or would-be mothers bear the brunt of the culture's anxieties about declining White birth rates, the behavior of younger generations, and the supposed decline of White privilege.

However, much like the possession film, the horrific child film wallows in the spectacle of White suffering only to offer clarity and redemption for many of the characters. The women come face-to-face with their own horrific offspring (sometimes figuratively, sometimes literally) and are given a chance to "mom up" and rejuvenate their maternalism, even if—ironically—they have to do so by murdering children, albeit evil ones. These narratives would seem to reveal the depravity of the nuclear family with their explorations of filicide, parricide, and the sins of families in the past, but as a whole, the films tend to torture White women just enough for them to get the message and find and embrace their maternal instinct.

HORRIFIC CHILDREN, SUFFERING MOMS, AND DEMOGRAPHIC ANXIETIES

Several classic films paved the way for the contemporary horrific child narrative, exploiting the uncanny imagery of evil children. Children should be symbols of innocence that affirm life and regeneration. But as icons of horror, they become uncanny reminders of death and the decay of the institution of the family. The 1956 psychological horror *The Bad Seed* and the 1960 British sci-fi horror film *Village of the Damned* (and its 1964 sequel, *The Children of the Damned*) are particularly important cinematic touchstones for creepy child stories, especially those involving unnaturally blond children. The narrative has popped up in popular culture periodically since then, with films such as *The Omen* (1976) and its 1978 sequel, *The Brood* (1979), the *Children of the Corn* series (1984, 1992, and a host of straight-to-video releases through the mid-2000s), including Macaulay Culkin's turn at villainy in *The Good Son* (1993), and others.[3]

Historically, these tales hinge on our fears around generational change and shifting social mores. Horrific children exaggerate the culture's fears that young people may fundamentally change the world that older people have grown accustomed to. This fear has been a particularly potent obsession in the US in the wake of the baby boomer generation, as each successive population wave terrifies the one that preceded it. First the boomers challenged the status quo through the youth counterculture of the '60s and '70s, and now Gen Xers and millennials are horrifying the boomers by challenging the cultural, political, and economic norms the boomers established, at least according to social-media clickbait that exploits these generational tensions. Soon millennials will be terrorized by the so-called Generation Z as they ascend to cultural and economic power. Cinematic horror stories about evil, demonic, or easily manipulated children who turn against the adult world tap into these ongoing generational tensions, exploring a grotesque vision of youthful rebellion.

For film scholar Vivian Sobchack, for example, the spate of "cannibalistic, monstrous, murderous, selfish, [and] sexual" children in the horror film in the early 1970s reflected "bourgeois society's negative response to the youthful movements and drug culture of the late 1960s and early 1970s."[4] In particular, these horrific children on film exposed the perceived decline of the patriarchal order and the inability of parents to contain and control their abhorrent offspring. These terrorizing youngsters threatened the stability of the White bourgeois nuclear family, and the films included revolting images of supposedly innocent children who, instead of reproducing patriarchy for the future, terrorize their fathers and mothers. Sobchack argues that these horrific children gave way in the late 1970s and early 1980s (starting with *Carrie* in 1976 as a transitional film) to stories of children from broken homes terrorized by their parents, dramatizing further the failures of the patriarchal family. In both cases, "the horror film shows us the terror and rage of patriarchy in decline (savaged by its children or murderously resentful of them)."[5]

Sobchack focuses particularly on fathers either terrorized by their children (e.g., *The Omen*) or terrorizing them (e.g., *The Shining*), but the contemporary horror film explores a decline in patriarchal values around the figure of the mother more than the father. In the Obama era, horror stories tend to put the blame for abhorrent or unnatural children on mothers—and White mothers in particular—and explore the supposed decline of the traditional White family in an age of multiculturalism.

These horrific child films explore the nightmarish inverse of White mom culture in the US. The impossible expectations that US culture places on mothers often morphs women—both real and represented—into horrible monsters who threaten the social order. Just ask Sady Doyle, whose book *Dead Blondes and Dead Mothers* traces a long history of US culture imagining women who defy social norms as terrible monstrosities. For Doyle, the strict expectations of patriarchal culture translate any kind of female deviance or, even more unsettling, female power into exaggerated stories of monsters, demons, or witches.[6] These expectations are often more pronounced for White women and mothers in particular, who bear the cultural burden of perpetuating White patriarchal culture; deviance from their delineated roles as wives and mothers within the nuclear family yields hyperbolic reactions and tales of evil afoot.[7]

The expectations for White mothers today are especially strict; the late 1990s saw the rise of the new momism, which asked White middle-class moms to embrace perfection,[8] and there has been a trend toward what Emily Matchar calls the "new domesticity,"[9] in which women are performing tasks associated with traditional domesticity—knitting, canning, or raising backyard chickens, for example. The new domesticity in particular has boomed among progressive White women, fueled by trendy social-media influencers.[10]

This new movement pressures women to publicly embrace traditional domesticity and motherhood in addition to holding successful careers (rather than, say, advocating for more equal divisions of household labor between men and women). In a neoliberal era that demands more from individuals in the capitalist economy, the new domesticity only increases the burden on women, expecting them to be educated, work full-time jobs, raise children, complete the lion's share of household chores, take up knitting, and post beautiful photos of their children frolicking with idyllic chickens on Instagram to appropriately demonstrate that you can "have it all."[11]

If the new domesticity establishes the idyllic benchmark for White motherhood in the contemporary US, the horrific child film reveals the nightmare of maternal failures, of being seen as a bad or tainted mother. Lurking behind the exaggerated wholesomeness of knitted beanies and gingham-topped mason jars lies a dark abyss of gendered pressures. In the US, we tend to place the

blame for most social ills—from crime to poverty to the generational conflicts mentioned above—on mothers and their parenting choices, so the culture's impossible standards on mothers are not simply fraught benchmarks but
threats: publicly embrace wholesome motherhood or face public scorn, a threat
made more common in a social-media era that has streamlined public shaming.
These impossible pressures to enact ideal motherhood find expression in horrific stories of violent, feral children and gory images of reproductive trauma,
animating the fear of failure and being seen as a bad mother—a failure that, in
US culture at least, is akin to being a bad woman.

The fear of being seen as a bad mother, moreover, is especially pronounced
in an era of racial resentment and declining White birth rates. Throughout
the Obama years, demographers and pundits speculated on the possibility of
White folks comprising less than 50 percent of the population, spurred on by
the US Census Bureau's 2014 report suggesting that just such a demographic
shift could occur by 2044, sooner than expected.[12] Demographers have debated
the veracity of that prediction, which hinges on whether multiracial or multi-
ethnic populations who identify as White actually count as White. But conservative commentators in particular latched onto the predictions to perpetuate a
narrative of White decline, or what columnist Charles Blow refers to as "White
extinction anxiety."[13] According to this logic, if Whites no longer outnumber
people of color in the US, White Euro-American culture will be decimated
and rooted out, leading White-nationalist conservatives such as Pat Buchanan
to claim that a failure to stem the tide of non-White immigration is a form of
"Western suicide."[14]

White mothers seem to bear the blame for these shifting demographics, as
they can't seem to keep up with their non-White, immigrant counterparts when
it comes to making babies, at least according to the logic of Republican Steve
King, who doesn't want "somebody else's babies" taking power in America
down the road.[15] In reality, fertility rates are declining across most racial and
ethnic groups in the US, but public discourse on race and birth rates focuses
primarily on the reproductive capacity of White women. For example, when
Census Bureau data from 2017 indicated that the US birth rate wasn't producing
enough babies overall to replace the population, right-wing media outlet Breitbart rhetorically laid the blame on women, claiming that "American women are
having less and less children needed to sustain the current population," while
hinting that White women in particular are at fault and announcing, "White
American births plummet in all 50 states and the District of Columbia."[16]

A major cause of these declining birth rates is women's equality; as women
attain more independence and autonomy, motherhood and the number of
children women have are seen as choices rather than social obligations.[17] In

essence, according to a conservative interpretation of the data, as White women have gained more social power and economic stability in the US over the past several decades, they have been derelict in their racial duty to maintain the White population for the next generation.

The horrific children lurking in the Obama-era horror film are grotesque manifestations of this worldview, there to punish White women for trying to determine the terms of their own motherhood by saddling them with horrific offspring. The contemporary horrific child cycle singles out White mothers who have failed—whether because of reproductive traumas such as miscarriages or infant deaths or because of their reluctance to choose motherhood over their own independence—and tries to reform them. First these women are relentlessly tormented and threatened with the loss of their social standing and affluence. Then they are offered the opportunity to redeem their maternal instincts and become the White mothers that the culture thinks it needs.

REPRODUCTIVE TRAUMA, WHITE MOTHERHOOD, AND SOCIAL CLASS

Horrific children are indicators of troubled parents in the horror film, the canary in the coal mine indicating the selfishness and degradation of parenting in the modern age, or really, the failures of mothers, who bear the burden of their children's bad behavior in Western cultures. The sinister, dead-eyed children who haunt the contemporary horror film express our fears that mothers today have failed not only their children, but society as a whole.

The suspect nature of modern motherhood often yields abject images of reproductive trauma on film. In the opening scenes of *Orphan*, for example, which are shot through a hazy filter, the protagonist dreams of her recent pregnancy that ended in a stillbirth. She checks into a hospital, ready to give birth, but as she is slowly wheeled across the floor, she starts hemorrhaging blood, which drips through the seat of her wheelchair (see fig. 5.1). An overhead shot reveals the long smear of blood she has left behind. She then dreams of a messy operation, after which the doctor hands her a mangled baby bundled in blood-stained cloths, as if it were still alive. We later learn that her real-life birth experience left her struggling with alcoholism, and while she was drunk, her two older children fell into an icy pond and almost died. Recovering from these crises, the family turns to an ill-fated adoption, and the mother has to confront a monstrous, sociopathic child in her home, as if her trauma and failures as a mother have birthed a horrible offspring that tries to tear the family apart.

The horrific child film is replete with similar stories of trauma and grief. In the 2009 film *The Unborn*, for example, a young woman is haunted by a

Fig. 5.1. Blood drips through a hospital wheelchair in a nightmare of traumatic birth at the start of *Orphan* (Dark Castle Entertainment, 2009).

pale-faced young boy dubbed Jumby, a Jewish *dybbuk* who has been trying to infiltrate her family since her grandmother was a young girl in the Holocaust and her twin brother became possessed by the demon during bizarre occult experiments. Now the young woman—who herself was a twin, though her twin brother died in the womb—sees visions of reproductive trauma everywhere she turns, from a blue-eyed fetus she discovers buried in the ground to a vision of Jumby plunging his hand through her stomach and into her womb. A similar pregnancy-possession narrative plays out in *Devil's Due*, in which an American woman back from her honeymoon in Latin America discovers she is pregnant. As her pregnancy becomes more traumatic and violent, her husband suspects she is carrying a demon child that she was impregnated with while they were abroad.

Less supernatural narratives of reproductive and maternal trauma present themselves in films like *The Boy*. In the film, a young American woman flees an abusive relationship by taking a job as a nanny at an isolated English estate, only to learn that her charge is really a lifelike doll whose elderly parents treat him like a real child. We later learn that the nanny had miscarried a child after being beaten by her ex-boyfriend, leading her to feel maternal toward the doll, which she increasingly feels might actually be alive. In *The Disappointments Room*, likewise, a mother struggles with her own sanity after accidentally smothering her infant daughter while they were sleeping together. After a failed suicide attempt, she moves her family from the city to a dilapidated country estate, where she begins seeing visions of a young girl being tormented by a ghostly dog.

The protagonist of *Annabelle*, meanwhile, is stabbed in the stomach while pregnant by Manson-style cultists who are in the midst of a murder spree in the late 1960s. She delivers her baby safely but struggles with early motherhood, especially when she begins to suspect that one of the dolls in her collection might be possessed with an evil spirit related to the cult attacks.

The persistent emphasis on bloody childbirths, demonic fetuses, and infanticide in the films reflects the long-standing obsession with abject mothers in the horror film. Scholars such as Barbara Creed explore the horror film's core fascination with what she calls the "monstrous-feminine," especially horrific and castrating mothers who express the culture's unease with female reproduction.[18] The stories and imagery comprising the monstrous-feminine reflect the broader cultural disavowal of menstruation, the messiness of childbirth, and other realities of the female body that mark it as impure or unclean in Western cultures. For the contemporary horror film, the female body and its reproductive capacity are still a source of horror and gore.

But the insistent imagery of grotesque reproduction in these films also indicates a kind of cultural guilt around White women's reproduction and maternalism, with the gory imagery of "motherhood gone wrong" suggesting that motherhood has gone wrong on a larger scale. These images of reproduction hint that motherhood today has become tainted somehow.

As I note above, this guilt reflects demographic anxieties about White women not having enough babies and the possible future of a White minority in the US. The blame we put on White women for declining fertility rates, after all, is intertwined with issues of privilege and social class: Will White folks retain their privileged position and the socioeconomic benefits they accrue in a White-supremacist society if Whites are no longer a majority in the US? That declining fertility rates are tied to economic and cultural equality for women only heightens these tensions. White women are choosing careers, independence, and economic stability over larger families or having any children at all, imperiling patriarchal White culture for their own individual gain, at least according to this conservative cultural logic.

In the films, this flight from motherhood has disastrous results, not only for the family, but for their affluence. The emergence of the horrific child in these films inevitably challenges the class standing of the afflicted families, as the creepy children set off a series of events that undermine the prosperity and independence White women have built for themselves. In this way, the films here function similarly to the first season of *American Horror Story*, in which images and narratives around dead or stillborn children evoke the stagnation of the US middle classes in the wake of the housing bubble, according to Dawn Keetley.[19]

In *Orphan*, for example, the family's sprawling home, nestled idyllically in the woods, becomes a site of terror as the seemingly sweet adopted daughter is revealed to be a thirty-three-year-old psychotic Russian woman with a hormone condition that gives her the appearance of a preteen girl. At the climax of her psychological assault on the family, she dresses herself provocatively in an attempt to seduce the husband, but her outfit also marks her low-class standing, evoking abject Eastern European Whiteness. Her somewhat tasteless appearance mars the affluent family home.[20]

Likewise, in *The Boy*, the protagonist's life in the wealthy estate is threatened when her abusive working-class boyfriend shows up, and the film reveals that the family's little boy, believed to be dead, is still alive and living in squalid conditions in hidden compartments in the mansion, where he clandestinely manipulates the doll to make it seem alive. Behind the veneer of old money and affluence lie corruption and squalor (see fig. 5.2). And in *The Disappointments Room*, the hidden room inside the estate, a vestige of White violence and White power that has fallen into disrepair, also signals the larger degradation of the White family over time. For the protagonists in these films, reproductive trauma initiates not only the horror of a creepy child, but also the loss of control of their class standing; the mother in *The Disappointments Room* can't keep hold of her wealth and privilege, while the woman in *The Boy* has her upwardly mobile aspirations dashed.

The strange behavior of creepy children (or creepy dolls) also casts aspersions on a family's attempt to maintain their social standing in other films. In *Don't be Afraid of the Dark*, the young girl's outlandish behavior (prompted by creepy elf-like figures) threatens to thwart the career advancement of her father and his fiancée when she embarrasses them in front of wealthy would-be investors. For the widowed single mother struggling to make ends meet in *Ouija: Origins of Evil*, the possession and subsequent strange behavior of her youngest daughter threatens their ability to maintain their middle-class lifestyle. And in *Annabelle*, the new mother struggles with her social position as a doctor's wife

Fig. 5.2. A squalid apartment lies inside the walls of a stately manor, hiding the violent and corrupt secrets of a wealthy White family in *The Boy* (Lakeshore Entertainment, 2016).

in the 1960s. Nice middle-class stay-at-home moms are supposed to put on a happy exterior, even while being haunted by a demonic doll.

For the protagonist of 2016's *Lights Out*, the relationship between low social standing and the ghost of an obsessed teen girl is explicit. The haunting and crazed antics of her mother leads a twenty-something daughter to leave her sprawling, affluent suburban home to live a gritty urban lifestyle on the edge of poverty (before her younger half brother ropes her back into the family's ghost issues).

Likewise, in the 2009 film *Case 39*, the introduction of a demonic child into the tidy life of a Portland social worker threatens to drag her back into the low social standing of her childhood, when her mentally ill mother terrorized her. Even though the social worker cares for vulnerable children as part of her career, she has made a middle-class life for herself that revolves around her job, not romance and family. She embodies cultural fears around young, middle-class White women who choose careers over family and reproduction. But when she takes in a seemingly sweet little girl, her independent life becomes a nightmare.[21]

Even as the films attempt more complex representations of issues like miscarriage, grief, mental illness, and postpartum depression, White women's bodies are envisioned as inhospitable and anti-maternal, prompting a psychotic or demonic child to infiltrate their fragile family unit and, by extension, tarnish White social standing.

REJUVENATING MOTHERHOOD

If the horrific child film acknowledges that pregnancy, childbirth, and motherhood in general can be traumatic for women today, those traumas largely exist in the narrative as challenges that devoted mothers will work to overcome. In the face of domestic anxieties and cultural concerns around appropriate motherhood, such films mostly affirm the need for White women to embrace motherhood. Whether they are young women who didn't want to have children or mothers who need to rejuvenate their commitment to mothering, the protagonists of the horrific child film—like the sad White men of the exorcism film—find renewed purpose by embracing maternalism with a vengeance.

That said, many narratives of horrific children do acknowledge the historical failures of the White patriarchal family. Films such as *The Boy* and *The Disappointments Room* explore the brutal evils of wealthy Whites who try to repress their depravity only to have it torment others over the years. Additionally, many horrific child films feature subplots around mentally ill mothers who prompt younger generations to avoid motherhood—*The Unborn*, *Splice*, *Case 39*, and *Lights Out*, for example. These storylines expose the nightmarish inverse of the nuclear family ideal in the US, signaling the brutality of White affluence and the lingering impacts of past traumas.

But by placing these traumas in the past or in older generations, most of the Obama-era horrific child films insist that women must overcome the moral decay of the White family and reinvigorate their maternal instincts. White patriarchal culture may have made a mess of family values, but White women today are still expected to clean up the mess.

For example, often in these stories, young women who had avoided motherhood for a variety of reasons (including tortured relationships with their own mothers) find themselves drawn into maternal roles. In *The Unborn*, the college-student protagonist has to work through her feelings about her mother—long dead after committing suicide while institutionalized—as she unravels the mystery of the demon stalking her. Eventually she discovers a long-lost grandmother (and Jewish heritage) and realizes that her mother was dealing with the same persistent *dybbuk* that now plagues her. In the end, she ends up pregnant with twins and knows that she must fight to protect her children from evil forces. In *Don't be Afraid of the Dark*, the young, pretty stepmother has to advocate for her fiancé's daughter when she starts behaving strangely, especially as the father puts his career over his family. Ultimately, the stepmother sacrifices herself to the evil elf creatures that enter the house through a portal in the basement, saving the child in a demonstration of her maternal instincts and dooming herself to be transformed into an evil elf. In *The Boy*, the young nanny runs away from relationships and motherhood after her abusive boyfriend's violence caused her to miscarry—fleeing from the US to her new post in the UK—but her experiences with the seemingly haunted doll lead her to the revelation that she wants to be a mother, a prospect hinted at through her budding relationship with the charming local grocer.

A young woman's commitment to family and maternalism is also at the center of *Lights Out*. Years after running away from her mentally ill mother, Rebecca is drawn back into her family drama when she gets a call from the school of her younger half brother about his chronic sleepiness, prompting an investigation into the family home by Child Protective Services. Although Rebecca is commitment-averse (she won't even let her boyfriend keep a single sock at her apartment), she decides to take her brother in, only to have CPS chastise her that she is not mother material. Eventually, she and her brother discover that the source of their mother's ostensible mental illness is the spirit of a young girl, Diana, who the mother met in a mental institution when they were children. In a bizarre experiment, Diana was killed, or really she became a shadowy entity that cannot be seen in the light and has latched itself onto the mother, driving away anyone who might take the love and attention of the mother away from her, even her children.

The film, then, doubles its maternal redemption stories. The mother, finally realizing the need to protect her children from Diana, discovers the only way to kill the evil spirit: the mother must kill herself, as Diana is attached to her life force. Her maternal self-sacrifice, witnessed by Rebecca, also redeems the daughter's faith in the mother, and at the film's end, Rebecca is now committed to making a new nuclear family with her younger brother and her boyfriend, who more than proved his commitment to her by helping her confront an evil spirit.

Other variations of this trope see moms whose motherhood has been called into question struggling to reassert their maternal responsibilities. In *Annabelle*, the demonic doll and its antics only punctuate the new mother's struggle to embrace motherhood. But the young mom finds her maternal groove thanks to the intervention of her neighbor Evelyn, an African American bookseller with a strangely vast knowledge of the occult, who is still grieving over the loss of her own daughter in a car accident years before (mirroring the magical non-White nanny in *The Other Side of the Door*, whose own story of grief plays second fiddle to that of the victimized White woman). Tempted to consider suicide, the mother in *Annabelle* is spared when Evelyn kills herself in order to keep the demon at bay, another example of maternal self-sacrifice, this time with a stereotypical wise Black mother sacrificing herself for the benefit of the middle-class White family.

This trope is repeated in *The Disappointments Room*, in which the White mother, plagued by guilt (and possible insanity), must reinvigorate her own sense of motherhood. By confronting the ghosts of a small girl and the stern father figure who murdered that girl decades ago, the mother is able to cathartically address her own guilt and failures, renewing her faith in her ability to be a mother to her older son.

The most dramatic instance of maternal rejuvenation comes in *Orphan*, however. When the mother, still grieving after a stillbirth, has to confront the sociopath posing as a young girl, she violently strikes back against her tormentor, who has already murdered her husband and is now coming after her children. The final confrontation comes at the pond in the backyard of their house—the same pond where her two children had almost drowned when she, drunk and grief-stricken, wasn't paying attention as they fell through the ice. This time, however, the pond becomes a site of redemption as the mother saves her children, kicking her psychopathic "daughter" into the icy depths of the water. Ironically, she redeems her motherhood by murdering a child—or at least what looks like a child.

Horrific children certainly express the culture's anxieties about motherhood, caregiving, and the responsibilities that we put on parents—especially mothers—to achieve perfection, but they also set the stage for women to rejuvenate their maternal instincts, rehabilitating the suffering White mother.

MAMA

The 2013 film *Mama* clearly illustrates these maternal tensions and the eventual rehabilitation of White mothers. *Mama* tells the story of a young, reluctant mother figure: Annabel (Jessica Chastain), whose boyfriend, Lucas (Nikolaj Coster-Waldau), adopts his orphaned nieces. When we first meet Annabel, she is taking a pregnancy test in the couple's messy urban apartment. The test comes up negative, and she expresses her relief at avoiding the domestic trap that would be motherhood. But motherhood comes calling anyway. Lucas has been searching for years for his two missing nieces, who disappeared into the woods with their father—Lucas's twin brother—after he went on a killing spree when his life fell apart following the economic crash of 2006–2007. Lucas has kept the desperate search for the two young girls going despite the odds, and one day it pays off. The men he pays to search the woods discover a small, dilapidated lakeside cabin in which the children have been living. The girls, Victoria and Lilly, have slowly turned feral and, unbeknownst to Lucas, have been kept alive by a strange, dark figure in the cabin.

That figure, Mama, has developed a maternal affection for the girls and follows them to their new home, a sprawling suburban house that a reluctant Annabel moves into with Lucas, after giving up her hip urban loft. Over time, Annabel begins to develop a maternal attachment to Victoria and Lilly, especially when the girls' aunt threatens to challenge the young couple for custody. But the dark figure's maternal attachment is just as strong and is revealed to be the spirit of a disturbed young woman, Edith, who escaped from a nearby asylum in the 1870s after nuns had tried to take her newborn baby away. Desperate, Edith jumped off a cliff. But in the fall, her baby got snagged on a protruding branch. Her spirit has haunted the area since, desperate and confused as to the whereabouts of her baby. Mama, then, had raised the young girls since they were young, having saved them from their unhinged and suicidal father.

In the end, Annabel musters up all the maternalism she has to confront Mama, who has taken the girls back to the same cliff near the lake and intends to repeat her suicide with them, this time ensuring that their spirits stay with her forever. The older girl, Victoria, however, chooses Annabel instead of death, affirming Annabel's status as a worthy mother. But the younger girl, Lilly, for whom Mama has been the dominant parent in her life, goes over the cliff. She and Edith dissipate into a beautiful cloud of dark butterflies after sharing a brief moment of quiet peace as they fall. The film ends before we get a chance to see Annabel and Lucas attempting to explain to the police how Lilly turned into butterflies.

Just as *Orphan* does, *Mama* indicates the need for women—in this case millennials who are reluctant to embrace nuclear family domesticity—to revitalize their maternal instincts. Throughout much of the film, Annabel can barely contain her annoyance that her hip urban lifestyle has been turned on its head because of Lucas's family responsibilities. With short black hair, tattoos, and a punk-rock style (to match her gig in a punk band), Annabel embodies the culture's stereotypes about selfish White millennials in the US, who supposedly only want to live in cities in hipster enclaves, playing in bands instead of settling down, buying homes, and starting families. The exceptionally bland suburban home that she and Lucas move into to raise the girls is stifling to Annabel's sensibility, especially as the malevolent Mama begins to torment her. Indeed, Mama acts as a kind of punishment for Annabel turning her back on family and domesticity; the recalcitrant Annabel is forced into a nightmare of suburbia, where she must parent near-feral children while a terrifying murderous entity proves to be a better mother than she is.

Of course, one could forgive Annabel for being wary of the supposed goodness of traditional family structures. The film opens with a seemingly wholesome and affluent father going on a killing spree and attempting to murder his own children when his social standing is threatened by the financial crisis of the mid-2000s. By invoking the crisis in the opening scenes, the film reveals the violence and brutality that lurk under the surface of the White nuclear family. For fragile White men like Lucas's brother, it only takes a personal economic downfall for that violence to bubble to the surface. The supposed threat to White male authority in the wake of the Great Recession uncovered the raw emotions of American manhood—and in this narrative, the raw brutality of men terrified of their own failures.

The dilapidated lake house where Victoria and Lilly are raised by Mama signals this decay of the moral and economic security of the White family. A 1950s or 1960s bungalow with wood paneling and modernist decor, the cabin has been abandoned and has fallen into disrepair (maybe thanks to the presence of Mama, who has roamed that forest since her death in the 1870s). Its style harkens back nostalgically to the postwar period often (mis)remembered as a period of domestic tranquility and economic prosperity for all. But its postwar quaintness has faded and literally fallen apart, leaving behind only a decrepit ruin of its former self. The cabin becomes the inverse of the American family ideal, a space where fathers attempt to murder their children, where unstable and obsessive mothers raise wild and filthy daughters (see fig. 5.3).

As in many haunted house narratives, the root of this moral decay can be found in the history of White patriarchal oppression. The family's ordeal actually begins in the 1870s, with White priests and nuns forcing an unruly young woman to give up her child in the name of traditional family values. Edith's trauma, while seemingly far removed from Annabel and Lucas, is actually part of a deeply interconnected history of violence underpinning the idea of the family in the US.

But while the patriarchal structures of the Catholic Church initiate the trauma at the heart of this story and the father's violence rends the family apart at the start of the movie, it is apparently Annabel's responsibility to restore the integrity of the family by embracing motherhood in the film's conclusion. The story of Mama—who so desires motherhood that she continues to kill in order to maintain her connection with Victoria and Lilly—seemingly helps Annabel realize the power of her own maternal instincts. She learns from Edith's story

Fig. 5.3. A dilapidated, mid-century cabin where Mama raises two feral children shows the degradation of White nuclear family domesticity in *Mama* (Universal Pictures, 2013).

that the choice of motherhood wasn't always a choice for women in the past and that she needs to see motherhood as a blessing. Despite exposing the long history of moral decay in the American family, the film still insists that Annabel must embrace motherhood to rejuvenate not only her own maternalism, but also the goodness of the family in general. She must recant her millennial selfishness by understanding that the fate of the family rests on the shoulders of mothers, at least according to the logic of the culture.

CONCLUSION

Not all horrific child films allow the mother to reclaim the White family's wholesomeness. For example, *Ouija: Origins of Evil* (2016) ends with the total destruction of the family when the single mother fails to hold her unruly daughters together. And in a common trope of the horror genre, several films offer ostensibly happy endings marred by last-second jump scares suggesting that the horror is still out there, including *The Woman in Black 2* (2014), *Sinister 2* (2015), and *The Other Side of the Door.*

The 2009 sci-fi horror *Splice* provides a particularly dark and critical perspective on motherhood. In *Splice*, Clive and Elsa are young hotshot geneticists who have built a splashy reputation as innovative and iconoclastic celebrity scientists. Living together but unmarried, they work as a team designing and producing new species that could produce medical breakthroughs for a massive pharmaceutical corporation. When their corporate bosses want them to spend more time on an older breakthrough to ensure that it yields profitable results, the couple secretly moves forward on a far more innovative and exciting project: the creation of a human-animal hybrid using an anonymous human DNA sequence.

The experiment results in the birth of Dren, a humanlike creature with a long prehensile and venomous tail, whom the two scientists raise as their own child in a secluded barn near Elsa's childhood home (a home that she had vowed never to return to because of her now-deceased mentally ill mother). But as Dren gets older—which happens quickly because she ages at an accelerated rate—the relationships between the three are strained. Clive, concerned about the ethics of their experiment, had never warmed to Dren and often considers whether she should be euthanized, straining his relationship with Elsa. Clive later discovers that Elsa used her own DNA to create Dren, using science to make herself an offspring rather than having a baby in the more traditional manner with Clive. Meanwhile, Dren becomes increasingly anxious to explore the outside world and experience life.

Elsa, then, exemplifies the would-be mothers throughout the cycle of horrific child films. A young woman who has devoted herself to her career instead of raising a family, thanks to the trauma of growing up with a mentally ill mother, Elsa must care for an abject offspring who tears her life and career apart. A narcissistic hipster who has carefully cultivated her own minor celebrity status, she is, like the White mothers across the cycle, punished for flouting her maternal responsibilities as a young White woman in the US.[22]

But the maternal rejuvenation for Elsa is a horrific nightmare as events spiral out of control. In a fit of anger over Dren's behavior (perhaps suggesting that the mental illness of Elsa's mother is genetic), Elsa coldly mutilates Dren by amputating the venomous stinger on her tail. Later, as Elsa and Clive's relationship deteriorates, Clive and a now-teenage Dren become attracted to each other and eventually have semi-incestuous sex (with Dren sprouting a new stinger while orgasming). Elsa walks in on them and is horrified. But when they both decide to end the experiment by killing their horrific (but sympathetic) offspring, Dren—seemingly dead—actually morphs into an aggressive male of her species as part of her life cycle. After raping Elsa, the now-male Dren attacks Clive and is killed by Elsa, but not before he can sting Clive, killing him.

While many other films in the horrific child cycle of this period end by asserting the power and wholesomeness of motherhood—with their protagonists embracing their newfound roles as mothers—*Splice* ends with Elsa, now pregnant as a result of being raped by her genetically modified offspring, essentially selling herself and her child to her corporate employers, who want to use her child to manufacture profitable pharmaceuticals. The film certainly follows through on the cycle's tendency to punish the young White women who shirk traditional families and maternalism, but there is no redemption for Elsa as her pregnancy and motherhood become corporate commodities.

Splice, however, is an exception that draws out the more cynical nature of this cycle. Suffering White mothers in most other horrific child films are given an opportunity to embrace maternalism and assuage the pressure we put on them to save the future of Whiteness in the US.

NOTES

1. Cynthia Prather, Taleria R. Fuller, William L. Jeffries IV, Khiya J. Marshall, A. Vyann Howell, Angela Belyue-Umole, and Winnifred King, "Racism, African American Women, and Their Sexual and Reproductive Health." See also Roni Caryn Rabin, "Huge Racial Disparities Found in Deaths Linked to Pregnancy," *New York Times*, May 7, 2019, https://www.nytimes.com/2019/05/07/health/pregnancy-deaths-.html?action=click&module=News&pgtype=Homepage.

2. For more on the long history of evil mothers in horror, history, and popular culture, see Sady Doyle, *Dead Blondes and Bad Mothers: Monstrosity, Patriarchy, and the Fear of Female Power* (Brooklyn: Melville House, 2019).

3. Andrew Scahill offers a detailed history and theory of the horrific child, including a useful discussion of childhood innocence and a taxonomy of how children are used in cultural representations. For Scahill, the horrific child is an important site to investigate queer spectatorship through such images distorting and unsettling bourgeois family norms. See Scahill, *The Revolting Child in Horror Cinema: Youth Rebellion and Queer Spectatorship* (New York: Palgrave Macmillan, 2015).

4. Vivian Sobchack, "Bringing It All Back Home: Family Exchange and Generic Exchange," in *American Horrors: Essays on the Modern American Horror Film*, ed. Gregory Waller (Urbana: University of Illinois Press, 1987), 182.

5. Sobchack, "Bringing It All Back Home," 185. For Sobchack, this shift in the representation of children in the horror film must be understood in relation to shifts in the family melodrama and science fiction genres of the same historical period, which took up similar narratives around patriarchal authority, imagining worlds of patriarchal ascendence that offset the patriarchal rage seen in the horror film.

6. Doyle, *Dead Blondes and Bad Mothers*.

7. This is not to deny that White patriarchal culture is not especially cruel to women of color and mothers of color. But in the cultural imagination in the US, White women and White mothers are so venerated as central to the mythology of the wholesome nuclear family that the rejection of traditional feminine roles by White women is met with especially reactionary responses.

8. See, for example, Judith Warner, *Perfect Madness: Motherhood in the Age of Anxiety* (New York: Riverhead Books, 2005); and Susan Douglas and Meredith Michaels, *The Mommy Myth: The Idealization of Motherhood and How It Has Undermined All Women* (New York: Free Press, 2004).

9. Emily Matchar, *Homeward Bound: Why Women Are Embracing the New Domesticity* (New York: Simon and Schuster, 2013).

10. Framed in environmental terms or as a response to a broken food system, the so-called new domesticity is celebrated by its practitioners as an extension of the feminist movement, rejecting the obsession of second-wave feminism with workplace advancement alone and reclaiming domestic tasks that empower women to make more environmentally friendly choices for their families.

11. Moreover, the resources and leisure time required for many of the pursuits of the new domesticity limit such hobbies to middle-class and more affluent households, making the new domesticity an affirmation of White social standing in the culture.

12. United States Census Bureau, "Projecting Majority-Minority: Non-Hispanic Whites May No Longer Comprise Over 50 Percent of the U.S. Population by 2044," accessed May 11, 2021, https://www.census.gov/content/dam/Census/newsroom/releases/2015/cb15-tps16_graphic.pdf.

13. Charles Blow, "White Extinction Anxiety," *New York Times*, June 24, 2018, https://www.nytimes.com/2018/06/24/opinion/america-white-extinction.html?action=click&module=Opinion&pgtype=Homepage.

14. Pat Buchanan, "Trump and the Invasion of the West," Patrick J. Buchanan: Official Website, June 19, 2018, https://buchanan.org/blog/trump-and-the-invasion-of-the-west-129497?doing_wp_cron=1556910904.9412651062011718750000. See also Jennifer Rubin, "The Demographic Change Fueling the Angst of Trump's Base," *Washington Post*, September 6, 2017, https://www.washingtonpost.com/blogs/right-turn/wp/2017/09/06/the-demographic-change-fueling-the-angst-of-trumps-base/?utm_term=.6e751361b6c6.

15. Jonathan S. Tobin, "Other People's Babies and American Values," *National Review*, March 14, 2017, https://www.nationalreview.com/2017/03/steve-king-other-peoples-babies-tweet-undermines-conservative-american-values/.

16. John Binder, "Data: White American Births Below Replacement Level in Every State," *Breitbart*, January 13, 2019, https://www.breitbart.com/politics/2019/01/13/states-birth-rate-2017/.

17. Claire Cain Miller, "Americans Are Having Fewer Babies. They Told Us Why," *New York Times*, July 5, 2018, https://www.nytimes.com/2018/07/05/upshot/americans-are-having-fewer-babies-they-told-us-why.html.

18. Barbara Creed, *The Monstrous-Feminine: Film, Feminism, Psychoanalysis* (London: Routledge, 1993).

19. Dawn Keetley, "Stillborn: The Entropic Gothic of *American Horror Story*," *Gothic Studies* 15, no. 2 (November 2013): 89–107. Keetley offers a rich and nuanced exploration of the ways that the stagnant economy intersects with the stagnation of life and motherhood in the film series.

20. In this way, *Orphan* and the horrific child cycle overall reflect an increasing media narrative around affluent White mothers who get more than they bargained for when they adopt troubled Russian kids with attachment disorders. News stories about Russian adoption problems tend to perform the same cultural work as the horrific child film, telling stories about middle-class White women who delay motherhood until later in life and pay the price. See, for example, Kate Pickert, "Russian Kids in America: When the Adopted Can't Adapt," *Time*, June 28, 2010, http://content.time.com/time/magazine/article/0,9171,1997439,00.html.

21. As films like *Lights Out* and *Case 39* indicate, the horrific child film often relies on the trope of the mentally ill mother to explain young women's aversion to maternalism, placing even more blame on White mothers.

22. In this way, films like *Splice*, alongside *Lights Out*, explore the fraught power relationships between young women and their troubled mothers, a clear pattern in these films, as many include narratives about mentally ill mothers. For more on the dynamics between White middle-class young women and their mothers in the context of post-feminism and the tensions of motherhood, see Kathleen Karlyn, *Unruly Girls and Unrepentant Mothers: Redefining Feminism on Screen* (Austin: University of Texas Press, 2011).

6

MOTOR CITY GOTHIC

White Youth and Economic Anxiety in
It Follows and *Don't Breathe*

AFTER THE HOUSING MARKET CRASH of 2007 and subsequent recession, the city of Detroit solidified its place in the US popular imagination as the exemplar of poverty and despair. Images of its once-thriving but now decrepit middle-class neighborhoods are frequently used in news, documentaries, and popular culture to signify the devastating economic fallout of the Great Recession and provide visual proof of urban decay and the failures of the American dream.

Such images appear in two recent Detroit-set horror films that tap into the Gothic potential of Detroit's crumbling neighborhoods: the critically acclaimed indie-slasher homage *It Follows* (2014) and the popular home invasion film *Don't Breathe* (2016).[1] Each film relies on the gorgeously shot spectacle of Detroit's crumbling neighborhoods to tell stories about young White women who must confront the horrors festering in the dilapidated ruins of the old middle class. Of course, despite the disproportionate impact of the Great Recession on people of color in the US and in Detroit in particular,[2] each film uses the images of a Gothic Detroit to tell stories of White Detroiters and the horrors they face in a postrecession world.

In both *It Follows* and *Don't Breathe*, the spectacle of a decaying Detroit exposes the nagging fear that White Americans were at risk of losing social standing in Obama's America. In *It Follows*, although the mysterious curse in the film is often interpreted as a reference to sexually transmitted diseases, the shape-shifting monster also dramatizes the stifling economic realities for millennials, especially White teens who face a far more precarious economy than their parents did. In *Don't Breathe*, the formerly middle-class family home becomes a trap (full of secret compartments and monstrous sexual threats) for the poor White protagonist seeking to escape Detroit and its poverty. In each film, the real horror is that young White folks might not be as out of place against the backdrop of Black poverty as they once were.[3]

These racial anxieties make Detroit the perfect Gothic setting for a postrecession America. The Gothic tradition in literature and cinema tends to focus on dilapidated mansions or castles as sites where the horrors of the past can never be truly laid to rest. British Gothic literature of the late 1700s and early 1800s challenged the narrative of progress emerging from the nascent Industrial Revolution, suggesting that a traumatic past will always haunt the present. Similarly, the Southern Gothic tradition focuses on sprawling Southern plantations, where the horrors of slavery continue to fester in the post–Civil War South.[4]

Detroit's landscape of urban decay provides a glaring reminder of the economic collapse of the mid-2000s, illustrating the persistent presence of this past trauma. But this landscape speaks more to a White nostalgia for a thriving suburban middle class than it does to the poor people of color who bore the brunt of the Great Recession. As David Church argues in his careful analysis of It Follows, the suggestions of "ruin porn" in the film (images exploiting the spectacle of urban decay) evoke an ambivalent kind of nostalgia, suggesting the decay of Detroit's former glory while simultaneously acknowledging that its glorious past was also full of inequality, racism, and community disinvestment. After all, the inequalities of neoliberal capitalism that left Detroit reeling in the mid-2000s hardly started with the Great Recession; as Church outlines, Detroit set itself on a path of racial inequality and urban decay almost immediately after World War II by shifting quality manufacturing jobs away from the cities and into predominately White suburbs.[5] In Detroit's contemporary Gothic imagery, the troubling, traumatic past of urban decay is a reminder of the neoliberal logic that at one time benefited the White middle classes but has now found its way into White suburbs. The horror of collapsing urban infrastructure intertwines White guilt and fear that the same processes of disinvestment that created White prosperity are now being applied to White suburbs.

In this version of a Motor City Gothic, then, the stagnant remains of formerly prosperous White neighborhoods are a warning to White youth vying for upward social mobility as they are engulfed by the kinds of urban poverty typically suffered by people of color in the US. Nostalgia for a whitewashed vision of past prosperity only reveals a haunting reminder of what White folks have done to communities of color in the past and what lies in store for young White people today. As Juan Valencia argues about It Follows and Don't Breathe,

the suburban home became "monstrous in these films because of the truthful unmasking of what capitalist greed has done to Detroit."[6]

IT FOLLOWS

The low-budget indie film *It Follows* (2014) introduces us to its protagonist, a teenage girl named Jay, as she wades into her family's aboveground pool, whose water, shaded by the surrounding trees, looks chilly and is peppered with dirt and debris. Enjoying the solitude, Jay notices a small bug crawling on her forearm and slowly immerses her arm in the water so the bug floats away.

Jay's pool is the perfect image of her precarious class status in the film. The idea of a built-in backyard swimming pool with the sun glistening off its pristine waters is a prevalent symbol of affluence in the US (see Clark Griswold's fantasies of installing one for his upper-middle-class family in *National Lampoon's Christmas Vacation* [1989]). But the aboveground pool, a cheaper imitation, perfectly represents lower social standing: Jay's family aspires to upward mobility, but a dirty aboveground pool is all they can attain.

Despite the pool's shortcomings, Jay uses it as a childlike respite from the pressures of the outside world, scoffing at the neighborhood boys who try to peep in on her swimming. But later in the film, as she waits for the demon that haunts her, the pool is inexplicably destroyed, a gaping hole in the side having let out all the water. Now, even the pretense of economic stability and the naive pleasures of childhood have gushed away.

It Follows made critical waves in 2014 with its minimalist, low-tech homage to slasher films of the '70s and '80s. In the film, Jay, who lives in the lower-middle-class suburbs of Detroit, becomes infected with a mysterious curse after having sex. Now, an entity that can take the form of any person (but can only be seen by those who have been infected) slowly stalks her. It can only walk slowly toward her, like a George Romero zombie, but it does so relentlessly. If Jay pauses, It will eventually catch up with her and kill her before turning its attention back to the person who initially infected her. With the help of her sister and neighborhood friends (adults exist only on the periphery of this story), Jay must decide if she will pass the curse along to someone else through sex or resort to a life of constant movement to keep It at bay.

Given the manner in which the curse is passed on, critics were quick to link the film to anxieties about sexually transmitted diseases and youth hook-up culture (although many critics and the director himself opt for more open-ended interpretations). Writing for the *Catholic World Report*, one reviewer even promoted the movie as a Christian parable about "tainted sex," one that highlights the failures of the sexual revolution.[7]

Cleary, sexual anxieties are central to the film's story, and the slasher genre has long intertwined its images of graphic death with anxieties about young people's forays into adult sexuality. But the real dread in *It Follows* centers less on sex than on a more general loss of childhood and the recognition that adulthood won't deliver on its promises of freedom and prosperity. Instead, adulthood in the film only delivers anxiety and a precarious existence. Jay herself articulates this dread just after she is infected by the young man she has been dating, Hugh. Lounging in the back seat of Hugh's car, a deserted building looming above them as a reminder of Detroit's economic ruin, she laments: "It's funny. I used to daydream about being old enough to go on dates and drive around with friends in their cars. I had this image of myself holding hands with a really cute guy listening to the radio, driving along some pretty road, up north maybe, when the trees started to change colors. It was never about going anywhere, really. It's having some sort of freedom, I guess. Now that we're old enough, where the hell do we go?" She is then violently chloroformed by Hugh and tied to a wheelchair in her underwear as he explains how the curse works, an abrupt end to her reverie about childish fantasies and a forceful reminder that she, in fact, now has nowhere to go without It.

The film is punctuated by similar wistful reflections on lost childhood. Jay's neighbor and friend, Paul, who harbors a not-so-secret crush on Jay, reminisces about being Jay's first kiss in a more innocent time before telling a story about the two of them finding porn and not realizing what the magazines depicted. Jay's flirty neighbor, Greg, recalls good times spent at the family lake house with his now-absent father as the teens flee to this once-safe place in a time of crisis. On his date with Jay, Hugh expresses a desire to be a carefree child again instead of facing the stress of young adulthood. All the while, their bespectacled friend, Yara, periodically reads them crushingly hopeless passages from Dostoevsky's *The Idiot* as their naive visions of childhood dissipate in the face of their banal present and future.

Jay is haunted not by the specter of casual sex, but rather by the plodding anxieties of becoming an adult in a world of dead-end opportunities. Sex is certainly part of these anxieties. Far from the promises of love and pleasure, sex here is fraught with danger, deception, and obligation.[8] But sex is only one part of a larger realization that the promises of adulthood are empty.

Specifically, *It Follows* explores the dread of White millennials facing a more uncertain economic future than their parents. As Katherina Lizza argues, the film "explores the vulnerabilities of a population obsessed with maintaining middle-class Whiteness,"[9] especially the vulnerabilities of young White people coming to grips with an uncertain economic future.

After all, the teens in the film live in a lower-middle-class White world suffering from economic stagnation. Their neighborhood is a Detroit suburb that appears to have been built in the 1960s, with largely brick, ranch-style houses that, while certainly far from derelict, are no longer homes for the upwardly mobile White families that used to occupy them. Jay's home in particular is decorated with '70s-style wood paneling and floral wallpaper and looks as if its last redecoration occurred in the mid-1980s. The teens lounge on sickly yellow couches from the '70s and watch old horror movies on a black-and-white TV (stacked on top of another, presumably broken, old TV). Hugh drives around in a 1970s sedan, while Greg drives an early 1980s station wagon. The film is peppered with anachronisms like these, juxtaposing landline telephones with Yara's sleek clamshell e-reader.

This retro aesthetic is part of the film's homage to the classic suburban slashers of the '70s and '80s, such as 1978's *Halloween*. But the anachronisms also draw attention to the economic stagnation of the neighborhood. The eclectic mixture of homages to different decades in the film suggests the realities of home decor for many suburban but economically precarious households, as David Church argues in his analysis of the film.[10] This is a neighborhood whose families, while not poor, have not made significant economic gains for decades and are barely treading water in the neoliberal economy. Its inhabitants are folks like Jay's mom, a single mother who is largely absent from her children's lives thanks to an unspecified job that requires her to wake at 5:45 a.m. and who struggles with alcoholism. She is often passed out in the evenings as the events unfold in her own home. If the film tries to emulate the visual style of '70s and '80s slashers, this technique only affirms how little progress middle-class Whites have made in recent years.

What really pursues Jay throughout the film, then, are a range of economic circumstances that haunt young people today: the prospect of student loan debts, low rates of homeownership, the need to move to high-cost cities to find low-paying jobs, a gig economy that won't provide stable employment, and a skimpy social safety net. Like It in its pursuit of Jay, these economic conditions creep along; they won't bankrupt you overnight, but they are steadily and relentlessly eroding young people's chances of social mobility. No matter how hard young people work, they can't shake the nagging threat of financial disaster that follows them.[11]

In this way, the conceit of *It Follows*—with its slow-moving but persistent threat—mimics the sensations of living near poverty for the working poor, the anxieties of living paycheck to paycheck. Jay is unsettled and exhausted by the constant cycle of frantic escape and restless waiting (as are her compatriots, who are frequently seen sneaking in naps when they can). Jay is constantly on the move, looking for opportunities and solutions, but she never makes headway.[12]

Gothic images of Detroit's crumbling neighborhoods are interspersed with scenes in which the teens struggle against their persistent foe. As they explore the city at different moments in the story, the film lingers on long tracking shots of run-down neighborhoods with crumbling, formerly middle-class homes and boarded-up storefronts. Sometimes, Black men stand on the corners of these neighborhoods. Such images highlight the racial anxieties that are intertwined with White economic anxieties. As the teens contemplate Jay's uncertain future, the images of a poor, implicitly Black Detroit taunt them, insinuating that the seemingly horrific poverty that is supposed to be endemic to Black communities may not be off-limits to them. They even contemplate these racial and economic borders as they wander through a poorer part of town:

> Yara: When I was a little girl, my parents told me I wasn't allowed to go south of 8 mile. I didn't even understand what that meant. It wasn't until I got a little older that I realized that was where the city started and the suburbs ended. I started thinking how weird and shitty that was. I had to ask permission to go to the state fair with my best friend and her parents just because it was a few blocks past the border.
>
> Jay: My parents said the same thing to me.

And yet, as they remember the old parental directives to avoid the poor (and Black) parts of Detroit, the teens transgress these borders, crossing through the city to get to the public pool to set a trap for It. The old boundaries that their parents so desperately enforced between White middle class and Black poverty are now meaningless to the teens.[13] And the swimming pool again marks Jay's downward social trajectory. Gone are the pretenses of even the aboveground pool, as she now seeks out the public pool, and one in the city to boot.

It is not simply social and economic standing that are at stake for Jay and her crew, but their racial standing, as well: their attempts to evade It are bound up in their efforts to elude the stigma of becoming so-called White trash. Because of persistent racial inequalities in the US, poverty is often imagined as being specific to people of color, especially in the specter of crime-ridden, mostly Black inner cities such as Detroit. The image of poor White people disrupts this racial vision of poverty; US culture stigmatizes poor Whites as White trash, people whose core Whiteness is called into question by imagining them as messy, uncouth, and lazy.[14] The Othering of poor White folks as trashy is an attempt to imagine them as somehow distinct from more affluent White people, whether culturally (poor taste, shoddy living conditions) or even physiologically (dirtier, more apt to be missing teeth).

Mirroring the culture's anxieties about trashy Whiteness, It almost always takes the form of abject White bodies. Although it sometimes appears as someone close to its victim (for example, as Yara or Jay's absent father), more often It manifests in White bodies that undermine cultural norms around Whiteness and beauty: naked middle-aged men and women; an unusually tall, gaunt man; a sallow-faced old woman in a ratty dress robe; a pale-faced, almost feral little man. Juan Valencia argues that the Whiteness of It reveals the facade of White innocence across most of the horror genre, especially the haunted house film, with the White-bodied monsters indicating the horrific actions of Whiteness in the past.[15] But the derelict White bodies of It also explore White fears of the effects of poverty on White bodies. Its manifestations are mostly grotesque White bodies that suggest low social class. One of the most memorable versions of It is a young woman, around Jay's age, with dark eyes and missing teeth, wearing a tattered bra with one side pulled down, a short skirt, and one tube sock. She pees down her leg as she walks toward Jay in her kitchen (see fig. 6.1). The missing teeth, repellant hygiene, and suggestions of sordid sexuality are all exaggerated White trash stereotypes, terrifying Jay with an image of what she might become.

As a result of their encounters with It and its specter of trashy Whiteness, the young people in the film are forced to linger in a world of unseemly poverty. Hugh—whose real name is Jeff—embraces a transient existence, squatting in dilapidated houses in abandoned urban neighborhoods and rigging up his hovel with makeshift security alarms built from empty bottles and cans. Once he has passed It onto to Jay, he, like so many other millennials, resides back in the suburbs with his mom. The last we see of him, he is sitting cross-legged in the grass of his parent's backyard, wearing sweatpants that resemble a child's pajamas.

Similarly, after the teens attack It at the city pool but are unsure about the entity's survival, Paul convinces Jay to pass the curse along to him. Once they have sex, he heads into an abandoned industrial zone in the city and contemplates sleeping with a poor White prostitute (who, with the dark shadows under her eyes, cheap push-up bra, and tube socks, bears a slight resemblance to the form that It took in Jay's kitchen). Because of It and its pursuit, Paul is forced to dally in the world of White poverty and trashy values while deciding whether he ought to buy some time and distance from It, with little thought for the

Fig. 6.1. "It" appears as a toothless, disheveled specter of trashy femininity in *It Follows* (Northern Lights Films, 2015).

lives of those he deems socially beneath him and therefore unworthy of his consideration.

In the final scene, Paul and Jay morosely walk hand in hand down their street. Unfocused in the background, a figure appears, following them. Is this It? We don't know, nor does it matter, because for the rest of their lives, Jay, Paul, and the other teens will always look over their shoulders, just as they will never escape the unrelenting horrors of the neoliberal economy. They grew up being promised the fantasies of constant upward mobility for White folks in the US economy, but instead they will always be on the move, seeking one dead-end job after another, entering into meaningless relationships as they attempt to keep the horrors of White poverty at bay.

DON'T BREATHE

It Follows tells a story about White teens on the bottom rung of the middle class, tormented by the possibility of poverty in their future, but *Don't Breathe* flips this story on its head. *Don't Breathe* focuses on poor White teens in Detroit who are struggling to move up in the world but are blocked by economic and moral decay. Directed by Uruguayan filmmaker Fede Álvarez and cowritten with frequent collaborator Rodo Sayagues, also Uruguayan, the film stands out against most other US horror films in this period for its frank depictions of White poverty and squalor. Its main character is not a suburban White teen clinging to the middle class, but rather a desperately poor young woman already enmeshed in the kinds of trashy poverty that Jay and her cohorts in *It Follows* feared.

The film first introduces us to Rocky, a young woman desperate to escape Detroit and her own poverty, as she breaks into a modern, upscale home. Rocky, her boyfriend, Money, and her friend, Alex—who provides access to the houses they rob through keys and security codes purloined from his father, an employee of a local home security firm—ransack the house in their own ways. Alex, wedded to strict rules and ethics (no cash, don't steal items totaling over $10,000), quickly and carefully grabs electronics that can be sold easily. Money, an impulsive borderline psychopath, purposefully breaks vases and masturbates on the kitchen floor.[16] But Rocky heads to one of the bedrooms in the house, clearly used by an affluent teen girl, and tries on her clothes. While the others rob the house, she flops on the bed in her new outfit, a cute stuffed bunny just over her shoulder. More than the others, she longs for escape, to become the carefree upper-middle-class young woman doted on by loving parents.

Rocky's wish to escape Detroit with her little sister and head to the beaches of California lead her, Money, and Alex to one last job, this one outside of the careful rules that Alex has established to protect them from more severe prosecution (and to protect his father's job). Money learns about an old man living alone in an abandoned neighborhood who won a huge settlement from a rich family whose daughter was driving drunk and killed the old man's daughter. The rich daughter avoided jail time, but the grieving father now supposedly keeps his settlement locked away in his house in cash. As they prepare for their home invasion, they also learn that the old man is a blind veteran who lost his vision in one of the US wars in Iraq. Alex at first wants nothing to do with the high-stakes job, but his simmering crush on Rocky and the idea of running away with her leads him to reluctantly accept.

Naturally, this is a huge mistake on Alex's part. Once inside, the heist goes wrong, and Money is shot by The Blind Man (we never learn his name), who is a well-trained army veteran able to masterfully navigate his own house. Alex and Rocky are locked inside the house with its owner, and a tense cat-and-mouse game ensues as the two try to find a safe route to escape. Although the audience might at first root for The Blind Man against his teenaged tormentors, soon Rocky, Alex, and the audience discover why The Blind Man has so much invested in security: he has kidnapped the wealthy young woman who killed his daughter and is keeping her in his basement, having artificially inseminated her with his own semen in the hopes that she will deliver to him a new child. Confronted with The Blind Man's horrific secret, Rocky and Alex have to decide what is more important to them: escaping with the money or getting caught by calling the police but bringing The Blind Man to justice.

Much like *It Follows*, *Don't Breathe* uses Gothic images of decaying, formerly middle-class neighborhoods as a backdrop to its violence. In a brief montage, the film makes a spectacle of Detroit's economic ruin and presents The Blind Man's neighborhood as a symbol of it. The houses, mostly two- and three-story brick homes that once housed the upper-middle classes of a more prosperous Detroit, are literally crumbling around The Blind Man's house, a last vestige of the White families that used to occupy the space. Boarded-up windows, collapsing roofs, and unclaimed furniture piled in yards are being slowly overrun with the vegetation that is reclaiming the land (see fig. 6.2). Whatever past prosperity these neighborhoods held is long gone, and the film shows that the remains of the White middle-class American dream are haunted by a tortured monster with a psychotically deranged sense of entitlement.

Rocky, meanwhile, lives the kind of squalid life that the teens in *It Follows* feared was in their future, one marked by the stereotypes of White trash. Rocky and her young sister share a tiny trailer with her abusive mother, whose lazy boyfriend is crashing with them while out of work. Lined with tacky wood paneling and ratty carpeting, the trailer is littered with Rocky's mother's empty beer and malt liquor bottles. Knowing that her daughter has been saving money on the side, the mother implies that Rocky has been giving blow jobs for money. And Trevor, the unemployed boyfriend, sports a swastika tattoo on the back of his hand, a reminder of their status as poor Whites who harbor a sense of racial superiority over Blacks, Latinos, and others.

This spectacle of horrific White poverty makes it easy to sympathize with Rocky's fantasy of escape, especially thanks to her adorable little sister, Diddy. But Rocky and the other teens soon find that the road to upward mobility is treacherous and passes through the remnants of the middle class that have been forsaken by the neoliberal economy. The Blind Man's neighborhood provides a visual reminder of the fickle economic forces that can devastate whole communities, but it also illustrates the monstrous effects of neoliberalism and the free market on morality, as well as the vicious competition at the heart of contemporary capitalism.

Fig. 6.2. The ruins of the former middle class in Detroit serve as a warning to the protagonists about the horrors of neoliberalism in *Don't Breathe* (Screen Gems, 2016).

What draws the teens to the neighborhood, after all, is its freedom from rules and regulations. While casing The Blind Man's house, they describe the neighborhood as a "ghost town," and Money notes that they won't have to worry about the police here: "No people means no five-o on patrol." On their other jobs, Alex enforces strict rules about whom they steal from and what they steal, hoping to create almost victimless petty robberies. But this job takes them to a space without those constraints, one with higher rewards but steeply higher risks, as they soon find out. By making the unethical decision to enter that space and steal from a blind war hero whose daughter was murdered, the trio enters a realm of unfettered greed and distorted morals. As the devastated neighborhood reminds us, though, the greed of the poor, desperate burglars exists alongside the greed of the capitalist system. The neighborhood is a visual reminder of the greed of executives, bankers, and brokers who would destroy whole neighborhoods in their quest for never-ending wealth during the housing bubble.

The Blind Man has also come to accept the failures of liberal systems to protect people from the excesses of capitalism. He has embraced the brutal freedoms of his abandoned neighborhood to pursue his own forms of monstrous justice. After capturing Rocky, like any good villain, The Blind Man delivers an extended monologue that indicts the freedoms of the wealthy in capitalism: "Rich girls don't go to jail," he notes. He has seen that systems designed to instill justice don't have meaning in neoliberal capitalism. Rich people don't follow the rules, so why should he? Freed from the logic and rules of civil society, he rejects all authority and morality, declaring the godlessness of his dilapidated world and, therefore, his right to unfettered violence to accumulate whatever he wants, in this case a new child. For critics like Valencia, The Blind Man's insistent logic that possessing Rocky inherently offers the right to inseminate her and possess her child lays bare the horrific logic of the White nuclear family in capitalism. The film exposes this logic "in a disturbing, subversive fashion that reveals the truly sickening nature of White wealth and power," a critical perspective missing from the haunted house genre, Valencia claims.[17]

The Blind Man's house is the perfect Gothic house for postrecession America. Like other houses in the Gothic tradition, it is full of labyrinthine passageways (his cluttered basement with rows and rows of metal shelves), hidden compartments (the unusually large ductwork through which Rocky attempts to escape, as well as his basement dungeon), and dark sexual secrets that have their roots in a traumatic past. A convoluted and treacherous space in which the horrors of the past impinge on Rocky's future, the creaky and dingy house is a microcosm of the economic collapse of Detroit and the moral collapse of neoliberal capitalism. The White middle-class home, once a symbol of stability and prosperity, is now a bastion of repressed fears about the degraded state of White patriarchal authority and the horrific challenges hindering upward social mobility.

In the face of the brutal logic of The Blind Man's world, then, Rocky and Alex must reevaluate their commitment to upward mobility and their own morality. At several points in the film, the teens have to choose between ruthless and dangerous individualism and the justice system of a civil society that they know doesn't have their best interests at heart: Should they try to make it out with the money or alert the police and save their life but face legal consequences? This dilemma assumes that upward mobility necessarily means abandoning one's morality, that the only path upward for poor young people is to embrace the same kinds of unethical behavior used by the capitalist elite to decimate Detroit's middle class in the first place.

This dilemma provides the tension in the film's final scene. After knocking The Blind Man down his basement ladder with a crowbar and seemingly killing him, Rocky escapes the house with the money. We then see Rocky, her face still bruised from her traumatic escape, and her sister, Diddy, waiting at the train station for their departure for California, when a news report catches her attention. The local news is reporting on her break-in, covering it as a remark-able survivor story in which a blind veteran killed two erstwhile robbers, show-ing that The Blind Man survived the home invasion but stating that "no goods were reported stolen by the victim." As Alex had suggested earlier, The Blind Man is buying Rocky's silence, knowing that reporting the money stolen would lead to Rocky and the revelation of his crimes.

Rocky's upward mobility, then, is contingent upon her silence, leaving The Blind Man to live, recover, and possibly strike again. Facing this dilemma, Rocky and Diddy march out of the station following the arrow toward "depar-tures," suggesting that she chooses ruthless individualism over morality. If she wants to move up in a competitive neoliberal world, she can't play by the rules, even if that means the denial of justice for The Blind Man.

CONCLUSION

In their explorations of White teens and economic standing, *It Follows* and *Don't Breathe* feature prominent shocking scenes of taboo sexuality. In *It Fol-lows*, Jay agrees to pass her infection to Greg to test its reality. While Greg at first says he hasn't seen any stalkers, one night, Jay sees a figure who looks like Greg wearing white long johns break into Greg's house. Fearing that the figure is It, she heads to Greg's house, where It has now taken the form of Greg's mom and is wearing a sheer nightgown with her breasts hanging out. When the real Greg opens his bedroom door, the entity pounces, and Jay watches in horror as It extracts the life from Greg by erotically rubbing its genitals on Greg while still in the form of Greg's mother.

In a similarly troubling scene in *Don't Breathe*, Rocky finds herself captured by The Blind Man after his former prisoner—the young woman who had acci-dentally killed his daughter—is shot when Rocky and Alex try to free her. Hung from the ceiling by a body harness, Rocky listens helplessly as The Blind Man tells her that he had artificially inseminated the young wealthy woman in order to extract a child from her. Now that his captive is dead, he plans to do the same to Rocky and approaches her with a turkey baster dripping with his semen, freshly defrosted over a nearby camp stove. He uses scissors to cut out the crotch of Rocky's pants and grips the squirming Rocky, but Alex arrives in time to knock The Blind Man to the ground and free Rocky as they make another escape attempt.

These scenes dramatize each film's concern with sex and power by using taboo sexual violence to highlight the generational tensions of the films. Both of these scenes graphically depict a member of an older generation committing unspeakable, implicitly incestuous acts of violence (Rocky is probably about the age that The Blind Man's daughter would be, had she lived). Underpinning each scene is a disturbing sense of betrayal, with parental figures becoming monstrous foes that must be overcome, a theme affirmed in *It Follows* when the entity takes the form of Jay's absent father in the film's climax at the city pool.

Images of Detroit's poverty and decay draw out this generational conflict in each film, providing stark visions of economic collapse and a deeply nostalgic musing on the perceived fall of the White middle class. The brooding shots of decaying neighborhoods in each film are a reminder of what the baby boomer generation threw away in its pursuit of neoliberal capitalism: thriving communities that could have supported the teens in these stories. Instead, like other millennials, the protagonists here must face a starkly different economic reality than the generation that came before them, and those scenes of incestuous violence underscore a sense of betrayal as millennials face the precarious economy created by their parents' generation.

This betrayal is felt mostly by White youth grappling with economic realities that are vastly different than what their parents' generation had promised. Detroit resonates not simply because of its poverty, but also because of its nostalgia for a time with a vibrant manufacturing base and thriving middle-class White communities. In the shadow of those stable communities, many of which are now decimated by the neoliberal economy, young White folks face dwindling opportunities. Young people of color, of course, face the same precarious economy as well as long-standing discrimination, but they had never really been promised the American dream. In the Motor City Gothic, however, the decaying ruins of the city's middle class haunt young White people as they mourn the loss of a past stability that their culture has taught them to feel entitled to claim.

NOTES

1. Similar images of a deteriorating Detroit are used in Jim Jarmusch's 2013 vampire film *Only Lovers Left Alive*, but as the film doesn't fit neatly into the horror genre, the primary focus here will be on *It Follows* and *Don't Breathe*.

2. United States Department of Labor, "The African-American Labor Force," February 29, 2012, https://www.dol.gov/_sec/media/reports/BlackLaborForce/BlackLaborForce.pdf.

3. For another comparison of the two films and their relationship to post-recession America, see Joni Hayward, "No Safe Space: Economic Anxiety and Post-Recession Spaces in Horror Films," *Frames Cinema Journal* 11 (2017), http://

framescinemajournal.com/article/no-safe-space-economic-anxiety-and-post
-recession-spaces-in-horror-films/.

4. Bridget M. Marshall, "Defining Southern Gothic," in *Critical Insights:
Southern Gothic Literature*, ed. Jay Ellis (Ipswich, MA: Salem Press, 2013), 3–18.

5. David Church, "Queer Ethics, Urban Spaces, and the Horrors of Monogamy in *It Follows*," *Cinema Journal* 57, no. 3 (2018): 3–28.

6. Juan Valencia, "The House Settling: Race, Housing, and Wealth in the
Post-Recession Horror Film," *Emergence*, November 25, 2017, http://emergence
journal.english.ucsb.edu/index.php/2017/11/25/the-house-settling-race-housing
-and-wealth-in-the-post-recession-horror-film/.

7. Nick Olszyk, "Pope Paul VI Makes a Horror Movie," *Catholic World
Report*, April 14, 2015, http://www.catholicworldreport.com/2015/04/14/pope
-paul-vi-makes-a-horror-movie/.

8. Church offers a compelling discussion of the sexual politics of the film as a
subversive, queer critique of heterosexual monogamy in "Queer Ethics."

9. Katherine Lizza, "*It Follows* and the Uncertainties of the Middle Class,"
in *Dark Forces at Work: Essays on Social Dynamics and Cinematic Horrors*, ed.
Cynthia J. Miller and A. Bowdoin Van Riper (Lanham, MD: Lexington Books,
2020), 294.

10. Church, "Queer Ethics," 20.

11. In "The House Settling," Valencia makes a similar argument about *It Follows*: the core dread explored in the film is not sexual as much as it reflects economic precarity.

12. For more on the representation of precarity in *It Follows*, see Casey Ryan
Kelly, "*It Follows*: Precarity, Thanatopolitics, and the Ambient Horror Film,"
Critical Studies in Media Communication 34, no. 3 (2017): 234–249.

13. This spatial dynamic is central to Lizza's argument in "*It Follows* and the
Uncertainties of the Middle Class"; Lizza argues that the geographic boundaries
between the middle-class suburbs and the derelict urban center are intertwined
with the racial boundaries of the protagonists' Whiteness, now under threat in
an era of neoliberal precarity. The blurred boundaries between the White suburb
and the multiracial city signals a foreboding sense of White economic decline.

14. Annalee Newit and Matt Wray, eds., *White Trash: Race and Class in America* (New York: Routledge, 1997).

15. Valencia, "The House Settling."

16. Coincidentally, Money is played by Costa Rican actor Daniel Zovatto, who
also played Greg in *It Follows*.

17. Valencia, "The House Settling."

7

SURVEILLING WHITENESS

The Horrific Technology Film

THE MARKED ONES, THE 2014 entry in the successful *Paranormal Activity* series, ditches the White suburbs to focus on Latinx teenagers in a working-class neighborhood in California. One of the teens has been gifted a new video camera to celebrate his high school graduation, the footage of which comprises most of the found-footage narrative. Early on in the film, the teens are playfully documenting their day-to-day lives with the camera when they accidentally record a local criminal. The tattooed tough guy spots the camera and mistakes the boys for narcs. He charges across the street and confronts them, leaving the boys to desperately plead with him and convince him they were just goofing around. It doesn't take ghosts to remind these particular teens that recording the wrong things at the wrong times can get you into trouble.

For a moment, this scene in *The Marked Ones* exposes the relationships between race, social class, and surveillance that the rest of the *Paranormal Activity* series takes for granted. The previous four films in the series showed middle-class White suburban homeowners who turn to video surveillance when confronted with seemingly supernatural occurrences. These White families assume that the supposedly neutral and rational documentation of the video camera will provide answers that explain the simmering terror they are feeling. These families willingly (and sometimes excitedly) deploy elaborate video surveillance systems in their own homes based on the assumption that only good things can come from such documentation. They eventually realize that the only thing all these cameras will document will be their own terror and deaths.

But the scene with the criminal in *The Marked Ones* establishes from the beginning that working-class people of color in the US should be wary of surveillance. For some folks, seeing and documenting too much can be inherently dangerous. The camera's gaze is not neutral but deeply tied to power and social location, something the entitled White homeowners could never grasp. For a brief moment, that early scene in *The Marked Ones* disrupts the supposed neutrality of surveillance culture, laying bare the White assumption that technology is a necessary tool for understanding the world. As the Latinx teens are drawn into the same demonic horrors that plagued the White homeowners who came before them, they at least do so without the same incredulity of middle-class Whites, who couldn't believe that surveillance wouldn't save them from the terrors of the world.

This chapter tracks the persistence of surveillance and media technologies in the narratives and visual styles of the Obama-era horror film. *The Marked Ones* aside, at the center of these films are White families or other White folks who either turn to technology to help them resolve their supernatural tribulations or find themselves haunted by possessed media technologies. Exploring dominant White perspectives on surveillance culture and the proliferation of media in our day-to-day lives, these films dramatize White anxieties that new technologies are no longer reassuring tools of social control, but rather a means through which White folks are shown the horrors that people of color have always known about (but White folks preferred not to see).

THE HORRORS OF SURVEILLANCE

The films discussed in this chapter are a subset of technology-based horror films, which proliferated after World War II in the US (and elsewhere). In these films, new technologies—whether real-world technologies like the atom bomb or imagined technologies like teleportation—unleash horrific outcomes on people, communities, or the whole world. Think of the science experiments gone wrong in *The Fly* (1958, 1986) or *The Lawnmower Man* (1992).

More recently, technology-based horror films have included a subset of films in which media technologies themselves are the source of horror, whether because mass media becomes a transmission device for violence and terror or because characters use media technologies to see the supernatural world in new ways. Examples include David Cronenberg's *Videodrome* (1983), a self-reflexive horror film about a sadistic snuff television program that infiltrates people's minds, and the Japanese and American version of *Ringu/The Ring* (1998/2002) and their sequels, which feature an evil spirit who climbs out of a TV set and attacks her victims if they watch a haunted video and fail to share it with others.

Since 1980, the broad category of technological horror has largely focused on stories of science gone too far, rather than narratives of haunted media. Around 10 percent of Hollywood's mainstream horror output between 1980 and 2007 featured horrific technology, mostly through narratives of unethical scientists who accidentally unleash horrors on themselves and the world, from 1980's *Altered States*, to *Flatliners* and *Braindead* in 1990, to *Mimic* in 1997, to *Hollow Man* in 2000, among others.

The percentage of technological horror in the Obama years remained relatively consistent (around 13 percent of mainstream horror from 2008 through 2016), but the technological horror category has largely shifted toward haunted media stories in place of science-gone-wrong narratives. This shift started with a trickle of movies in the 1980s, like *Videodrome* (1983) or *976-Evil* (1988), in which Satan lures his prey using a phone hotline. The 1990s saw more haunted media with the video game–themed films *Brainscan* (1994) and *eXistenZ* (1999), and the early 2000s featured even more, including *The Ring* and its sequel (2002, 2005), *Feardotcom* (2002), *White Noise* (2005), and *Pulse* (2006), all of which involve elements of the supernatural infiltrating mass media to find new victims.

Then, from 2008 until 2016, haunted media stories accounted for sixteen out of nineteen technological horror stories,[1] thanks in large part to the proliferation of found-footage horror, which often depicted characters attempting to use any available video equipment to document the terrors all around them.[2] According to scholars and critics, this subgenre of horror cinema dramatizes post-9/11 paranoia around government surveillance and the corporatization of digital networks in the social-media era. For example, Linnie Blake and Xavier Aldana Reyes's book *Digital Horror* explores the recent trend toward found footage in global horror cinema. They argue that these films explore the new fears and paranoias stemming from constant digital surveillance and self-surveillance, whether as part of the War on Terror or as part of neoliberal capitalism. For the essays in *Digital Horror*, the aesthetic of found footage is not simply a stylistic gimmick applied to existing narrative tropes in the horror genre, but rather a new way for audiences to grapple with the relentless monitoring of the digital era.[3]

Similarly, Catherine Zimmer shows how the intersection of surveillance systems and cinema has yielded a set of postmillennial films utilizing new styles, logic, and forms of engagement based on expanding surveillance regimes, especially in the US and Europe. For Zimmer, horror films—from post-9/11 torture porn to found-footage thrillers—employ images of surveillance technology to explore new visions of national politics and consumer identities in the 2000s in the midst of the War on Terror and new forms of digital consumption. These new forms of cinema and narrative, Zimmer argues, are explicitly racial, using images of surveillance to produce White subjectivities in the midst of geopolitical crises.[4]

Of course, while social media and the War on Terror brought critical attention to the role of surveillance in our day-to-day lives, the roots of this surveillance culture extend back far before Facebook or the USA PATRIOT Act. As Simone Browne has documented, the contours of today's surveillance culture have largely been shaped by the long history of White surveillance of Black bodies in the US. Linking the design of slave ships, eighteenth-century lantern laws, the Book of Negroes (an eighteenth-century ledger that documented self-emancipated slaves in New York City), and FBI surveillance of civil rights leaders, Browne stipulates that regulating and controlling Blackness in the US has been a central (but critically neglected) force in the development of contemporary surveillance culture.[5] Today's debates around surveillance culture tend to cluster around government spying or the confluence of advertising and big data (as seen in the insightful discussions of horror and surveillance in Blake and Reyes's book), but these debates are often implicitly White debates that sometimes ignore the racial histories and racial biases of contemporary surveillance.

After all, the histories that Browne documents have yielded a massive system of surveillance and big-data algorithms that present themselves as neutral but impact people of color with far more severity than they do middle-class and affluent Whites. New research is beginning to reveal that the big-data revolution, far from providing a rational corrective to racial and other biases, only provides a technocratic manifestation of those already-existing inequalities. Safiya Umoja Noble's book *Algorithms of Oppression*, for example, exposes the kinds of data discrimination that inform the functions of search algorithms used by major search engines.[6]

These kinds of data-driven discrimination inform a range of digital practices that exacerbate inequalities in areas such as banking, education, and social services,[7] but a particularly problematic example of big data's contributions to racial discrimination are new forms of technocratic policing. In the face of public concern that policing is based around the racial prejudices of officers and institutions, more police departments are turning to scientifically informed techniques intended to remove human bias from the practices of law enforcement. But as Jackie Wang argues, programs like PredPol—a data-based algorithm intended to help police predict where crimes might occur—offer a facade of technological neutrality behind which racially discriminatory police work still thrives.[8]

While contemporary surveillance culture is certainly varied and complex, this emerging research highlights how certain forms of surveillance should be seen as essentially White projects of social control, not simply by-products of modern technology. As cultural theorist John Fiske has suggested concerning surveillance culture, "Today's seeing eye is White."[9] Such surveillance practices are presented as ostensibly race-neutral but, in fact, participate in larger cultural forces that privilege Whiteness at the expense of people of color. After all, these technologies of surveillance did not emerge in a vacuum—they were developed out of a long history of White surveillance by White institutions organized around White assumptions about capitalism, property, and social values.

It shouldn't be surprising, then, that aside from *The Marked Ones*, the mainstream haunted media film tells the story of White people and their relationship to technology. These films explore ordinary (middle-class, often suburban) White people as they struggle not only with supernatural events, but with their own strategies for coping with personal upheaval. As these White characters grapple with their assumptions about technology and documentation—how can what I'm seeing be real?—the films dramatize White fears that surveillance culture might not be the solution they had made it out to be.

For example, the found-footage film hints that the new technocratic age might erase the kinds of privileges White people have historically enjoyed. While researchers have explored the racial biases underpinning surveillance culture, surveillance and big-data monitoring continue to be promoted as race-neutral. The idea of race-neutral systems is both reassuring and terrifying to White culture. On the one hand, contemporary neoliberal capitalism celebrates its own supposed color blindness, valorizing the idea of pure meritocracy and reassuring White folks that their successes are their own, free from the explicit systems of White privilege that supported past generations. Most White folks know that this isn't really true, but the neoliberal insistence on color blindness assuages White concerns that they might have unearned advantages. However, when more and more systems are turned over to data-based algorithms that are supposedly race-neutral, the idealistic rhetoric of the big-data revolution gives the appearance that White privileges might actually be reduced or eradicated, a terrifying proposition for White culture. What if the found-footage genre is documenting just how un-special White people are in a seemingly race-neutral, technocratic system?

Luckily for White folks, these systems are not actually race-neutral, but the new systems of surveillance and big data do require more participation from the White mainstream. Older visions of surveillance culture typically entailed the monitoring of Black and poor bodies, whether through policing and surveilling alleged high-crime areas or through extensive monitoring of individuals receiving social services. But today's neoliberal surveillance draws almost everyone into its orbit. Coupled with the imperative for every person to self-discipline, self-monitor, and self-promote, today's digital culture means that White bodies are regulated and documented in ways that were largely confined to at-risk bodies in the past. The found-footage film emerged just at the moment when White bodies became subject to the same kinds of systemic monitoring and surveillance typically reserved for people of color in the US.

In this way, the haunted media film plays out a set of White contradictions concerning surveillance, as White people assume at first that technological monitoring will provide them and their families with a sense of security. But when the technology does nothing to help them, the characters find that they are now just like all the other vulnerable and precarious populations in the US, subsumed into technological systems that cannot save them.

The racial implications of the White characters' predicament also reflect contemporary debates around both surveillance and *sousveillance*, the use of recording technologies by those outside of official power structures to document the world, often as a corrective to official surveillance. These debates have become particularly important in the era of Black Lives Matter and discussions of policing, as sousveillance has brought much-needed attention to issues of police brutality (thanks to the proliferation of video cameras in the hands of ordinary people).

Because systems of surveillance have been deployed to protect private property or to enforce White culture's vision of social control (often against Black bodies), such systems are often regarded as a necessary evil within White culture. But sousveillance has challenged those assurances of benevolence and neutrality by documenting racial violence. Today's sousveillance culture shows that other institutions, like the police, may not be as race-neutral as White culture would like to believe. Surveillance culture promises that more surveillance and documentation will only provide more security and oversight, but the wave of smartphone videos on the streets of America's cities is instead revealing a world in which White police officers might shoot unarmed Black folks in the back. Far from stabilizing social institutions, the use of video technologies by everyday folks has only undercut White assumptions about their own privileged place in the world. These technologies often show White people a horrific and racially charged world they wish they could unsee.[10]

Of course, the fallout from this glut of video evidence around police brutality has not been a thoughtful national conversation around race and injustice, but rather a general assault on the idea of truth and image-making. When confronted with evidence of injustice that had been long invisible to them, the White middle class simply insisted that you can't really trust what you see on the media, eventually embracing a president who frequently lies and denies in the face of credible evidence. This is perhaps why the White characters in the haunted media film seem so incapable of altering their stories: they doggedly insist on documenting everything but then can't believe what the footage so plainly reveals to them. Incredulous that affluent White folks could be so blatantly victimized, they keep the cameras rolling all the way to their deaths.

REVELATIONS AND REDEMPTIONS

This cynical perspective on haunted media was not always the dominant narrative in US horror cinema. During the 2008 election year, several films on the cusp of the Obama era explored the possibility that, while scary, the new regimes of visual surveillance might just save us.

These films were international horror remakes, with American producers reimagining international stories of horrific media for American audiences. Prompted by the financial and critical success of the US remake of *The Ring* and its sequel (2002, 2005), a flurry of international horror remakes was released in 2008 that told stories of haunted media technologies. These films helped spur a sense of crisis among horror fans and scholars, who feared that the US horror industry had run out of original ideas, but as a group they reveal a fascinating obsession with media, with each film inserting anxious White people into a global set of stories about seeing (or hearing) too much. The core of this group is *The Eye* (the American remake of a Hong Kong/Singapore coproduction that was also remade in Tamil and Hindi), *One Missed Call* (a remake of the 2003 film by Japanese director Takashi Miike), and *Shutter* (a remake of a Thai horror film from 2004). The year 2008 also saw the release of *Quarantine* (a found-footage viral zombie film based on the Spanish film *REC*) and *Mirrors* (a very loose remake of the South Korean horror film *Into the Mirrors*).

In each film, some kind of media technology, most often technologies of vision, enable a character to glimpse the world of the supernatural. In *The Eye*, a blind musician gets a cornea implant that allows her to see for the first time in her life, but the surgery leads to unsettling visions that she isn't sure are real.

In *One Missed Call*, spirits have infiltrated their victims' cell phones, leaving them voice mails containing the sounds of their deaths, foreshadowing the freak accidents that later kill them. And in *Shutter*, an American living abroad in Japan with her husband is drawn into the world of spirit photography when she starts seeing a strange figure in her pictures.

As remakes of international horror films, these US films take on global anxieties about the horrific possibilities of media as cell phones and cameras reshaped everyday life not only in the US, but around the world. Like their international inspirations, these US films turn to the interconnections of personal media and the expansion of photo-video image culture as fraught with the potential to see and reveal too much. The US films, though, tend to be somewhat more bullish about a hypermediated world, populated now with White characters who find more redemption through their brush with haunted media than their global counterparts. While the revelations of each film are horrific, offering the characters (and the audience) a set of unsettling images and sounds, in each case, the haunted media in US films serve as a warning to the living, helping the characters navigate the supernatural world that they now have access to.

The heroine of *The Eye*, for example, learns that her corneas came from a young Mexican woman with psychic abilities who could not only see the spirits of the dead, but could also predict horrible deaths in the future. The young woman died trying in vain to save workers from a fire in an unsafe factory that she knew was going to burn down. Now the formerly blind musician can not only see, she can also help lost spirits and save people's lives, a possibility that isn't fully explored in the original film.

Likewise, in *Shutter*, the young protagonist keeps seeing the creepy image of a Japanese woman in her pictures and discovers that the woman was her husband's ex-girlfriend who had committed suicide. The American woman assumes that the spirit is coming after her because she is still obsessed with her husband, even beyond the grave. In actuality, the spirit has come to warn the woman of her husband's misdeeds and the horrible cruelty he perpetuated that led to the ex-girlfriend's death. By appearing in the woman's pictures, the spirit eventually directs her to a compartment in their home containing secrets that the husband had intended to keep hidden. This mirrors the plot of the original film, but in the US version, the intent of the spirit is clearer (and the separation of the woman from the corrupt man made more explicit in the end).

Similar stories of supernatural warnings are used in *One Missed Call*. In this film, the final girl initially suspects that the demonic force behind the calls is the spirit of an abusive mother who finds victims in the contact lists of people's cell phones. But eventually the young woman discovers that the mother's ghost is simply trying to warn her and other potential victims. The mother's psychotic (and possibly demonic) daughter had an asthma attack, and while she tried to call her mother for help before she died, her evil energy somehow got into the phone lines. While the technology was still haunted and fatal—reflecting concerns about digital networks and contamination—the mother's spirit was also able to infiltrate the technology and aid the young woman being targeted. The original film ends quite darkly, with the demonic spirit possessing the protagonist and starting a new cycle of violence and abuse, but in the US version, the protagonist is spared, thanks to the timely intervention of the mother's spirit at the climax (though the film suggests that the demonic daughter will continue to find other victims via cell phone contacts).

The insertion of White characters into these global stories of haunted technology highlights White anxieties around the nature of invasive media technologies. As each character faces her own vulnerability—a blind woman, a White woman struggling to acclimate to a foreign culture, a millennial dealing with her history of abuse and trauma—they each find their vulnerability exaggerated by their interactions with media and their ability to see more thanks to changing technology.

In this way, these stories are organized around a general apprehension of media culture and new technologies, building on earlier films such as 2006's *Pulse* (about haunted computer viruses, another US remake of an international horror film) or *The Ring* (about haunted VHS tapes) to call attention to the dangers of intensifying media connectivity and regimes of surveillance. As our day-to-day lives become increasingly mediated, monitored, and tied to technology, these stories depict a deep sense of unease about these new patterns of everyday life.

Of course, as I note above, the regimes of surveillance and big data that would come from these technologies would impact people of color with much more severity in the years after these films were released, and the global origins of these stories suggest a deeply transnational set of concerns about the ways that media connects people as new communication technologies proliferate. But these mid-2000s remakes insist that these are essentially White-people problems, as White culture seeks to manage its relationship to new technologies and the trade-offs of seeing more and being more connected to the rest of the world.

For films such as *The Eye* and *Shutter*, in particular, the horrors of surveillance culture are mitigated by the usefulness of the information gleaned from peering into the supernatural world. The films suggest that, yes, people will see things that disturb them deeply with these technologies of vision, but those with the courage to truly see can help themselves and others.

Both films, then, feel like relics from the Bush-era War on Terror discourses around privacy and torture, especially since both films explicitly tell stories of White Americans abroad struggling with horrors that are rooted in foreign countries. While torture-porn films such as *Hostel* and *Saw* deployed surveillance styles that negotiated the logic and justifications of torture and violence,[11] films such as *The Eye* and *Shutter* suggest that surveillance might yield horrific images, but the images are essential for coping with a chaotic world.

The Eye, for example, sends its heroine across the border to investigate the origins of her new corneas, as the source of her disturbing visions is located in a poor, rural Mexican village. Like many other horror films of this period, the protagonist's haunting undermines her sense of privilege and social standing, linking her to a desperate, racialized poverty. These connections are all the more compelling because the protagonist of *The Eye* is played by Jessica Alba, an actress who has Latinx roots (her father's parents were the children of Mexican immigrants to California) but frequently plays White characters on-screen and who became the subject of controversy in the mid-2000s for allegedly downplaying her Latinx ancestry. Her character's journey in the film mirrors somewhat Alba's public turmoil in this period, with a seemingly White, middle-class woman being forced to explore her connections to Mexico and Mexican identity that have been repressed.

The character's international adventure, however, yields new insights not simply into her anxieties around race and class privileges, but also into the potential benefits of her supernatural surveillance powers. Just as in the original film, in the US remake, the protagonist and her therapist/love interest are stuck in a traffic jam when many of her horrific visions seem to come to life, including an army of shadowy figures that presage many deaths in a fiery accident (the traffic jam is stuck behind a gasoline truck about to explode while waiting at the US-Mexico border). In both the original film and the US remake, she tries to warn those around her, banging on car windows and compelling people to run for their lives. In the original film, her actions are in vain, and hundreds die grisly deaths, but in the US remake, the heroine invokes the threat of terrorism to get people's attention, and the crowd listens. People flee their vehicles just in time, thanks to the character's supernatural insights, and the heroine even rushes back into danger to save a small blond child trapped inside an RV before the explosion destroys all the cars (and sends glass shards into the protagonist's eyes, making her blind again). Placing the action on the border and raising the specter of a threat to national security, the film insists that seeing too much of

Fig. 7.1. Spirit photography reveals the presence of a ghost, who offers a warning to the living about toxic masculinity in *Shutter* (New Regency Productions, 2008).

the horrors of the world helps these particular Americans save innocent lives while abroad, a sentiment absent from the original film.

The lives of Americans abroad are also at stake in the remake of *Shutter*. In the original Thai film, the story unfolds entirely in Thailand with Thai characters. But the US remake, directed by Japanese filmmaker Masayuki Ochiai, tells the story of White American expatriates in Japan, retaining an Asian backdrop for its tale of spirit photography but focusing on the perspectives of a White couple adjusting to life in a foreign culture. The international power dynamics of White Americans abroad become the centerpiece of the remade film.

These power dynamics become tantamount when the film's heroine discovers her husband's secret: he had photographed his best friends (also White Americans) raping his Japanese ex-girlfriend and had done nothing to intervene, keeping the photos locked away after the ex-girlfriend's suicide following the trauma. The images of young, entitled Americans inflicting sexual violence on foreigners while other Americans simply recorded the attack for posterity brings to mind the atrocities of the Abu Ghraib prison torture scandal. And the final image of the film—the husband, now in a mental hospital, weighed down, literally, by the ghost of his ex-girlfriend on his shoulders—evokes the failed and now traumatized masculinity of so many young Americans abroad. The secret recordings of sexual violence may have initiated the horrific acts of revenge that followed in the film, but the ex-girlfriend's haunting of the heroine provides a kind of solution. Though spirit photography leads the heroine to see things that trouble her, ultimately it helps her learn from the horrors of the world and move on from her own personal monster, which she now realizes is toxic manhood (see fig. 7.1).

Both films mirror neoconservative discourses around surveillance and torture in the late War on Terror years; such practices might seem horrific and terrify us, but the world is a scary place, and knowledge of its horrors is ultimately beneficial, even if we will never see the world in the same way again.

PARANORMAL ACTIVITY AND WHITE INCREDULITY

The haunted media cycle would be transformed in 2009 with the release of *Paranormal Activity*, a low-budget found-footage film directed by newcomer Oren Peli. Produced in 2007, the film didn't receive a major release until 2009, when it grossed $107 million in the theatrical box office, a tidy profit for a film that reportedly only cost around $15,000 to produce. While *The Blair Witch Project* from 1999 ushered in the modern era of found-footage horror, *Paranormal Activity* turned found footage into a commercial juggernaut. *Paranormal Activity* was the highest-grossing horror film of 2009 and spawned a franchise, with sequels quickly released in 2010, 2011, and 2012 and then two more entries released in 2014 and 2015. The films were able to create a unique style of found-footage horror that led to commercial success, not to mention imitators as the popularity of the found-footage film surged in the Obama era.

The first *Paranormal Activity* from 2009 established a narrative and visual pattern that would be deployed fairly consistently across the sequels. In the original, a young couple begins hearing strange sounds in their suburban tract house. The man, a friendly day trader named Micah, decides to use his camcorder to investigate the unsettling sounds and experiences that are terrifying his girlfriend, Katie. At first, Micah hopes to simply find a rational explanation to assuage Katie's fears, but as the supernatural events increase in intensity, he hopes to get documented proof that there really is something unexplainable happening in their home. For much of the film, the audience watches Micah's surveillance, looking for little discrepancies or signs of ghosts in the footage. Unlike the somewhat reassuring endings of *The Eye* or *Shutter*, however, the end of *Paranormal Activity* depicts the unraveling of Micah's tidy little life: Katie becomes possessed by a dark spirit, kills Micah, and flees, her whereabouts unknown.[12]

The films that follow rely on remarkably similar plots. *Paranormal Activity 2* (2010) is actually a prequel, or rather a parallel plot, to the first film, focusing on Katie's sister, Kristi, and her family, consisting of a husband; their new baby, Hunter; and the husband's daughter from a previous marriage. Slightly before the events of the first film, Kristi and her family also experience strange occurrences, starting with the ransacking of their home, which they assume is the work of would-be robbers, so they install an elaborate home security system. As in the first movie, the family is systematically terrorized by the spirits until they are dead, possessed, or kidnapped.

The third movie in the franchise (2011) pulls the story back even further, taking us to Kristi and Katie's childhood in the 1980s, when they first make contact with a dark spirit, anticlimactically named Tobi. This time, their mother's boyfriend starts documenting the strange events, only to end up dead alongside Katie and Kristi's mother, at the hands of a mysterious California-based coven. The fourth movie (2012) takes us to an unrelated family in present-day Nevada whose teen daughter and her boyfriend capture much of the action on video chats, bringing social media into their paranormal investigations. Ultimately, the girl discovers that her adopted little brother is, in fact, young Hunter, and Katie comes to collect him for a bizarre ritual. This storyline is picked up in the sixth film, *The Ghost Dimension* (2015), in which a suburban family finds that their McMansion was built on the site of Katie and Kristi's childhood home. Now Tobi has come for their daughter, who is needed to complete a ritual (alongside Hunter) that will bring Tobi, possibly the antichrist, into material form. As in all the other films, everyone ends up dead.

By and large, the White terrors in the *Paranormal Activity* franchise stem from the anxieties of White homeownership after the housing bubble burst, and the films focus on White families struggling to assert control over the domestic spaces that have inexplicably turned against them. As I discuss in chapter 1, the housing crisis impacted people of color far more severely than White folks in the US, but the crisis disrupted the cultural narrative of homeownership as a reliable means for White folks to become upwardly mobile. The housing market crash produced an acute fear in White culture in the Obama years that Whites were losing their privileged social standing because property ownership had lost is value, both culturally and literally. The *Paranormal Activity* series came along at just the right moment to probe these fears around White proprietorship. As Julia Leyda argues, the first film—produced just before the housing market collapsed but released just after—perfectly encapsulates the anxieties of debtor capitalism in the Great Recession, as young people find that their dreams of homeownership are actually a nightmare of unpaid debts.[13]

As Leyda notes, these tensions around homeownership are particularly central to *Paranormal Activity 2*, which brings issues of race and proprietorship to the foreground of its story. In the prequel, when their home gets trashed from what the family presumes was a robbery, the husband invests in a home security system complete with an array of hidden cameras. Surveillance here is enacted in response to White anxieties around personal safety and the protection of private property, reflecting the long histories of racialized surveillance culture that Simone Browne discusses. Naturally, the first victim of these systems is the Hispanic housekeeper, who is caught on camera attempting to cleanse the house of evil spirits against the wishes of the husband, who promptly fires her. Of course, as the family's surveillance regime yields only more bizarre and unexplainable images, the husband brings back the housekeeper to exploit her knowledge of the occult (playing out a very tired racial trope in the horror film). This leads to even more unethical behavior in the name of protecting one's home: the husband uses a ritual to send the demon away to his sister-in-law's home, setting the events of the first film in motion. The systems of surveillance used in the film are overtly aligned with White paranoia around the sanctity of the home and White desperation to maintain control in domestic spaces.

The visual style of the *Paranormal Activity* series sutures the audience into these White assumptions around the power of surveillance. Much of the series is comprised of wide, long camera takes resembling security footage, most often with a time and date log running in the corner (see fig 7.2). Our job as a viewer is to scan the footage, closely examining its details for anything out of the ordinary. Is that pot supposed to be gently swaying? Was that door opened or closed in the previous shot? As the film toggles the audience through the various camera setups, we take on the role of night watchman, surveilling the home for anything out of the ordinary. Like the families, we assume that these cameras will reveal something useful to us, something that will allow us to really understand what is happening, even if we know that the footage has been meticulously staged by the filmmakers to only reveal bits and pieces as they unfold the plot.[14] To watch the film, we must buy into the family's assumptions that subjecting oneself to intense surveillance produces something useful, something that might protect the home, even if we know that their efforts will be fruitless.

These visual dynamics animate other found-footage films of the period. In *The Last Exorcism* (2010), a documentary crew hopes to prove that exorcisms

11:50: 10 PM

Fig. 7.2. Surveillance footage from the suburban home doesn't actually save the family but simply documents their deaths in *Paranormal Activity 2* (Paramount Pictures, 2010).

are faked but instead comes face-to-face with the occult. In *Devil's Due* (2014), a young husband attempts to document the strange behavior of his pregnant wife, who might be carrying a demon. In *The Visit* (2015), two young children hope to discover why their grandparents—who they only just met—are acting so strangely. And the reporters in *Quarantine* and *The Bay* (2012) hope to document the strange stories of viral infection unfolding around them. In these stories and across most of the *Paranormal Activity* series, incredulous White folks assume that the unbiased documentation of video surveillance will provide clear and scientific explanations for the world, only to find chaos, evil, and the occult. Unused to the vulnerable positions they find themselves in, White people attempt to assuage their hysteria through surveillance, assuming that it will protect their interests. Instead, their forays into surveillance culture affirm their worst fears: they are being victimized and can't control their homes or their communities.

Against this backdrop, *Paranormal Activity: The Marked Ones* stands as a fascinating counterpoint to these stories of White anxiety. Not only does the film leave behind the White suburb as a paradigmatic space for hauntings, moving the action from suburban McMansions into apartment complexes in a working-class Latinx neighborhood, it also highlights the perspective of young Latinx folks who use cameras to document the strange phenomenon impacting them, not to protect the family home.

In the film, eighteen-year-old Jesse Arista starts investigating the mysterious murder of an old woman in his family's apartment complex in Oxnard, California. After seeing a classmate, Oscar, flee from the scene of the crime, Jesse enlists the help of his friends Hector and Marisol to investigate, documenting the whole time with a new camera gifted to him as a high school graduation present. As they probe the mystery of the old woman, Ana, who was rumored to be a witch among the neighbors, Jesse begins to develop mysterious powers before slowly becoming possessed by an unseen force. Hector and Marisol try to save Jesse, discovering an occult scheme to possess young men for a demonic ritual (organized by the same coven revealed in *Paranormal Activity 3*). As is typical in the series, however, any attempts to stop the coven are futile, and everyone is presumed dead at the end.

The found-footage style of *The Marked Ones* deviates from the obsession with surveillance in the previous (and subsequent) *Paranormal Activity* films. The rest of the series fixates on the sanctity of the suburban home, with a heavy reliance on security-style footage that the White homeowners have installed themselves, certain that surveillance technology will somehow protect the home. But the footage in *The Marked Ones* is much more mobile and subjective, as Jesse and his crew explore not only their apartments, but also the city, running into non-supernatural danger along the way (such as their run-in with local criminals). And while the intent to document the strange phenomenon is shared with other films in the series, the context of this documentation is vastly different: instead of using the camera to maintain the safety of a family home, Jesse and Hector use it to record Jesse's growing supernatural abilities in one scene, hoping to produce a viral video. There is no space in which Jesse and his friends might presume to feel safe—not their small apartments, nor the streets or parks of the city they explore—so their camerawork instead captures their vulnerability as they unmask the dark forces at work. The found footage in this film feels much more like the grainy cell phone footage, circulated via social media, of violence in US cities that challenges the dominant narratives proffered by authorities.

Moreover, *The Marked Ones* shifts the normal focus of the series away from the vulnerabilities of White children targeted by demonic forces because of their heritage, offering instead a narrative about White exploitation of Latino bodies. In the film, Jesse discovers that Oscar had murdered Ana because Ana was helping the coven of White witches possess the bodies of young men, including Oscar and then Jesse. By contrast, the rest of the *Paranormal Activity* series dabbles in White guilt, showing White families terrorized because their forebearers made some unethical pacts in the past. But in *The Marked Ones*, young Latino boys are targeted by wealthy White folks to do the heavy lifting for their satanic rituals, providing a loose commentary on the exploitation of Latinx bodies in US culture for difficult labor that middle-class White folks can't or won't do.

Of course, whatever disruptions *The Marked Ones* provided to the series didn't seem to interest the producers, who quicky moved back to the standard White-family-in-distress formula in the next film in the series, *The Ghost Dimension*, released one year later. *The Marked Ones* demonstrates that the found-footage demonic horror film need not obsess over the sanctity of the White suburban home, but the subgenre overall remains fixated on the anxieties of Whiteness.

SURVEILLING WHITE MASCULINITY

Non-found-footage horror films in the Obama years also tell stories of White folks dabbling in the supernatural with the aid of technology, with mixed results. In the haunted house film *Oculus* (2013), a twenty-something young woman and her brother rig up their family home with cameras to document the supernatural realities of a haunted mirror that had possessed her father when she was a child. But the mirror has the ability to warp the minds of those around it, and in the end, the cameras clearly document the brother murdering his sister in an attempt to destroy the mirror. Likewise, in *Poltergeist*'s 2015 remake, paranormal scientists use a host of inexplicably complicated gadgets to track and study the family being tormented by agitated spirits. But in *Poltergeist*, the characters get their happy ending: with the aid of the technology, the nuclear family is restored. In both films, just as in the *Paranormal Activity* series, the use of technology is intertwined with narratives of families in crisis.

Such narratives tend to be particularly invested in White male authority. Note that in all the *Paranormal Activity* movies except part 4, it is a man who instigates the surveillance schemes, most often a White father or father figure whose control in the house is challenged by supernatural events he cannot explain or stop. Likewise, *Poltergeist* features a recently fired father struggling to support his family, and while the main character of *Oculus* is a young woman, her goal in the film is to vindicate her father, who was accused of murdering his wife all those years ago. Given that masculinity in US culture is often linked with science and rationality, the use of technology to document and explain away the irrational in these films highlights a bevy of fears around White manhood and authority.

As I discuss in chapter 3, cultural debates around White male authority intensified in the Obama era, as multiculturalism and feminism seemed to challenge the centrality and privileges of White manhood, all while the Great Recession further eroded the economic stability of working-class Whites. The haunted media cycle of US horror cinema, then, staged stories of White men in decline who were desperate to reclaim their former authority through careful investigation and documentation.

A variation on this theme runs through the meta-slasher film *The Cabin in the Woods* (produced by Joss Whedon in 2011). The film offers a playful commentary on the generic conventions of the slasher film by making the film's main action—a group of college students being murdered while visiting a remote cabin in the woods—all part of a government-sponsored ritual to appease ancient gods that dwell deep underground. The young people are monitored and manipulated by a team led by two older White bureaucrats (played by Bradley Whitford and Richard Jenkins), who desperately attempt to make the events unfold according to a preordained script, lest the ancient ones rise up and destroy all of humanity. What's more, these US bureaucrats compete with an international set of teams, each of whom provides a different horrific narrative in the hopes of appeasing the gods. But as each of the other teams fail, it is the sole responsibility of White men from the US to save the world.

The blandly dressed bureaucrats take to the task like they are in the cast of *The Office*, instead of enmeshed in a life-or-death scenario, cracking jokes and making bets as the film pokes fun at bureaucratic culture. As the teens make a mockery of this year's ritual, however, the film becomes a kind of generational dispute, pitting the upstart and cynical millennials against the expertise and authority of aging White bureaucrats who just want to clock in, clock out, and do their jobs. Using an elaborate series of surveillance cameras to track the college students, the bureaucrats in *The Cabin in the Woods* mirror the other White men in horror cinema, as they rely on the trappings of surveillance, technology, and bureaucracy in a desperate attempt to hold on to whatever authority they have left.

A more explicit example of haunted media plaguing the authority of White men is the 2012 haunted house film *Sinister*, discussed briefly in chapter 1. The film follows a once-successful true-crime writer, Ellison Oswald, who hasn't been able to reproduce the success of his first book, which vindicated a wrong-fully accused man. His subsequent books floundered, and now he hopes to rejuvenate his career by investigating the gruesome murder of a small-town family. Unbeknownst to his own family, he moves them into the site of the crime (the house was a bargain, given its recent bloody past).

As he delves into his investigation, he discovers a box of 8 mm films in the attic of the crime scene that link the murders to a series of crimes in which whole families are murdered, save one child who disappears. Oswald hopes he has stumbled across the pattern of a deranged serial killer that will make him rich and famous again, but he instead has discovered an ancient demon that inhabits pictures and migrates from house to house, possessing one of the children and forcing them to murder their families.

Like many of the fathers in the *Paranormal Activity* series, Oswald hopes that intensive study of the footage will yield rational clues explaining the bizarre deaths, but instead the footage only further erodes his patriarchal authority; the demon inspires strange behavior in his children, and his wife becomes increasingly frustrated with his withdrawal from the family. For Oswald, his careful and meticulous investigation is intertwined with his efforts to rejuve-nate his authority, but the haunted media makes a mockery of him as his family falls apart (see fig. 7.3).

The slow crumbling of his own family is also strangely mirrored in the foot-age he finds in his attic, which purports to show typical White suburban family activities, with titles such as "Pool Party '66" or "Lawn Work '86." The 8 mm films at first evoke the wholesomeness of home movies from the past, show-ing families having fun and goofing off before the playful titles become grue-some jokes. "Pool Party '66" ends with the family duct-taped to lawn chairs and tossed into the pool, where they drown. "Lawn Work '86" offers a POV shot of a riding lawn mower running over bound family members in the grass. The grainy 8 mm footage nostalgically conjures a supposedly simpler time for American families—a time when White male authority was more stable—but undercuts that nostalgia with shocking images of brutality that literally destroy those White families.

Oswald's quest to solve the crime and restore his manhood ultimately dooms his family. He seemingly makes the right decision to leave the investi-gation behind and move his family back to their old house, a sprawling country mansion he bought off the proceeds of his first book. But he discovers that the demon only strikes once it has driven the family to a new home, ensuring that the demon has a new house to haunt. Oswald finds out too late, and his young daughter poisons the family before murdering them all with an ax and

Fig. 7.3. Ellison Oswald carefully studies the horrific 8 mm footage found in his attic, hoping the research will resuscitate his career in *Sinister* (Summit Entertainment, 2012).

joining the demon and his army of ghost children. Oswald had hoped that his investigation would restore his masculine authority and a sense of rationality and provide a clear explanation for the murders that he had investigated so doggedly. Instead, he became the subject of yet another haunted film, another White patriarch made into a joke by the demon's haunted movies.

CONCLUSION

The real horror of the haunted media film, then, is that the White middle classes have lost their hold on rationality as an ideological cudgel. Challenges to bourgeois worldviews in the US (from women, people of color, or other disenfranchised groups) are dismissed for being hysterical, angry, or unhinged. Calm rationality is supposedly the domain of White men, and anyone who challenges White patriarchy must clearly be irrational.

Technocratic systems of surveillance are a natural extension of this rationality, but today's systems of surveillance and sousveillance don't offer the assurances that such systems did in the past. Surveillance and data-based systems are perceived as race- and gender-neutral (even if they aren't), suggesting that White folks aren't as special as they once were. And the proliferation of cameras in the hands of diverse populations reveals new and damning perspectives on the state of inequality in the US. Today, White folks are the hysterical ones offering emotional, unhinged perspectives on their own victimization and the unreliability of media.

The *Paranormal Activity* series and other haunted media films document this supposedly horrific descent into irrationality for the White men in the films. Assuming that technology and surveillance will assuage their vulnerability and affirm their rational position of privilege, the men in such films instead slowly begin to panic, fruitlessly running about while holding a camera as we watch them slide into oblivion.

NOTES

1. The other three films in this period were more standard science and technology gone astray films: *Splice* (2009), *Chernobyl Diaries* (2012), and *The Lazarus Effect* (2015).

2. Not all found-footage films are examples of "haunted media," of course. But in many found-footage films, the style is justified by storylines in which people (almost always White people) decide that documenting the intrusion of the supernatural into their everyday life is a key strategy for coping with the horrors of the world. The *Paranormal Activity* series exemplifies this trend, as does the 2016 remake of *The Blair Witch*.

3. Linnie Blake and Xavier Aldana Reyes, eds., *Digital Horror: Haunted Technologies, Network Panic and the Found Footage Phenomenon* (London: I. B. Tauris, 2016).

4. Catherine Zimmer, *Surveillance Cinema* (New York: NYU Press, 2015).

5. Simone Browne, *Dark Matters: On the Surveillance of Blackness* (Durham, NC: Duke University Press, 2015).

6. Safiya Umoja Noble, *Algorithms of Oppression: How Search Engines Reinforce Racism* (New York: NYU Press, 2018).

7. A number of authors have explored how automation and big data exacerbate, rather than alleviate, social inequalities. See Meredith Broussard, *Artificial Unintelligence: How Computers Misunderstand the World* (Cambridge, MA: MIT Press, 2018); Virginia Eubanks, *Automating Inequality: How High-Tech Tools Profile, Police, and Punish the Poor* (New York: St. Martin's Press, 2017); and Cathy O'Neil, *Weapons of Math Destruction: How Big Data Increases Inequality and Threatens Democracy* (New York: Crown, 2016).

8. Jackie Wang, "'This Is a Story About Nerds and Cops': PredPol and Algorithmic Policing," *E-Flux* 87 (December 2017), accessed May 13, 2021, https://www.e-flux.com/journal/87/169043/this-is-a-story-about-nerds-and-cops-predpol-and-algorithmic-policing/.

9. John Fiske, "Surveilling the City: Whiteness, the Black Man and Democratic Totalitarianism," *Theory, Culture and Society* 15, no. 2 (1998): 67–88.

10. For example, the increased use of surveillance cameras and the ability of bystanders to record police interactions have brought attention to the practice of "testilying," which is when police officers lie on the stand to justify illegal actions on the job. See Joseph Goldstein, "'Testilying' by Police: A Stubborn Problem," *New York Times*, March 18, 2018, https://www.nytimes.com/2018/03/18/nyregion/testilying-police-perjury-new-york.html.

11. Zimmer argues in *Surveillance Cinema* that the surveillance imagery in torture-porn films of the mid-2000s elicit embodied perspectives that supported the national imperatives toward torture in this period.

12. This is the ending of the theatrical version, at least. An alternate ending shows Katie slashing her throat, and the film's original ending has Katie being shot by police when they enter the house. Those endings would upset the continuity of the franchise, however, which wanted to build on the story of Katie and her sister, Kristi.

13. Julia Leyda, "Demon Debt: *Paranormal Activity* as Recessionary Post-Cinematic Allegory," *Jump Cut* 56 (Winter 2014–2015), accessed May 6, 2021, https://www.ejumpcut.org/archive/jc56.2014-2015/LeydaParanormalActivity/index.html.

14. The visual style of the *Paranormal Activity* series mirrors the spectatorship patterns of online "ghost" videos purporting to capture supernatural events that we are supposed to scrutinize.

8

~m~

MAKING HORROR GREAT AGAIN

The Horror Remake

HORROR REMAKES SUCH AS 2010's *A Nightmare on Elm Street* often seem more cynical than the original films; they take on a darker visual style and weigh the plot with a sense of seriousness. The newer *Elm Street* self-consciously asserts that our contemporary world is much worse than the 1980s of the original—more somber, more socially disconnected, more traumatic—as it tells the story of exhausted and burned-out teens coming to grips with the knowledge that they were molested as children (a sentiment only hinted at in the original). Freddy was originally a witty and campy antagonist who cracked jokes as a counterpoint to his gruesome torment of suburban teenagers. He "could make us groan and chuckle simultaneously with his half-witty commentary directed more toward the viewer than the victims he teased before the slaughter," as film scholar Adam Lowenstein puts it.[1] But in 2010, Freddy is a deadly serious stalker who reminds his prey of sexual traumas that they have tried desperately to forget.

The newer film includes all the bleakness of the original without any of the wit or campy charm. Its darker tone makes the original seem more lighthearted, even if the original film integrated historical concerns around child molestation and Satanic cults into its narrative.[2] Indeed, as Lowenstein argues, the original film places much more emphasis on the larger community surrounding the characters in the film, highlighting the role of parents as the teens find themselves tormented by Freddy's deadly dreams. The newer *Elm Street*, by contrast, pushes the parents and the larger community to the sidelines, wallowing in the desperation of its young protagonists. For Lowenstein, the newer film's nostalgic fixation on classic slasher conventions removes the story from the larger cultural debates around families, parents, and divorce from the 1980s, contexts that gave the original such resonance. The newer film offers instead an empty nostalgia that "overwhelms opportunities to confront the communal politics of the present."[3]

Of course, the absence of parents and the larger community in the 2010 *Elm Street* is central to its bleakness. By suggesting (erroneously) that the past was somehow tamer and more lighthearted, the newer film wallows in its own vision of the present as grittier, more traumatic, and more isolating for the millennials it focuses on, tapping into today's fears that overworked and anxious young White people will never attain the stability of previous generations. The isolation and exhaustion of its young protagonists, in its own way, does confront the communal politics of the present by presenting a deadening vision of isolation: the teens in the newer film don't even seem capable of forming meaningful relationships with one another. In this way, the excessively dark tone of the newer film tries to rewrite history, framing the original as a fun slasher lark instead of a film deeply invested in the cultural politics around families, communities, and sexual trauma. The implication seems to be that if the 2010 *Elm Street* can be depressing and desperate enough, we'll forget that the 1980s were also complex and, at times, traumatic.

The recent cycle of films remaking or reimagining classic US horror movies offers similar meditations on the past in the US. The films are gleefully nostalgic for past horror films from supposedly simpler times (the low-budget, independent horror classics from the 1970s or the campy slashers from the 1980s, typically). And yet, rather than trying to capture the pleasures from the past, they obsessively insist that today's world is far more dangerous and fraught, especially for White people. Despite the filmmakers' clear love and veneration for the originals, they approached classic slashers as artifacts of simpler and easier times that can be transformed and leveraged into illustrations of how much more horrific the US has become.

It hardly seems a coincidence that the US horror remake cycle coincided with a rising tide of White nostalgia that Donald Trump would harness in his 2016 presidential campaign. As horror filmmakers persistently looked back to the past for inspiration, White racial resentment in the US encouraged a vague nostalgia for a supposedly simpler time, when the cultural position of White folks and White men in particular was more secure. With Obama in the White House as a powerful symbol of multiculturalism, conservatism in the US became increasingly organized around White nostalgia and a return to unabashed White cultural dominance. As Ronald Brownstein wrote in *The Atlantic* during the 2016 election, Trump's persistent promises to make America "win again" or to "bring back" jobs and stability were explicit references to this

White nostalgia, "evok[ing] a hazy earlier time when American life worked better for the overwhelmingly White, heavily blue-collar coalition now drawn to him."[4]

Trump's Electoral College victory demonstrated the power of this nostalgia, as not just blue-collar Whites, but Whites across the socioeconomic spectrum voted for Trump and his claims that he would "bring back" an era of White stability.

Interestingly, though, Trump's brand of nostalgia is hardly uplifting or utopian. While Trump's rhetoric references a vague and idyllic past—as illustrated by his campaign promise to "Make America Great Again"—he spends much of his time painting a bleak picture of America's recent past and present, decrying what he and his supporters see as the travesties of multiculturalism, environmentalism, and liberalism in the contemporary US. As president, Trump spent almost all of his time pointing to the perceived failures and betrayals of past presidents (especially Obama) instead of outlining when exactly America was great and how to achieve his vision of greatness. It is far easier to make monsters out of your political enemies than to articulate a cogent vision of the future. As Trump and his supporters responded to (and recoiled from) the changing cultural conditions of the modern US, they balanced nostalgia and horror, yearning for an imagined and idyllic past of White centrality while also obsessing over the imagined horrors stemming from a monstrous Obama that constantly haunts them.

This tendency masquerades as a form of nostalgia but is really a cynical assertion that our present is worse than our past. The yearning for an imagined past in Trump's conservative rhetoric is often subordinate to a desire to see political and cultural opponents punished for their role in cultural change. Vague nostalgia is most often a rhetorical cudgel used in the service of insults or deliberately cruel policies meant to mock the political and cultural left in the US. There is no real desire or vision for achieving a supposedly lost greatness. Instead, these discourses use the idea of lost greatness to engender cynicism about the present.

This kind of faux nostalgia animates the horror remake cycle. In their attempts to make horror great again, filmmakers are certainly not engaging in the exact same nostalgia for White dominance evidenced in the rise of Trump. But the persistent recycling of '70s and '80s horror starting in the mid-2000s does engage in the same kinds of cynicism at the core of conservative nostalgia, rewriting the past to wallow in the seeming desperation of the present. Based on the products they made, horror filmmakers did not turn to the past for inspiration in the 2000s and 2010s because of a wistful longing for classic horror, but rather to build comparisons showing how much more horrific the contemporary world is. No matter how complex, political, or gruesome the original film, the remakes desperately insist the world today is far worse off.

In particular, these films participate in a general exploration of Whiteness and social class in America's past and present. The horror remake cycle revisits stories of Whiteness from the recent past and reimagines them, offering cynical reflections on the changing perceptions of race and social class in the US.

These films are particularly prominent in the Obama era, but really the horror remake cycle starts in the mid-2000s. Horror remakes only accounted for around 3.5 to 5 percent of total mainstream horror output in the '80s and '90s. But the commercial success of the 2003 remake of *The Texas Chainsaw Massacre* sparked a cycle of remakes centered primarily on 1970s independent horror or campy 1980s slasher films.[5] By the end of the Bush era, remakes accounted for around 10 percent of total mainstream horror output, a trend that would continue in the Obama era, as sixteen remakes were released between 2008 and 2016. Examining all twenty-six mainstream Hollywood remakes between 2005 and 2016, this chapter compares the original films to their newer versions, looking for changes made in narrative and imagery in order to analyze how these films reimagine classic narratives from the past.

Two major trends are evident in this cycle of films. First, many films imagined the present as notably worse than the past when compared to the original narratives. The newer films develop narrative worlds rooted in class anxiety for White communities in particular. If the older films featured stable White communities that were tormented by ghosts, monsters, serial killers, or what have you, their newer counterparts imagined a world of White instability that was made worse by the tormentors in the plot, where the monsters might be seen as extensions of White economic precarity.

Second, a group of films created worlds in which the characters *seemed* far better off and more affluent than their counterparts in the older films, but this conspicuous success was only a veneer under which anxieties lurked about the costs of achieving prosperity for Whites and the fate of those left behind by the modern economy. Some of these affluent Whites are literally tormented by working-class and rural White trash monsters who were not present in the original narratives and remind the characters of class divisions in the US. There might seem to be a semblance of progress and prosperity in these narratives, but that success cannot obscure the ways that many White folks have been left behind.

A MORE HORRIFIC PRESENT

The recent horror remake cycle has been a source of hand-wringing for horror fans and scholars alike since the mid-2000s, when Hollywood's remake obsession turned its attention to horror.[6] As with other high-profile Hollywood remakes, horror remakes spawned accusations from fans and critics that the newer films were simply crass commercial calculations aimed at wresting profits from established intellectual property rather than investing in new and innovative stories. There were also the usual concerns that the remakes would never be able to capture the innovation and ingenuity of the original films, which were often low-budget cult classics.[7] The commercial and critical resurgence of horror throughout the Obama era has largely quieted these critiques of Hollywood's horror output. The success of original horror content has outpaced the reliance on remakes. But early in the remake cycle (which includes remakes of successful international horror films), fans and critics worried openly about the dearth of creativity in mainstream horror cinema. One scholar even wrote an insightful study devoted to the failures of newer films to engage and disturb audiences as the originals did.[8]

However, rather than exploring remakes as a commentary on Hollywood's supposed lack of creativity, I want to explore how horror remakes (very creatively) took up issues of Whiteness and social class in Obama's America. This chapter, then, explores remakes as a kind of conversation about White communities, White men, and White economic status over time.

One the major trends across the remake cycle, for example, is to insert the narrative of the original film into the present day. But the present day in the newer films is far more uncertain and anxious than the world of the original films, especially when it comes to social class.

For example, consider the 2009 3-D remake of *My Bloody Valentine*, based on the 1981 Canadian slasher film. The original film tells the story of young Canadian miners who vow to put on a Valentine's Day dance in their small mining town, despite local lore saying that if they hold the dance, a miner who went insane after a grisly accident on Valentine's Day would come back to town for his revenge. Sure enough, while the town prepares for the dance, people start dying as a mysterious killer in mining gear cuts out their hearts.

While setting the film in a working-class mining community certainly adds a fascinating twist to the typical suburban-set slasher (as does the fact that the original mining accident was caused by neglectful supervisors who attended the dance instead of doing their safety checks), the class politics of the original film are largely implied. The young miners are a generally carefree group who just want to have a party and hook up, much like their suburban teen counterparts in other slashers of the period.

In the 2009 US remake, however, the story is laden with the class anxieties of working-class White communities. Set in a Pacific Northwest mining town named Harmony, the newer film centers on Tom, the young son of the mine's recently deceased owner. Tom reluctantly comes back to town years after he witnessed an attack by a deranged miner that left many young people dead. Having inherited the family business, Tom intends to close the mine and sell the property as soon as possible, which would devastate the economy of the already struggling community. Right on cue, a series of murders grips the community, leaving the town and the audience to guess who might be behind the attacks.

The newer film offers a vacillating perspective of small working-class communities. The town is picturesque and filled with wholesome families in well-kept homes; even the sheriff and his wife in this working-class town can employ a Hispanic housekeeper. But the town cannot repress the moral and economic decay enmeshed in the community, from the seedy truck-stop hotel, where the mysterious killer gruesomely murders a prostitute and a crass truck driver, to the dilapidated cabin, where the unsavory sheriff has trysts with his mistress. Mirroring the Trumpian rhetoric that would come later, the film insists that small mining communities are at once the wholesome core of American values and crumbling dystopias, thanks to liberal politics.

Compared to the original *My Bloody Valentine*, the remake sees the struggles of working-class White communities far more cynically, with the murders acting as an extension of the town's economic anxiety. Even though the mine is operating and jobs are being created, poverty and economic decline are still creeping into the fringes of the town. Closing the mine would devastate the town, but keeping it open isn't exactly a lifeline either, especially as the opening scene reveals how dangerous the jobs provided actually are. A maniac miner on the loose highlights these tensions, drawing attention to the town's moral decay through his violence but pointing to mining—dangerous and fickle in the global economy—as an agent of this decay. In the original, the murders *disrupted* a sense of communal belonging and stability in the tight-knight community. In the new version, the murders only exacerbate the slow decay of the town in the global economy.[9]

This tendency to set horror remakes against a more fraught cultural and socioeconomic backdrop extends across the cycle. In the original *The Evil Dead* (1981), the characters are ordinary college students simply hoping to have a fun vacation in the woods when they are beset by an ancient demon who possesses them one by one. In the remake (2013), the main character is an addict who brings her friends and estranged brother to the cabin to help her get clean. The remake dwells on the possible upward mobility of White folks who have been dragged into poverty and bad choices by drugs. Likewise, the original *Don't Be Afraid of the Dark* (1973) tells the story of a middle-class housewife who is terrorized by evil creatures that emerge from the basement of the country estate she inherited from her grandparents. In the remake (2010), the family takes possession of the house as a desperate investment by the father, whose plans to save his career in house remodeling are threatened by his daughter's strange antics as she deals with the evil creatures from the basement. In each retelling of these stories, the characters are inserted into narrative worlds more clearly rooted in gendered and class-based anxiety for White folks.

Sometimes, the addition of class anxiety into the remakes references the Great Recession and the sluggish economic recovery that followed. For example, the 2011 remake of *Fright Night* (1985) inserts the imagery and anxiety of the housing market crash into the original narrative about a teen boy who confronts the vampire living next door. The original *Fright Night* was set in a generic tree-lined middle-class community, with the charming vampire Jerry Dandrige moving into a stereotypical rundown Victorian mansion for his new lair. The remake sets the action in a small subdivision on the outskirts of Las Vegas, with cookie-cutter tract homes carving a few blocks out of the desert (see fig. 8.1).

The Las Vegas suburbs featured so prominently in the film were one of the major epicenters of the mid-2000s housing crisis, with huge numbers of suburban homes falling into foreclosure when the housing bubble burst. *Fright Night*'s setting alludes to these anxieties, which are reinforced even further by the mother in the film, a realtor trying to get people to move into their neighborhood while "legions" of people are fleeing it, she says. In this way, the newer *Fright Night* takes up the original film's concern with teenage manhood, this time placing the film's teenage male protagonist against the backdrop of economic instability for the White middle class.

Fright Night is not the only remake in this period to reimagine the tensions of White manhood in the contemporary world. Consider the remake of *The Wicker Man*, which sought to update the classic British folk horror film from 1973. Both films dramatize the struggles of White authority figures confronted with worldviews that challenge their power, but the remake radically alters the backdrop of the story. In the original, an uptight, by-the-books English policeman investigates the disappearance of a small child on an isolated island that dislikes outsiders. The prudish policeman (a devout Christian and a virgin

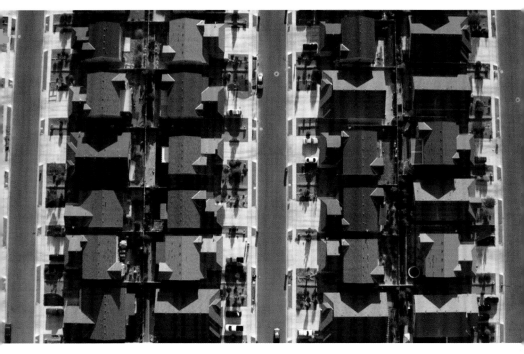

Fig. 8.1. An isolated stretch of tract housing, seen from above, is the source of both economic decline and vampiric horrors in the remake of *Fright Night* (DreamWorks Pictures, 2011).

who is saving himself for marriage) is shocked to discover that the island follows a pagan folk religion that celebrates sexuality and reproduction. As the policeman investigates the disappearance without the support of the hostile community (all while resisting the sexual temptations of the locals), he makes the horrific conclusion that his investigation is all a ruse put on by the islanders themselves, who want the virginal authority figure as a human sacrifice to save their failing apple orchards.

Somewhat shockingly, the remake of *The Wicker Man* in 2006 makes almost no references to sexuality. Following a similar storyline, the newer version features a troubled California police officer (played by Nicolas Cage) who travels to an island off the coast of Washington to investigate the disappearance of a small girl—later revealed to be his daughter—who had been kept secret from him by his ex, who lives on the island. But instead of finding a sexually liberated neo-pagan community like his predecessor in the 1973 film, the policeman finds a matriarchal community that privileges women and femininity over manhood. He grows increasingly hostile throughout his investigation as he realizes that the men of the community, when allowed to stay on the island, are treated as second-class citizens and that none of the women of the island respect his authority as a police officer or as a man. What makes this vision of the neo-pagan community horrific is not their lusty disregard for Christian mores, but their disenfranchisement of men and masculinity.

Just as in the original, the investigation is a ruse to lure the policeman to the island for ritual sacrifices, but in the newer version, the island's women have been priming their unsuspecting target for years, manipulating his life on the mainland to prepare him psychologically for his role in their pagan rites. The film presents a paranoid fantasy of an evil feminist conspiracy targeting good-hearted men to appease their bizarre anti-male beliefs. The original film toyed with the audience's sympathies, presenting the police officer as overly rigid and the islanders as seductive and free-spirited, only to see those sympathies challenged as the narrative reveals the islanders' intents. In the remake, by contrast, the police officer is simply a well-intentioned public servant attempting to do the right thing, while the matriarchal islanders are prickly, strange, and oppressive. In this way, the newer version dramatizes a heightened sense of White male victimization in contemporary culture.

These anxieties around White manhood, of course, are entwined with concerns around White economic precarity in the Obama era. The relative financial instability of White middle-class families in the Great Recession challenged the traditional authority of White patriarchs (as discussed in more detail in chap. 4). The prospect of economic instability pushes horror remakes to dwell on the authority of men in a changing economy, a tendency most apparent in the 2015 remake of *Poltergeist*.

Tobe Hooper's 1982 horror blockbuster *Poltergeist* (written and produced by Steven Spielberg) is already deeply concerned with manhood and capitalism. In the film, a typical middle-class family has recently moved into a home in a new subdivision because the father (Steven, played by Craig T. Nelson) has a successful job selling homes in the development. The family, however, is soon faced with a crisis when supernatural forces kidnap their daughter through a mystic portal in their new home. Steven's professional life falls apart as the family enlists a series of supernatural experts to try to help them recover their daughter. Steven eventually discovers that the housing development he works for was built on an old cemetery, but rather than relocating the bodies, the greedy developer simply removed the headstones, leaving a horde of angry spirits to haunt the neighborhood.

The original *Poltergeist* helped popularize the use of seemingly normal, modern suburbs as the site of hauntings, demons, and other supernatural events in cinema and the use of ghosts to dramatize cultural fears that wholesome White suburbs masked corruption and dark secrets. In this case, the greedy developers in the film and their unwitting release of evil spirits imply that middle-class White prosperity may be (literally) built upon the unethical behaviors of the corporate elite. But the family is economically secure, and the father doesn't suffer from the personal or financial crises that would become common in the Obama-era haunted house film (although these issues do arise in the 1986 sequel, in which the father's career has stalled out thanks to the events of the first film). Rather, the original film explicitly focuses on White prosperity and the unethical practices that support it.

When *Poltergeist* was remade in 2015, however, the evil spirits targeting the family became a dramatic extension of the White patriarch's fragile manhood and declining economic fortunes. Taking its cues from other popular haunted house films from the 2010s, the remake opens with a struggling White family who has been forced to move into a much smaller and cheaper tract home in a suburban development because the father, Eric (Sam Rockwell), lost his job at the John Deere corporate headquarters (a nod to the economic struggles of rural Whites, even if the father isn't one). And the father isn't alone in his struggles. The family can only afford this smaller house because foreclosures have hit the neighborhood hard. The nearby mall is boarded up because of the economic downturn (much to the chagrin of the family's teenage daughter). Rather than tackling White prosperity, this version of the *Poltergeist* story establishes a clear backdrop of White socioeconomic decline.

The family's precarity is also depicted as a direct challenge to the father's sense of authority and identity. Their declining economic fortunes stem from his failures as a breadwinner, and this torments him, as he takes their economic crisis as a threat to his manhood. He is publicly humiliated when his credit card is declined at a local store, and his humiliation continues when he and his wife are invited to a dinner party at a wealthy friend's house. The father drinks too much at the party when confronted with the successes of others, losing face by acknowledging his struggles to find more work. The film explicitly links the impacts of the Great Recession on White men's self-worth, imagining the contemporary world as far more difficult for White men than the world depicted in 1982.[10]

The father in the newer film, however, is allowed to redeem his flailing manhood. In the original, the family saves their daughter but ends up essentially homeless, their assets literally liquidated when their house gets sucked into the spirit world. Worn down and despondent (but happy to be alive), they check into a cheap motel. The remake, however, culminates in the triumph of the father as he takes his wife shopping for a new house, this time much nicer, because he has found a personally fulling job as a high school baseball coach. The family's encounter with the supernatural has essentially resuscitated their class standing, a hopeful ending suggesting that White families who are able to endure the torment of the bad economy will eventually persevere and reclaim a privileged place in the culture.

ESCAPING A HORRIFIC PAST

The 2009 remake of *Friday the 13th* also imagines a world with more class tension compared to its source material. The first two films of the *Friday the 13th* series largely focused on middle-class White teens and twenty-somethings working at Camp Crystal Lake, without any significant references to their social class or class divisions in the narrative (at least until part III in 1982). But in the 2009 film (which loosely remakes *Friday the 13th II* from 1981), the narrative weaves together a set of characters from different social backgrounds that conflict with one another in the film. Largely organized around a group of wealthy college students whose ringleader's family owns a vacation home on Crystal Lake near the site of the old camp, the film also features a working-class hero, Clay (Jared Padalecki), as he searches for his missing sister, who was abducted by Jason Voorhees. Adding more complexity to an already messy plotline, the teens also get creeped out by the local redneck Whites, who embody a host of "poor White trash" stereotypes before getting killed off by Jason as well. The film situates itself within a host of class tensions and stereotypes instead of simply dwelling on the fates of middle-class teens trying to party and have fun.

But the remake also exhibits another tendency of the Obama-era cycle: it scales up the social class of the main characters in order to depict the corruption of White elites who have left poor Whites behind. The 2009 remake of *Friday the 13th* goes out of its way to depict the wealth of the affluent college students as obnoxious and toxic. The ringleader, Trent (Travis Scott Van Winkle), is a materialistic asshole who uses his family's wealth to get friends, and the drugged-up debauchery of his group (a staple of the slasher genre) is more of an indictment of their spoiled class standing than a depiction of fun-loving teen antics. Trent, for example, gleefully cheats on his girlfriend while she's out helping the working-class hero search for his missing sister. So we aren't that concerned when Trent gets gruesomely impaled by Jason's machete after he is too reluctant to get a ride from a run-down pickup truck that evokes the killer hillbilly trope used frequently in mid-2000s horror. His class stereotypes cost him his life, not that we had any expectations that his character might live.

These kinds of class-based critiques of White wealth find their way across the remake cycle. Many of the films include imagery of excessive White affluence, often linking that excess to the horrors that befall the characters. Similar to the White guilt evidenced in the home invasion cycle (see chap. 2), these changes in the storylines draw attention to the disparate fates of White folks in the global economy, where the prosperity of some leaves others behind.

The 2009 film *Sorority Row*, based on the 1983 slasher *The House on Sorority Row*, for example, exaggerates the class standing of the original characters. While the original film's focus on college students certainly speaks to class discourses around privilege in the '80s, the remake puts those discourses on steroids, depicting the women as more affluent, spoiled, and privileged. The film is filled with markers of class and consumption (their cars, their clothes), and the antics involving sex, drink, and drugs suggest the immoral excesses of wealth.

A similar effect is seen in 2008's *Prom Night*, which features the excesses of more affluent teens than those featured in the 1980 Jamie Lee Curtis slasher. However, a more prominent example is the 2013 remake of the 1976 horror classic *Carrie*. Class divisions are certainly displayed in the original film between the middle-class suburban community and the eccentric protagonist, Carrie White, with her run-down home and shoddy clothes. But the remake changes Carrie's teenage tormentors into exaggerated clichés of rich mean girls. Their ringleader, Chris, still launches mean-spirited attacks on Carrie, but this time those attacks are more explicitly linked to her class privilege. She is a spoiled rich girl who threatens and demeans teachers because she knows her rich father will come to school and threaten lawsuits to keep her out of trouble. More than in the original, Carrie's assault on the school and its bullies feels like a form of class warfare, a punishment for the excesses of White affluence in the modern world.

A number of other films in this cycle depict affluent characters being tormented by the specter of poverty. The 2006 remake of *Black Christmas*, for example, develops an elaborate backstory for the serial killer hiding out in the sorority house that used to be the killer's family home (in contrast to the 1974 original, which doesn't reveal much about the killer from their nonsensical rantings over the phone calls that are coming from inside the house). This time around, we learn that the serial killer—a psychopath with jaundiced skin who recently escaped from a mental hospital—was raised in the home by an uncaring, incestuous mother who murdered the boy's kindly father when he was young and locked the boy in the attic to keep him from reporting the murder to the police. When a tryst between the budding killer and the drunken mother leads to the birth of a little girl who is doted on by the mother, jealousy drives the young man to murder his family and make gruesome Christmas cookies out of their flesh.

Visually, the killer's roots in *Black Christmas* suggest stark class differences from those of the sorority girls, who are mostly from privileged or middle-class families. The sorority house in the present may suggest wealth and comfort, but in the flashbacks, the home is dingy and unkempt. In this derelict space, the mother, with dark rings under her eyes and stringy hair, drinks too much and glares at the offspring she hates. The house in the present, by contrast, is a haven for affluence (as suggested by one of the young women's townie boyfriend, who calls the sorority girls "spoiled bitches"). But the upward mobility of the house's current occupants is a sharp contrast to the economic struggles of poor White folks like the killer, whose jaundiced skin indicates that his poverty and desperation make him not quite White. He never had the normal middle-class Christmas that he could see other White families celebrating (with the aid of a telescope in his attic prison), so he comes back on Christmas for his revenge on the affluent college students.

Similar narratives of class-based horror are common early on in the remake cycle, building on the rural horror trend of the Bush years to focus on horrific hillbillies who torment more prosperous Whites. These stories feature economically secure White folks who are violently reminded about the precarity of inequality in the US.

Chief among these films is the 2006 remake of Wes Craven's low-budget film from 1977, *The Hills Have Eyes*. The original film, of course, is itself a striking work of class consciousness; it tells the story of a middle-class White family, helmed by a retired police officer, who gets stuck in the Southwest desert on a road trip and has to face off with a band of mutated White cannibals.[11] The remake takes on the same conceit, this time adding more class conflict within the middle-class family between the hardened, conservative patriarch and the liberal and more affluent son-in-law, who owns a cell-phone store and wears glasses, always a sign of effete manhood in Hollywood. As the family gets drawn into a conflict with the mutated clan—who are represented as more deformed and grotesque in the newer version—the film gives more space in the narrative to the backstory of the murderous mutants, who are the offspring of poor miners in the area who refused to leave their homes when the desert became a site for nuclear testing. Linking the mutants more clearly to structural inequity in the US, the newer film suggests that the effete son-in-law must violently confront the horrific inequalities of the country in order to *man up* and take the mantle of middle-class patriarchy in the new economy.

The 2005 reimagining of the 1953 Vincent Price classic *House of Wax* develops a similar narrative about upward mobility and the hidden inequalities of White poverty. Set in the present, *House of Wax* tells the story of a struggling but upwardly mobile twenty-something young woman on a road trip with her downwardly mobile twin brother, recently out of jail for auto theft, along with a few friends. Just as in *The Hills Have Eyes*, the protagonists get lost and have car trouble somewhere in rural America, leading to a violent confrontation with poor Whites who remain hidden from the rest of the world. This time, those poor Whites are another set of twins—brothers, one of whom is horribly deformed, the other of whom is a psychopath—who have inherited their mother's long-forgotten city of wax, a perfect simulacrum of small-town Americana populated with realistic wax figures in a series of tableaus. As the vulnerable twenty-somethings discover, the figures are actually real people who were murdered by the twins and coated in wax in order to speed up their work bringing their mother's vision to life. The twin heroes face off against the wax artists and survive, and the brother redeems himself with his sister, suggesting that he might get his life back on track.

Interestingly, both *House of Wax* and *The Hills Have Eyes* use decaying and dilapidated replicas of wholesome White American towns as sites of horrific violence between poor and more affluent Whites in the new economy. *House of Wax* features an artificial town with wax figures originally built as a tourist attraction, while in *The Hills Have Eyes*, the son-in-law must rescue his infant daughter from an artificial American town built by the military for radiation testing but now occupied by mutants (see fig. 8.2). These settings both suggest that the nostalgic fantasy of economic and cultural stability for the White middle class is now a ruse, a horrific joke juxtaposing the promises of the American dream with the cutthroat realities of inequality in the US. Poor rural Whites were promised those wholesome and stable communities, but now they struggle to survive in the nightmarish shadow of those promises, clinging to the deception of the American dream while enacting a gruesome charade of White Americana. And the middle-class heroes must visit these spaces and grapple with the unkept promises of the American economy in order to survive.

While not as explicit as these mid-2000s remakes, a similar narrative trope around poor Whiteness is used in the 2016 version of 1999's *The Blair Witch Project*. While ostensibly a sequel, the newer film reboots the story of the original about a group of college students making a documentary about supernatural folktales in the Maryland woods. This time, the much younger brother of the original documentary filmmaker, Heather, heads into the woods to investigate his sister's disappearance, spurred on by new footage found by a couple

Fig. 8.2. The protagonist explores a simulated American town from the 1950s used to test the effects of nuclear radiation, now occupied by cannibalistic mutants, in the remake of *The Hills Have Eyes* (Craven-Maddalena Films, 2006).

of poor, rural Marylanders who are online conspiracy-theory fanatics of the Blair Witch folklore. Class tensions keep the college students and the poor locals from trusting one another in the woods, especially since the locals hung a confederate flag in their run-down trailer, which didn't sit well with the young Black couple helping the filmmakers. But there is no survival this time for the middle-class millennials, no hardened cynicism that helps them persevere in their confrontation with rural horrors. This time, both the rural Whites and the upwardly mobile millennials are consumed in the decaying home hidden from the world.

ROB ZOMBIE'S *HALLOWEEN*

These confrontations with the specter of poor Whiteness are perhaps most pronounced in Rob Zombie's reimagining of the 1978 slasher film *Halloween*. Like other slashers that became the fodder for remakes, the original *Halloween* is mostly devoid of class conflicts. The teens terrorized by Michael Myers are average middle-class teenagers looking to have a good time. And while the abandoned Myers home in the original implies a bit of class anxiety—suggesting what could be simmering beneath the surface of middle-class normalcy—Michael Myers himself is just another offspring of those White suburban families, a middle-class child who inexplicably became an almost-supernatural killer. But as Rob Zombie tells the story, the saga of Michael Myers dramatizes White fears that White poverty and low social class may still haunt a seemingly prosperous White middle class.

Zombie's version of the story expands the original film's opening scene (in which a young Michael Myers, dressed in a clown costume for Halloween, stabs his older sister to death after she has sex with her boyfriend) into a forty-five-minute meditation on the psychological factors that may have made Myers become a psychopath, from bullying, to an unstable family home, to suggestions of anxiety around his sexual identity. Film scholar James Kendrick argues that Zombie's fixation on what made Myers a monster is a hallmark of the 2000s remake cycle, with Zombie and many other filmmakers desperate to build elaborate backstories that can explain the horrific violence in the films. For Kendrick, the obsession with explanations and knowledge about horror monsters demonstrates a post-9/11 desire to grapple with and understand the senseless violence of the contemporary world.[12]

Kendrick makes a compelling case, but, as demonstrated above, our desire to understand and explain this violence most often hinges on narratives of White decline as the foundation for contemporary horrors. After all, in Zombie's film, Michael Myers becomes a monster because of his roots as poor White trash. In a major change to the original, the Myers family in the 2007 version is not an average middle-class family in the Illinois suburb of Haddonfield, but a desperately poor family embodying all the culture's stereotypes about White poverty (see fig. 8.3). Myers's mom, while loving, works as a stripper to make ends meet while her lazy and crass boyfriend recuperates from an injury that supposedly keeps him from working. The mother's boyfriend bullies Michael incessantly and ogles Michael's promiscuous older sister, who also calls Michael names. Set in an undetermined past, the Myers home brings together all of the culture's worst assumptions around White poverty, linking it to dirt and slovenliness, disrupted and unhealthy families, and crass sexuality.[13]

When Michael viciously murders his sister, her boyfriend, and his mother's abusive boyfriend one Halloween night, sparing only his beloved baby sister, Angel, the audience is happy to cheer him on as he cleanses his trashy household. But when a grown Michael (played by hulking former professional wrestler Tyler Mane) finally escapes from the state mental hospital and returns to Haddonfield, the class politics get more complex. The Haddonfield that Myers returns to hardly seems like the same community that could have once fostered the desperate Myers clan. Just as in remakes like *Sorority Row* or *Friday the 13th*, the world of the *Halloween* remake is now more obnoxiously affluent,

Fig. 8.3. The Myers family home—an average middle-class suburban home in the original film—is now a bastion of low social class in the remake of *Halloween* (Dimension Films, 2007).

filled with bigger, more opulent homes and spoiled rich teens. While the teen babysitters originally targeted by Myers drank and wanted to have sex with their boyfriends, they were still essentially fun-loving youngsters the audience could sympathize with. But in the remake, teens like Lynda highlight the crassness and immorality of affluence. Lynda is a brat who jokes about flirting with her male teachers and gets suspended from the cheerleading squad for suggesting that they "flash some snatch" instead of doing the same old routine. She calls the head cheerleader a cunt but knows that she'll never get in trouble because her recently divorced father is easily manipulated. Today's Haddonfield may look fancier than the Haddonfield that Myers knew, but teens like Lynda exhibit the same vulgarity that was supposed to be rooted in the Myers clan's poverty.

The film's central character and final girl, Laurie Strode, bridges Haddonfield's White trash past and more affluent present when we discover that she is, in fact, Angel Myers, now adopted into the Strode family (a revelation that comes later in the original *Halloween* series). She now has a stable, loving upper-middle-class family with a fancy home. But while Laurie is less crass than her friend Lynda, she is far more foul-mouthed than the Laurie played by Jamie Lee Curtis back in 1978. In one scene, the 2007 Laurie makes a joke about child molestation over breakfast while she graphically fingers a bagel, leaving the audience to wonder if her tactless sexual comments stem from her spoiled affluence or if she can't help but be vulgar because she is, by birth, a Myers.

This ambiguity provides the dramatic conflict in the last act of the film, when Myers seeks out Laurie, who he idealized as a child as a source of purity in his chaotic world. Is he planning on saving her from a modern world that seems better off but is still as corrupt as their poor family? Or is he planning on killing her because she has been corrupted, just like the rest of his family?

At its core, Zombie's *Halloween* enacts many of the same anxieties animating the remakes of *The Hills Have Eyes*, *House of Wax*, and others, namely that the White middle class in the contemporary US can never escape the menacing specter of the poor Whites left behind by the new economy. While a young White millennial like Laurie Strode may have moved up in the world by being adopted out of the Myers clan and into the affluent Strode family, the inequities that kept the Myerses mired in poverty and immorality will come for her someday.

CONCLUSION

It is important to note, of course, that the revisions to classic horror enacted in these remakes often distort the past, attempting to paint the world of the 1970s and 1980s as a supposedly simpler time that would need to be made more complex in a modern retelling of these stories. Just as in the seemingly nostalgic call to "Make America Great Again," the attempts to reimagine horror classics often assume that the past was somehow easier and less fraught than the present, especially for White folks. But the 1970s and 1980s were not necessarily a less complex time for the White middle classes. Clearly, many of the films selected for remakes already evinced strong anxieties around Whiteness and prosperity, imagining the ostensibly stable and wholesome space of the White middle-class suburbs as spaces where violent or supernatural brutality lurks just beneath the surface.

Moreover, not all remakes engage in this distortion. *The Amityville Horror* (1979), for example, already encapsulated fears of White economic decline and White male fragility, and those same fears are addressed in the 2005 remake. The 1979 film links the demonic forces in the house to the economic precarity of the family patriarch, who struggles to make ends meet when the family buys a dream house just out of their budget. As the patriarch in the original descends into madness, his crisis reflects the White middle class's struggle—and frequent failure—to attain the American dream during the recession in the late 1970s in the US.[14] The remake only brings these concerns into the mid-2000s housing bubble, indicating some anxiety around homeownership a few years before that bubble would burst.

Likewise, the 2005 remake of John Carpenter's 1980 horror film, *The Fog*, offers a similar condemnation of White prosperity. Both films tell the same story of a small coastal town on the verge of celebrating its anniversary when a supernatural fog heading toward town leads to a horrifying discovery: the beloved founders of the town deceived the wealthy leader of a leper colony, stealing his money and murdering the lepers in order to finance the success of the community. In both 1980 and 2005, this story dramatized White fears that their success and prosperity might come at the expense of disenfranchised others.

However, the insistent trend of filmmakers inserting class anxieties for middle-class Whites into their updated visions of classic stories suggests that many folks today see the contemporary US as necessarily more complex for White folks. Whether these newer stories imagine a world that is more economically precarious for White families (and White men in particular) or acknowledge that the success and stability of the White middle class is based on the exclusion of more working-class Whites from the promise of the American dream, the horror remake buys into the common assumption that life is harder for White folks today.

NOTES

1. Adam Lowenstein, "Alone on Elm Street," *Film Quarterly* 64, no. 1 (2010): 18–22.

2. David Kingsley offers a nuanced and compelling reading of the original *Elm Street* that explores the themes of incest and molestation in the film, seeing it as an essentially Gothic text. Kingsley's reading aligns with the cultural anxieties around the Satanic childcare moral panic of the 1980s, a context that clearly informed the original film. See Kingsley, "*Elm Street*'s Gothic Roots: Unearthing Incest in Wes Craven's 1984 *Nightmare*," *Journal of Popular Film and Television* 41, no. 3 (2013): 145–153.

3. Lowenstein, "Alone on Elm Street," 18.

4. Ronald Brownstein, "Trump's Rhetoric of White Nostalgia," *The Atlantic*, June 2, 2016, https://www.theatlantic.com/politics/archive/2016/06/trumps -rhetoric-of-White-nostalgia/485192/.

5. A range of older horror films were also remade starting in the mid-2000s, from the 1953 Vincent Price film *House of Wax*, to made-for-TV films such as *Don't be Afraid of the Dark* (1973), to big-budget Hollywood films such as *Poltergeist* (1982).

6. For a more detailed account of the industrial factors driving the remake cycle, see Kevin Heffernan, "Risen from the Vaults: Recent Horror Film Remakes and the American Film Industry," in *Merchants of Menace: The Business of Horror Cinema*, ed. Richard Nowell (New York: Bloomsbury, 2014), 61–74.

7. Steffen Hantke outlines (and debunks) this perceived crisis in horror cinema in "They Don't Make 'Em Like They Used To: On the Rhetoric of Crisis and the Current State of American Horror Cinema," in *The American Horror Film: The Genre at the Turn of the Millennium*, ed. Hantke (Jackson: University of Mississippi Press, 2010), vii–xxxii.

8. David Roche, *Making and Remaking Horror in the 1970s and 2000s: Why Don't They Do It Like They Used To?* (Jackson: University of Mississippi Press, 2006). Several other book-length studies have explored the Hollywood horror remake. See James Francis, *Remaking Horror: Hollywood's New Reliance on Scares* (Jefferson, NC: McFarland, 2013); and Christian Knöppler, *The Monster Always Returns: American Horror Films and Their Remakes* (New York: Columbia University Press, 2017).

9. Appropriately enough, the film reveals that Tom—the new, young mine owner—is the killer, having invented the maniac miner as an alter ego after all the trauma and violence he witnessed years ago. The fickle management, vacillating between selling the mine and keeping it, is also an agent of chaos and violence.

10. Paul Doro's discussion of *Poltergeist* and its remake would counter this assessment. Doro argues that the original film, with its emphasis on a seemingly stable White family whose life is turned upside down by the haunting, more authentically engages with class anxieties than the remake, whose depiction of economic precarity he finds unconvincing. I disagree and feel that there is a very specific effort on the part of the remake's creators to engage with contemporary fears around White middle-class economic stability. See Doro, "Thirty-Five Years of Middle-Class Fears: How Two *Poltergeists* Address Race, Class, and Gender," *Frames Cinema Journal* 11 (2017), http://framescinemajournal.com /article/thirty-five-years-of-middle-class-fears-how-two-poltergeists-address -race-class-and-gender/.

11. For further discussion of the class politics of the original film and how they intersect with environmental discourses, see Carter Soles, "Sympathy for the Devil: The Cannibalistic Hillbilly in 1970s Rural Slasher Films," in *Ecocinema Theory and Practice*, ed. Stephen Rust, Salma Monani, and Sean Cubitt (New York: Routledge, 2013), 233–250.

12. James Kendrick, "The Terrible, Horrible Desire to Know: Post-9/11 Horror Remakes, Reboots, Sequels and Prequels," in *American Cinema in the Shadow of 9/11*, ed. Terence McSweeney (Edinburgh: Edinburgh University Press, 2017), 249–268.

13. Jacqueline Morrill also explores the degradation of the White family home as a source of horror in Zombie's *Halloween* remake and *The House of 1000 Corpses*. See Morrill, "The Hovel Condemned: The Environmental Psychology of Place in Horror," in *Dark Forces at Work: Essays on Social Dynamics and Cinematic Horrors*, ed. Cynthia J. Miller and A. Bowdoin Van Riper (Lanham, MD: Lexington Books, 2020), 267–278.

14. For further discussion about the original *Amityville* and its engagement with class politics, see Joseph Maddrey, *Nightmares in Red, White, and Blue: The Evolution of the American Horror Film* (Jefferson, NC: McFarland, 2004).

—ᴡᴡ—

CONCLUSION

Horror in the Trump Era

THROUGHOUT THE TRUMP ADMINISTRATION, FILM critics insisted that horror would become the most important genre of this new political era. As women's marches galvanized anti-Trump sentiment—especially in the wake of the contentious Supreme Court nomination hearings in 2018 for Brett Kavanaugh, during which he was accused of sexual misconduct in his youth—horror filmmakers responded with films such as *The Invisible Man* (2020), a taut thriller in which a domestic-abuse survivor is harassed and gaslit by a system that won't believe her. And as the Black Lives Matter movement has reshaped public opinion about police violence in the wake of (even more) tragic deaths of Black folks such as George Floyd and Breonna Taylor at the hands of the police, horror storytellers are turning more to the horrors of racial violence, as seen in the 2021 remake of *Candyman*, which explores histories of race, violence, and poverty in Chicago.

Rather than fixating on the stagnation of the White middle classes, horror films in the Trump years tackled issues of race, social justice, and the corruption of the powerful in much more overt ways.[1] After a long spell of haunted houses, possessed dolls, and creepy children dominating the genre, several of the highest-profile horror films of the Trump years took the horror genre in sometimes radical new directions.

Chief among these innovators was Jordan Peele, whose contributions to the genre, *Get Out* in 2017 and *Us* in 2019, brought a critical perspective on race relations and the corruptions of prosperity in today's world. *Get Out* tells the story of a young Black photographer who visits his White girlfriend's seemingly progressive parents only to discover a horrific plot in which rich White people appropriate the bodies of young Black folks. The main character, Chris, has

Fig. C.1. Chris sits powerless in the affluent White family's basement game room in *Get Out* (Universal Pictures, 2017).

been targeted by his girlfriend and her diabolical family, who auction off his body in a modern-day slave market to an older White art dealer who is blind and desperate to have not just his sight back, but the sight of a talented young Black artist. Using hypnosis to prime Chris for brain surgery—performed in the family's wood-paneled basement—the White family attempts to make Chris a powerless spectator of his own exploitation on a distant screen as White folks take control of his body (see fig. C.1).

In this way, *Get Out* explores the feelings of powerlessness of the Black community in the face of continuing discrimination and exploitation and, importantly, holds White liberals accountable for their role in racial inequality, rather than vilifying the explicit racism of conservative rhetoric and policy. The evil White family is not *pretending* to be Obama-loving liberals who value diversity; they *are* Obama-loving liberals who value diversity, which leads them to grotesque acts of violence and cultural appropriation.[2] The film deftly uses the conventions of horror to explore something other than terrified White families worried about being victimized. In this way, it became a transformative film for the genre, highlighting the ways that horror conventions can engage with racial violence and inequality in meaningful ways (and be profitable).

Likewise, Peele's 2019 follow-up, *Us* (discussed in more detail at the end of chap. 2), reimagines the home invasion trope popular in Obama-era horror. The film addresses race and consumerism in the US by focusing on a middle-class Black family terrorized by mysterious doppelgängers. These shadow selves have been forced to live out a degraded and despairing version of their counterparts' lives, and the upwardly mobile Black family must face the injustices that middle-class prosperity is based on in the US.

Through each film, Peele has demonstrated the capacity for the horror genre to engage with fears beyond those felt by the White mainstream and be commercially successful at the same time. Thanks in part to the successes of Peele's films, there were more high-profile horror stories that presented themselves as politically charged in Trump's America, including on television. *American Horror Story*'s seventh season, *Cult* (2017), directly engages with the political tensions in Trump's America, and the AMC horror anthology *The Terror* set its second season (2019) in a Japanese internment camp during World War II. *The Terror* addresses the racialized atrocities of the past, all while the US ramped up its hostility toward immigrants in the present. Likewise, HBO's horror/fantasy series *Lovecraft Country* (2020) uses the racial violence of the 1950s in the United States as the backdrop to its horrific world, imagining a space in which its Black characters must be vigilant against White country sheriffs as much as against demons, monsters, and secret societies. *Lovecraft Country*'s depiction of horrific violence against Black bodies (both supernatural and historical) is used to explore many of the same issues at the core of the Black Lives Matter movement, whose massive protests would spur new discussions of race and policing in the US. And the 2020 thriller *Antebellum* imagined a horrific theme park in which contemporary Southern Whites reenacted the brutality of slavery against kidnapped Black folks. Even more standard horror fare, like 2019's *Ready or Not*, feels deeply political in Trump's America, depicting US wealthy elites as bloodthirsty sociopaths.[3]

But the cinematic horror of the Trump years wasn't all quite as engaged with racial justice and racial violence. A continued focus on White victimization yielded the top-grossing horror film of 2018, *A Quiet Place*. In a postapocalyptic future where mysterious creatures have decimated most of the human population, a White family attempts to survive on their isolated farm. The creatures are blind but hunt using their acute hearing, so the family has created a new life for themselves designed to reduce as much sound as possible, and a pretty stylish one at that, as their woolen attire, neatly organized jars of food, and outdoor string lights closely resemble the White hipster homesteading movement's style (see fig. C.2). The family only communicates using sign language. Instead of dishes, they eat using large leaves of kale as plates. They have created

Fig. C.2. The independent White family leads a hip and stylish postapocalyptic life in their bunker in *A Quiet Place* (Paramount Pictures, 2018).

sand walking paths throughout their compound to dampen the sounds of their footsteps. And, given that the mother is pregnant and about to have a baby, they have built a soundproof crib (with an oxygen mask to the keep the little one from suffocating). Of course, all of their precautions are put to the test when the mother goes into labor and their home is invaded by the grotesque monsters.

In an insightful review of the film, Katherine Fusco links the hipster DIY aesthetic of *A Quiet Place* with the bunker mentality of the White middle classes. The paranoid fantasy that the White middle classes can't rely on the government leads many to become homesteaders (moving to the country to attempt life off the grid), preppers (stockpiling food and other supplies to prepare for the collapse of society), or anti-vaxxers or to adopt some combination of isolationist worldviews built around the independence of the White nuclear family. *A Quiet Place* exploits these anxious worldviews, suggesting that White identity is under siege and only self-determination will enable the White family to prevail.[4] The plot device of their silence could also be read as a veiled critique of political correctness and the cancel culture of the social-media era: look at these sympathetic White folks who are too terrified to speak out. This plot device is also taken up in the Netflix film *The Silence* (2019), and a variant appears in another postapocalyptic horror film, *Bird Box* (also from Netflix, 2018), only this time the characters must survive while blindfolded to escape from monsters that, should you look at them, will drive you to suicide.

In these narratives, only the rugged individualism of the White family will enable survival.

Looking only at individual films or small sets of cherry-picked examples, therefore, can't provide a full picture of a possible sea change in the horror genre as US culture adapts to the Trump era. Putting films like *Get Out* and *A Quiet Place* side by side only reveals the diversity of perspectives within the genre and the capacity for horror to both critique and exploit the fears of White folks. What, then, are the larger trends and patterns across US horror production during the Trump years? Have we seen a shift in the kinds of horror stories told and the persistence of certain narrative tropes?

Although three years of US horror production make up a rather small sample size (2020 and 2021 were difficult to measure using the same metrics, thanks to the COVID pandemic), there are some noticeable trends in Trump-era horror in 2017, 2018, and 2019.[5] When it comes to race and ethnicity, for example, there does seem to be increased attention given to people of color in the horror genre, although the bar was set fairly low. As I note in the introduction, the mainstream Obama-era horror film featured very few people of color as central characters, focusing heavily on White people and their encounters with psychopaths or the supernatural. Only 7.4 percent of mainstream US horror from 2008 to 2016 featured non-White central characters (11 films out of 147), and of those, nearly half were either horror satires or films in which ambiguously ethnic actors play essentially White roles.

By contrast, 2017, 2018, and 2019 saw nineteen mainstream US horror films featuring non-White central characters out of fifty-eight total films produced, representing 32 percent of all horror productions. More films featuring people of color in leading roles were released in those three years than throughout the entire Obama era. Now, of those nineteen films, one was a horror satire (Tyler Perry's sequel, *Boo 2: A Medea Halloween*, from 2017) and seven featured actors of color in roles that don't necessarily engage with the race or ethnicity of the character in a meaningful way (for example, Mexican actor Demián Bichir's role in *The Nun* [2018] or the diverse cast of young people in *Unfriended: The Dark Web* [2018]). Nevertheless, the inclusion of people of color within the genre at these much higher numbers draws the horror film's focus away from the trials and tribulations of the White middle classes.

Moreover, several films in this period offer meaningful explorations of race and violence, from *Get Out* to *The First Purge* (2018), the latter of which continues that franchise's emphasis on racialized violence orchestrated by White elites. The indie horror film *It Comes at Night* (2017) features an isolated family struggling to survive in the woods in a postapocalyptic America, similar to

A Quiet Place. It Comes at Night, however, explores the paranoia of and psychological toll of survival on an interracial couple and their mixed-raced son, rather than focusing on the purity of an off-the-grid White family. While it is only reflected in a small group of films, this trend does seem to suggest at the least the rumblings of change, dangling the prospect that horror over the next decade will explore issues of race and ethnicity with more nuance or at the very least will include more people of color in its vision of terror in the US.

Other notable horror films engaging with race in this period include the 2019 remake (or re-remake?) of *Black Christmas,* which explicitly takes on issues of racial and gender inequality on college campuses, following a group of woke, multiracial sorority girls challenging White patriarchy on campus. These heroines have to face off with violent frat bros possessed by the spirit of one of the college's racist, sexist founders. The appetite for racial horror films was so pronounced, in fact, that the 2019 film *Ma,* starring Octavia Spencer, was heavily marketed as a provocative narrative about race in America akin to *Get Out,* despite the fact that the film often goes out of its way to avoid acknowledging race in its story of an obsessed woman punishing the children of bullies who tormented her in high school.

This possible shift might mean that horror is finally catching up to the shifting demographics of the US, and not simply because horror producers want to capture growing non-White audiences. While these trends toward more diversity in the genre certainly reflect shifting market forces, these new, racially conscious horror films also speak to cultural concerns around the growing prosperity of historically disempowered groups. If the mainstream horror film articulates the plight of those who have privilege but fear losing it, these new entries to mainstream horror explore the fears of people of color who find themselves more squarely in the traditionally White middle classes. Horror still speaks from the perspective of the privileged, but we are seeing more and more horror films told from the perspective of people of color who find themselves negotiating their relationships to Whiteness and privilege.

The fears of the non-White middle classes, after all, may have been more acute in the Trump era in response to the shifting culture and politics of post-2016 America. Mainstream media discourse in the Obama era, after all, was often defined by feel-good narratives of diversity and inclusion, celebrating the hopeful power of multiculturalism. Even if these optimistic stories belied continuing inequalities in the US, they promoted an uplifting narrative of progress and diversity. Change was coming, even if it was slow.[6] These discourses, of course, fanned the flames of racial resentment for White folks across socioeconomic classes, suggesting to many that Obama's political efforts only sought to aid people of color in the cities. These resentments found their way into the White-centric horror of the Obama era.

By contrast, media discourse in the Trump era was largely defined by stories pointing out the inherent racism and sexism that continue to impact US culture and society. Stories unearthing the racist or misogynist comments of celebrities, politicians, and everyday folks, while common throughout the Obama years, increased dramatically in the early Trump years. The increasing power and relevance of #MeToo and #BlackLivesMatter on social media continued to draw attention to stark inequalities that have persisted in a supposedly multicultural era.

This trend was spurred by the higher profile of racism in the US. White supremacists and racist political provocateurs, emboldened by Trump's election, dramatically increased their public profile and garnered more attention from the media once their racist agenda—previously considered fringe—was brought into the mainstream by Trump and the new Republican Party. Additionally, government policies such as the inhumane incarceration of lawful asylum-seekers from Central America brought the country's xenophobia into clearer focus. The achievements of prominent Latinx people in the US are far less resonant and uplifting when the government is forcibly separating children from their families as punishment for daring to hope that they might find a better life in the US. After decades of more polite, coded, and implied racism in public discourse, the US found itself (again) reckoning with explicit racism in public discourse and government policy.

Against the backdrop of such atrocities, the Trump-era horror film is tentatively more engaged with issues of race and the fears of people of color—not necessarily poor people of color or the most vulnerable populations in the US, but the non-White middle classes and their hopes for economic stability or upward mobility. What does the rejuvenation of explicit racism mean for more prosperous people of color who had felt the pangs of hope in the Obama years that they might share in some of the privileges usually reserved for prosperous White folks?

Jordan Peele's films, for example, explore race relations from the perspective of Black folks who find themselves enmeshed in a world of the White elite. In *Get Out*, the young Black photographer is upwardly mobile, with a successful career, a swanky urban loft, and a White girlfriend who wants him to meet her parents. But his foray into seemingly progressive White affluence only exposes the horrors of White culture, revealing how White folks continue to exploit the Black body. Likewise, the college-educated Black family in *Us* is financially successful and spends their time with obnoxious, wealthy White friends. But their

Fig. C.3. The daughter of a struggling mixed-raced Latinx family is attacked in the bathtub by La Llorona in *The Curse of La Llorona* (Atomic Monster, 2019).

encounter with their murderous doppelgängers forces them to reckon with the costs of prosperity and the horrors on which their privileges are based. Both films explore the challenges and dangers for upwardly mobile Black folks and their relationship to White culture.

These tensions are also at the heart of the 2019 film *The Curse of La Llorona*. The most recent entry in *The Conjuring* extended universe, the film tells the story of a struggling single mother raising two mixed-race children in Los Angeles in 1973. Her late husband was a Hispanic LAPD officer who was killed in the line of duty, leaving her to frantically try to maintain the stability of her family on her salary as a social worker. But the mother's work with poor Hispanic families in the city puts her own family at risk when La Llorona, a Mexican spirit who murders vulnerable children, targets her children (see fig. C.3). Seeking help from the Church, the mother learns of a local Hispanic faith healer, formerly a priest, who agrees to help the family confront the evil entity.

As in other haunted house films, the supernatural activity in *The Curse of La Llorona* threatens the class standing of the family. The unexplained burns that La Llorona leaves on the children's wrists cause the mother to be investigated by her social worker colleague. The protagonists—already teetering on the edge of solid middle-class standing—are becoming more like the poor Spanish-speaking families that the mother normally investigates. Their close contact with impoverished Hispanic folks leads to their supernatural affliction, which taints the family and challenges their upward mobility. Can this mixed-race family become part of the normally White middle classes? Of course, they can only save themselves with the help of Hispanic folk rituals, suggesting that Hispanic traditions and identity are indispensable to their family, as long as they can escape the curses that normally afflict poor Latinx populations.[7]

As *The Curse of La Llorona* suggests, the debates around the class standing of people of color are being integrated into the existing narrative trends of the contemporary horror film, in this case modifying the wildly popular haunted house cycle of the Obama years. Similarly, the possession and exorcism film *The Possession of Hannah Grace* (2018) continues one of the major trends of the past decade but adjusts the formula somewhat. This time, instead of exploring the trials and tribulations of sad White men, *Hannah Grace* features a struggling young female morgue worker (played by mixed-race Canadian actress Shay Mitchell) whose encounters with demons help her recover from past traumas. Reworking the possession film's preoccupation with White male authority, this new entry to the cycle indicates the capacity for the exorcism trope to speak to the fears of vulnerable women of color.

Moreover, even if the dominant cycles of horror in the Obama years continue to focus on White folks in the early Trump era, some show interesting modifications, like a recent entry in the home invasion genre, *The Strangers: Prey at Night* (2018). In this sequel to the 2008 home invasion film, the action is now set in an isolated trailer park, raising concerns around poverty and economic stagnation for White folks. Of course, this shift might simply be a continuation of the logic of Obama-era horror, where the most terrifying outcome for many White families was the prospect of poverty and low social standing.

The highest-grossing US horror film in recent years—*It, Chapter 1*, from 2017, based on the 1986 Stephen King novel—also explored the anxieties of Whiteness and corruption. Told from the perspective of seven preteens living in Derry, a seemingly idyllic small town in Maine, in the mid-1980s, the film chronicles a strange entity gripping the town that takes the form of a creepy clown named Pennywise and awakens every twenty-seven years to kill children and devour their fear. The children who investigate and confront It are all social outcasts in one way or another—a stutterer whose younger brother was killed by It, an overweight new kid to town, a young woman living with a sexually abusive father, a poor hypochondriac stifled by his overweight and overbearing mother, a Jewish young man with a distant rabbi for a father, a wisecracking bespectacled nerd, and an orphaned Black kid who lives outside of town on a sheep farm. This self-proclaimed Loser's Club has to navigate not only the supernatural threat of It, but also a pack of sociopathic bullies that the authorities in the small town seem to tolerate.

The film's focus on social outcasts struggling with a brutal world seemed to resonate in the early years of the Trump administration. As the preteen characters navigate the terrors of It—who makes them hallucinate their greatest fears—the group finds no support from the adult world, as all authority figures in the film are repressive, abusive, or just uncaring. In other words, a team of outcasts bands together to face their fears and resist the brutality that corrupt authorities will not, mirroring the kinds of resistance rhetoric popular in the early Trump years as activists stepped up to advocate against a wide range of injustices.

Of course, It, Chapter 1 doesn't represent a radical break from the mainstream US horror film. It still fundamentally addresses issues of Whiteness and social position. The mainstream US horror film has historically prioritized the perspective of those who have something to lose, those who have relative social power but are worried about that power receding. Throughout the Obama years, this has most often meant middle-class White families who find their social and economic stability under siege or else White teens whose hopes to inherit the middle-class stability of their parents are threatened. The mostly White outcasts of It might not have access to that social and economic stability yet in the late 1980s, but that seems to be the point: Will these mostly White "losers" have the opportunity to achieve success and stability in the neoliberal economy that will unfold before them?

This very question, in fact, becomes the foundation for the next installment, It, Chapter 2, from 2019, which picks up the story twenty-seven years later. The members of the Losers Club have all left Derry behind and have found material success in the outside world (as authors, comedians, architects, businesspeople, etc.), but they have also lost vital memories from their childhoods, including their battle with Pennywise the clown. The only one who hasn't is Mike, the African American young man raised on the sheep farm, who stayed behind in Derry studying the clown and waiting. Mike thinks that the town itself has been so long corrupted by Pennywise that when people finally leave it, their memories of the horrors stay behind. But when Pennywise emerges again after his hibernation, Mike calls the rest of the gang back for a final confrontation, not only with Pennywise but with the traumas that they had repressed: the abusive parents, the bullies, the humiliations, the guilt, and the fear.

Essentially, then, the second instalment takes up the narrative of rural displacement, so familiar in small towns in the neoliberal economy, in which young folks are forced to leave for larger cities, either because of a lack of economic opportunities or stifled cultural opportunities (on display in *It, Chapter 2*, which opens with a rural hate crime against a gay couple in Derry). The White losers have all fled the horrors of small-town America, with Pennywise standing in for the bigotry, callousness, and corruption of cloistered White communities. Their new lives are marked by opulent successes—Bill is married to a movie star, Ben has an enormous modernist mansion that he presumably designed himself, Beverly packs out of a massive closet filled with high fashion, Eddie drives a shiny black SUV, Richie packs auditoriums with his stand-up, and Stanley is literally in the process of booking a trip to Buenos Aries with his wife from his elegant apartment when we meet him in middle age—but the film demands that they come home to reckon with their pasts as trashy losers before they can be fully at home in the upper-middle classes. In this way, the core of the *It* films still probes our anxieties around White social position and victimization.

Not all the Obama-era cycles show signs of transformation, however. The horrific child genre remains small but consistent in the Trump era, with films such as *Anabelle: Creation* (2017), *Hereditary* (2018), and *The Prodigy* (2019) continuing to explore the fate of White motherhood (although *Annabelle: Creation* does tend to focus more on fatherhood). Likewise, technological horrors remain popular and generally unchanged, the more diverse cast of *Unfriended: The Dark Web* notwithstanding.

The Trump-era horror also seems to be charting several new narrative directions that keep Whiteness centered in the horror film. While some of the dominant cycles of the Obama era are slowing down or drying up, several older cycles are resurgent, such as slasher films (focusing on teens or college-aged students being targeted by a killer while negotiating their relationships and sex lives) and monster movies (in which a nonhuman monster threatens a community, a city, a nation, or the whole world).

The slasher film, for example, was once the most dominant cycle of horror in the 1980s, representing around 20 percent of all mainstream horror output. But starting in the 1990s, the cycle slowed, dwindling to around 10 percent across the 1990s, 2000s, and the first half of the 2010s. While a sample of only three years is not really predictive, Hollywood did produce nine mainstream slashers in 2017, 2018, and 2019, around 15 percent of all the major theatrically released horror during those years.

Given the increasing generational conflict in US politics—with Trump's brand of Republicanism most commonly associated with older White men—the resurgence of the slasher film could signal a renewed interest in the anxieties and paranoia of young people. Millennials and Gen Zers face an economy that, even when it is good, still requires far more sacrifices from the young than from those who came before them (see chap. 6 for a lengthier discussion of generational anxieties in the horror film). Of course, while it has become commonplace to feature a diverse cast of young people in the contemporary slasher genre, it still largely remains a narrative world in which people of color are killed off first, leaving the tribulations of young White women as the primary focus. This is still largely the case with the Trump-era slashers, which are mostly concerned with the fate of young White women.[8]

Similarly, monster movies were once the dominant cycle of the 1990s, representing around 20 percent of all mainstream horror output in an era marked by rapid technological change. But the output of monster movies slowed down in the 2000s and early 2010s, and such films accounted for only 7 percent of mainstream US horror in the Obama years. But a slate of ten new monster movies in the Trump era has raised the prospect of a rejuvenation of the monster cycle.[9]

Monster movies have historically involved stories of cities, nations, or international enterprises that are threatened by monsters capable of destroying communities. Closely related to disaster films, monster movies tend to use ensemble casts or a small group of characters who muster a resistance to the nonhuman forces that threaten whole communities.

With the exception of *The Meg* (2018), the Trump-era monster movie tends to be more insular, focusing on smaller groups with no recourse to authority figures, most often White folks under siege. *A Quiet Place* and *It, Chapter 1* exemplify this trend, but it also manifests in films such as *47 Meters Down* (2017) and its sequel, about divers trapped by sharks, or *Jeepers Creepers III* (2017), the third installment of a series about a monster tormenting a rural White community. It is unclear how (or if) this trend will develop, but for now it only perpetuates the horror film's fascination with White folks—especially White women—under siege from outsiders who often threaten the social order.

These are, of course, still nascent trends in US horror production. Only time will tell if these slight surges in certain types of horror stories will yield longer-term cycles. And it remains to be seen if the mainstream horror film will stay more political in its vision of Whiteness and race relations in the US. While there is some credence to the argument that horror in the Trump era addresses the national traumas around race that have been absent from the genre in the recent past, these changes are occurring alongside a continuing obsession with White victimization and fragility in the new economy.

In discussing these possibilities, however, we shouldn't lose sight of the fact that the horror film has *always* been concerned with White guilt and the histories of White corruption. This book has probably too often highlighted US horror's more conservative tendencies to cater to the fears of privileged White folks. But there has always been a lively tradition of political critique within the genre that draws out all the brutality and degradation of the White middle classes in the US, although sometimes this tendency is more subdued. In the Obama-era horror film, this tendency is probably best expressed in the home invasion cycle, which has quite cynically expressed the rot at the core of affluent White society. Spinning off from this trend, *The Purge* franchise is almost radical in its messages about systemic violence waged against the poor and people of color. And I have tried to single out films throughout the book that challenge the more conservative directions of the genre, including *The Witch* (2015), *Splice* (2009), *Don't Breathe* (2016), *Silent House* (2011), and others.

In doing so, of course, I don't want to suggest that political critique is the unique domain of *highbrow* or *intellectual* horror, popular terms for film critics today to describe indie horror films such as *Get Out* and *It Follows* (2014) or *Midsommar* (2019). These films highlight the capacity of horror to make artistic and often political statements about the world around us, but this capacity has nothing to do with their elevated status. Rather, these films simply get the most attention from the critics for doing what horror always seeks to do: unsettling the bourgeois norms and values of those with privilege.

In the age of Obama, however, horror primarily seized on White paranoia. The most dominant horror cycles of the Obama years focused on

- the sanctity and stability of the White family home;
- the authority of White men;
- the failures of White motherhood;
- the fear that surveillance culture exploits rather than protects White folks; and
- the fears that Whites are worse off than they were in the past.

While many films mined this paranoia to critique those who exploit their power, such attempts were overshadowed by an obsessive concern with the idea that Whiteness isn't as privileged as it once was. As the specter of a popular, upwardly mobile Black family living the White House haunted the cultural imagination of White America, the horror film became preoccupied with the dread of White people that they might not be as special as they thought.

When the White House was occupied by a bombastic White president who openly espoused the perspectives and conspiracy theories of White supremacists, horror filmmakers were handed an opportunity to explore a new set of fears. But how will they rise to that challenge now that Trump has left the White

House? Will there still be an urgency around issues of race and injustice with the new Biden administration? Or will the fears of White victimization again become the core narrative concern of US horror storytellers? Time will tell, especially as the country grapples with the continuing horrors of polarization, racism, and misinformation.

NOTES

1. Brandon Tensley, "Horror Films Emerge as Best Political Commentary of Our Times," *CNN*, September 1, 2019, https://www.cnn.com/2019/09/01 /politics/ready-or-not-horror-movies-trump-politics/index.html?fbclid =IwAR1EC_kEc_ziGWElPDec35ZZ0E5b-XmZ9H9-E9_HcAKH0PA5E ohjIruI3bs.

2. For a range of scholarly and critical responses to the film, see Crystal Boson, "Horror Blackademics: The *Get Out* (2017) Syllabus," *Graveyard Shift Sisters*, June 15, 2017, https://www.graveyardshiftsisters.com/2017/06/horror -blackademics-get-out-2017.html.

3. Tensley offers a discussion of *Ready or Not* in "Horror Films." See also Clarisse Loughery, "*Ready or Not*: Horror-Comedy Doesn't Mess Around with Its Social Commentary," *The Independent*, September 26, 2019, https://www .independent.co.uk/arts-entertainment/films/reviews/ready-or-not-review-film -comedy-horror-samara-weaving-cast-a9120696.html?fbclid=IwAR0To Ocln6D44_cMj7Tj1k_cv6V5dbgcoTuXl4xxjDWBxtmEwlwTLrGVyYA.

4. Katherine Fusco, "DIY Whiteness in the Age of Apocalypse," *Los Angeles Review of Books*, May 24, 2018, http://avidly.lareviewofbooks.org/2018/05/24/diy -whiteness-in-the-age-of-apocalypse/.

5. As a reminder, these numbers are based on the following criteria: US films that grossed at least one million dollars in the theatrical box office and were tagged as horror on the International Movie Database (IMDB).

6. For further discussion of these Obama-era media discourses, see Russell Meeuf, *Rebellious Bodies: Stardom, Citizenship, and the New Body Politics* (Austin: University of Texas Press, 2017).

7. For further discussion of *La Llorona* and its reliance on stereotypes, see Tyler Unsell, "In the Age of Trump, 'The Curse of La Llorona' Is Not Helpful," *Signal Horizon*, April 25, 2019, accessed November 2019, https://www.signal horizon.com/single-post/2019/04/24/In-the-Age-of-Trump-The-Curse-of-La -Llorona-is-Not-Helpful?fbclid=IwAR2IkBfDxK1XzyV2h7kscMk9iH -Wei-kLjSwTJ9n_yYYBKojeXQCdty30NQ.

8. An exception would be the 2018 *Halloween* sequel, which featured typical slasher teen characters but remained focused on an older Laurie Strode, still traumatized from her encounter with Michael Myers decades ago.

9. These figures are complicated by the messiness of the monster movie category. Films like *Godzilla* from 2014 or 2019 aren't categorized as horror films by IMDB and thus aren't included in these numbers. The downturn in monster movies in the 2000s could simply be that many monster movies simply weren't categorized as horror and therefore weren't included in my numbers. There was, however, a recent uptick in *horror* monster movies in 2017 and 2018.

BIBLIOGRAPHY

Appelbaum, Binyamin. "The Vanishing Male Worker: How America Fell Behind." *New York Times*, December 11, 2014. https://www.nytimes.com/2014/12/12 /upshot/unemployment-the-vanishing-male-worker-how-america-fell-behind .html.

Báez, Jillian, and Mari Castañeda. "Two Sides of the Same Story: Media Narratives of Latinos and the Subprime Mortgage Crisis." *Critical Studies in Media Communication* 31, no. 1 (2014): 27–41.

Bailey, Dale. *American Nightmares: The Haunted House Formula in American Popular Fiction*. Madison: University of Wisconsin Press, 1999.

Bakke, Gretchen. "Dead White Men: An Essay on the Changing Dynamics of Race in US Action Cinema." *Anthropological Quarterly* 83, no. 2 (2010): 400–428.

Banco, Lindsey Michael. "Recession Horror: The Haunted House Crisis in Contemporary Fiction," in *Dark Forces at Work: Essays on Social Dynamics and Cinematic Horrors*, edited by Cynthia Miller and A. Bowdoin Van Riper, 79–98. Lanham, MD: Lexington Books, 2020.

Baumgaertner, Bert, Juliet E. Carlisle, and Florian Justwan. "The Influence of Political Ideology and Trust on Willingness to Vaccinate." *PLoS ONE* 13, no. 1 (2018). https://doi.org/10.1371/journal.pone.0191728.

Binder, John. "Data: White American Births Below Replacement Level in Every State." *Breitbart*, January 13, 2019. https://www.breitbart.com/politics/2019 /01/13/states-birth-rate-2017/.

Blake, Linnie, and Xavier Aldana Reyes, eds. *Digital Horror: Haunted Technologies, Network Panic and the Found Footage Phenomenon*. London: I. B. Tauris, 2016.

Blow, Charles. "White Extinction Anxiety." *New York Times*, June 24, 2018. https:// www.nytimes.com/2018/06/24/opinion/america-white-extinction.html?action =click&module=Opinion&pgtype=Homepage.

Boson, Crystal. "Horror Blackademics: The *Get Out* (2017) Syllabus." *Graveyard Shift Sisters*, June 15, 2017. https://www.graveyardshiftsisters.com/2017/06 /horror-blackademics-get-out-2017.html.

Briefel, Aviva, and Sianne Ngai. "'How Much Did You Pay for This Place?': Fear, Entitlement, and Urban Space in Bernard Rose's *Candyman*." In *The Horror Film Reader*, edited by Alain Silver and James Ursini, 71–91. New York: Limelight, 2000.

Brodkin, Karen. *How Jews Became White Folks and What That Says About Race in America*. New Brunswick, NJ: Rutgers University Press, 1998.

Broussard, Meredith. *Artificial Unintelligence: How Computers Misunderstand the World*. Cambridge, MA: MIT Press, 2018.

Browne, Simone. *Dark Matters: On the Surveillance of Blackness*. Durham, NC: Duke University Press, 2015.

Brownstein, Ronald. "Trump's Rhetoric of White Nostalgia." *The Atlantic*, June 2, 2016. https://www.theatlantic.com/politics/archive/2016/06/trumps-rhetoric -of-white-nostalgia/485192/.

Buchanan, Pat. "Trump and the Invasion of the West." Patrick J. Buchanan: Official Website, June 19, 2018. https://buchanan.org/blog/trump-and-the -invasion-of-the-west-129497?doing_wp_cron=1556910904.9412651062011718750000.

Chang, Justin. "Has Horror Become the Movie Genre of the Trump Era?" *Los Angeles Times*, October 13, 2017. http://www.latimes.com/entertainment/movies /la-ca-mn-horror-movies-trump-20171013-story.html.

Church, David. "Queer Ethics, Urban Spaces, and the Horrors of Monogamy in *It Follows*." *Cinema Journal* 57, no. 3 (2018): 3–28.

Clasen, Mathias. *Why Horror Seduces*. New York: Oxford University Press, 2017.

Clover, Carol. *Men, Women, and Chainsaws: Gender in the Modern Horror Film*. Princeton, NJ: Princeton University Press, 1992.

Coleman, Robin Means. *Horror Noire: Blacks in American Horror Films from the 1980s to Present*. New York: Routledge, 2011.

Conley, Dalton. *Being Black, Living in the Red: Race, Wealth, and Social Policy in America*. Berkeley: University of California Press, 2009.

Cowan, Douglas. *Sacred Terror: Religion and Horror on the Silver Screen*. Waco, TX: Baylor University Press, 2008.

Creed, Barbara. *The Monstrous-Feminine: Film, Feminism, Psychoanalysis*. London: Routledge, 1993.

Curtis, Barry. *Dark Places: The Haunted House in Film*. London: Reaktion Books, 2008.

DeLamotte, Eugenia. "White Terror, Black Dreams: Gothic Constructions of Race in the Nineteenth Century." In *The Gothic Other: Racial and Social Constructions in the Literary Imagination*, edited by Ruth Bienstock Anolik and Douglas L. Howard. Jefferson, NC: McFarland, 2004.

Desmond, Matthew. "How Homeownership Became the Engine of American Inequality." *New York Times*, May 9, 2017. https://www.nytimes.com /2017/05/09/magazine/how-homeownership-became-the-engine-of -american-inequality.html.

Dias, Elizabeth. "Her Evangelical Megachurch Was Her World. Then Her Daughter Said She Was Molested by a Minister." *New York Times*, June 10, 2019. https:// www.nytimes.com/2019/06/10/us/southern-baptist-convention-sex -abuse.html.

Dixon, Wheeler Winston. *Hollywood in Crisis or: The Collapse of the Real*. New York: Palgrave, 2018.

D'Oleo, Dixa Ramírez. "The Hills Are Alive: *Pet Sematary* and the Horror of Indigenous Sovereignty and Black Freedom." *LA Review of Books*, May 17, 2019. https://lareviewofbooks.org/article/the-hills-are-alive-pet-sematary-and-the -horror-of-indigenous-sovereignty-and-black-freedom/.

Donahue, Anne T. "In 2018, Horror Movies Are the Most Comforting Things I Watch." *Marie Claire*, November 19, 2018. https://www.marieclaire.com /culture/a25058660/horror-movies-2018-trump/?fbclid=IwAR2FJTSpdkHzcKf LPqiKkb_9N2jmidV2xXKjTnXw2O7zo8sfPuS2PZw5P2Y.

Doro, Paul. "Thirty-Five Years of Middle-Class Fears: How Two *Poltergeists* Address Race, Class, and Gender." *Frames Cinema Journal* 11 (2017). http:// framescinemajournal.com/article/thirty-five-years-of-middle-class-fears-how -two-poltergeists-address-race-class-and-gender/.

Douglas, Susan, and Meredith Michaels. *The Mommy Myth: The Idealization of Motherhood and How It Has Undermined All Women*. New York: Free Press, 2004.

Doyle, Sady. *Dead Blondes and Bad Mothers: Monstrosity, Patriarchy, and the Fear of Female Power*. Brooklyn: Melville House, 2019.

Dyer, Richard. *White: Essays on Race and Culture*. New York: Routledge, 1997.

Eddie Murphy Delirious. Directed by Bruce Gowers. Aired August 17, 1983, on HBO.

Erwin, Elizabeth, and Dawn Keetley, eds. *The Politics of Race, Gender and Sexuality in* The Walking Dead: *Essays on the Television Series and Comics*. Jefferson, NC: McFarland, 2018.

Eubanks, Virginia. *Automating Inequality: How High-Tech Tools Profile, Police, and Punish the Poor*. New York: St. Martin's Press, 2017.

Fiddler, Michael. "Playing *Funny Games* in *The Last House on the Left*: The Uncanny and the Home Invasion Genre." *Crime Media Culture* 9, no. 3 (2013): 281–299.

Fiske, John. "Surveilling the City: Whiteness, the Black Man and Democratic Totalitarianism." *Theory, Culture and Society* 15, no. 2 (1998): 67–88.

Francis, James Jr. *Remaking Horror: Hollywood's New Reliance on Scares.* Jefferson, NC: McFarland, 2013.

Fusco, Katherine. "DIY Whiteness in the Age of Apocalypse." *Los Angeles Review of Books*, May 24, 2018. http://avidly.lareviewofbooks.org/2018/05/24/diy -whiteness-in-the-age-of-apocalypse/.

Fuster, Jeremy. "Horror Movies Have Grossed Over $1 Billion at the Box Office in 2017." *The Wrap*, October 31, 2017. https://www.thewrap.com/horror-movies -grossed-1-billion-box-office-2017/.

Goldstein, Joseph. "'Testilying' by Police: A Stubborn Problem." *New York Times*, March 18, 2018. https://www.nytimes.com/2018/03/18/nyregion/testilying -police-perjury-new-york.html.

Gonyea, Don. "Majority of White Americans Say They Believe Whites Face Discrimination." *NPR*, October 24, 2017. https://www.npr.org/2017/10/24 /559604836/majority-of-white-americans-think-theyre-discriminated-against.

Haltinner, Kristin, and Dilshani Sarathchandra. "Climate Change Skepticism as a Psychological Coping Strategy." *Sociology Compass* 12, no. 6 (2018).

Hamilton, Lawrence C. "Education, Politics and Opinions about Climate Change Evidence for Interaction Effects." *Climatic Change* 104 (2011): 231–242.

Hantke, Steffen. "They Don't Make 'Em Like They Used To: On the Rhetoric of Crisis and the Current State of American Horror Cinema." In *The American Horror Film: The Genre at the Turn of the Millennium*, edited by Steffen Hantke, vii–xxxii. Jackson: University of Mississippi Press, 2010.

Hayward, Joni. "No Safe Space: Economic Anxiety and Post-Recession Spaces in Horror Films." *Frames Cinema Journal* 11 (2017). http://framescinemajournal .com/article/no-safe-space-economic-anxiety-and-post-recession-spaces-in -horror-films/.

Heffernan, Kevin. "Risen from the Vaults: Recent Horror Film Remakes and the American Film Industry." In *Merchants of Menace: The Business of Horror Cinema*, edited by Richard Nowell, 61–74. New York: Bloomsbury, 2014.

Hochschild, Arlie Russell. *Strangers in Their Own Land: Anger and Mourning on the American Right.* New York: New Press, 2016.

Hunt, Darnell, Ana-Christina Ramón, Michael Tran, Amberia Sargent, and Debanjan Roychoudhury. *UCLA Hollywood Diversity Report 2018*, February 27, 2018. http://documents.latimes.com/ucla-hollywood-diversity-report-2018/.

Hutchings, Peter. *The Horror Film.* New York: Pearson, 2004.

Jensen, Robert. *The Heart of Whiteness: Confronting Race, Racism, and White Privilege.* San Francisco: City Lights, 2005.

Karlyn, Kathleen. *Unruly Girls and Unrepentant Mothers: Redefining Feminism on Screen.* Austin: University of Texas Press, 2011.

Karlyn, Kathleen. *The Unruly Woman: Gender and the Genres of Laughter.* Austin: University of Texas Press, 1995.

Keetley, Dawn, ed. *Jordan Peele's* Get Out*: Political Horror.* Columbus: Ohio State University Press, 2020.

Keetley, Dawn. "Stillborn: The Entropic Gothic of *American Horror Story.*" *Gothic Studies* 15, no. 2 (November 2013): 89–107.

Kelly, Annie. "The Alt-Right: Reactionary Rehabilitation for White Masculinity." *Soundings* 66 (Summer 2017): 68–78.

Kelly, Casey Ryan. "*It Follows*: Precarity, Thanatopolitics, and the Ambient Horror Film." *Critical Studies in Media Communication* 34, no. 3 (2017): 234–249.

Kendrick, James. "The Terrible, Horrible Desire to Know: Post-9/11 Horror Remakes, Reboots, Sequels and Prequels." In *American Cinema in the Shadow of 9/11*, edited by Terence McSweeney, 249–268. Edinburgh: Edinburgh University Press, 2017.

Kimmel, Michael. *Angry White Men: American Masculinity at the End of an Era.* New York: Nation Books, 2013.

Kingsley, David. "*Elm Street's* Gothic Roots: Unearthing Incest in Wes Craven's 1984 *Nightmare.*" *Journal of Popular Film and Television* 41, no. 3 (2013): 145–153.

Knöppler, Christian. *The Monster Always Returns: American Horror Films and Their Remakes.* New York: Columbia University Press, 2017.

Leyda, Julia. "Demon Debt: *Paranormal Activity* as Recessionary Post-Cinematic Allegory." *Jump Cut* 56 (Winter 2014–2015). https://www.ejumpcut.org/archive/jc56.2014-2015/LeydaParanormalActivity/index.html.

Lizza, Katherine. "*It Follows* and the Uncertainties of the Middle Class." In *Dark Forces at Work: Essays on Social Dynamics and Cinematic Horrors*, edited by Cynthia J. Miller and A. Bowdoin Van Riper, 293–304. Lanham, MD: Lexington Books, 2020.

Loughrey, Clarisse. "*Ready or Not*: Horror-Comedy Doesn't Mess Around with Its Social Commentary." *The Independent*, September 26, 2019. https://www.independent.co.uk/arts-entertainment/films/reviews/ready-or-not-review-film-comedy-horror-samara-weaving-cast-a9120696.html?fbclid=IwAR0ToOcln6D44_cMj7Tj1k_cv6V5dbgc0TuXl4xxjDWBxtmEwlwTLrGVyYA.

Lowenstein, Adam. "Alone on Elm Street." *Film Quarterly* 64, no. 1 (2010): 18–22.

Lowenstein, Adam. *Shocking Representation: Historical Trauma, National Cinema, and the Modern Horror Film.* New York: Columbia University Press, 2005.

Maddrey, Joseph. *Nightmares in Red, White, and Blue: The Evolution of the American Horror Film.* Jefferson, NC: McFarland, 2004.

Marshall, Bridget M. "Defining Southern Gothic." In *Critical Insights: Southern Gothic Literature*, edited by Jay Ellis, 3–18. Ipswich, MA: Salem Press, 2013.

Matchar, Emily. *Homeward Bound: Why Women Are Embracing the New Domesticity.* New York: Simon and Schuster, 2013.

Meeuf, Russell. *Rebellious Bodies: Stardom, Citizenship, and the New Body Politics.* Austin: University of Texas Press, 2017.

Miller, April. "Reel-to-Reel Recessionary Horrors in *Drag Me To Hell* and *Contagion.*" In *The Great Recession in Fiction, Film, and Television: Twenty-First Century Bust Culture,* edited by Kirk Boyle and Daniel Mrozowski, 29–50. Plymouth, UK: Lexington Books, 2013.

Miller, Claire Cain. "Americans Are Having Fewer Babies. They Told Us Why." *New York Times,* July 5, 2018. https://www.nytimes.com/2018/07/05/upshot /americans-are-having-fewer-babies-they-told-us-why.html.

Miller, Cynthia. "Making the Hard Choices: The Economics of Damnation in *Drag Me to Hell.*" In *Elder Horror: Essays on Film's Frightening Images of Aging,* edited by Cynthia Miller and A. Bowdoin Van Riper, 108–118. Jefferson, NC: McFarland, 2019.

Morrill, Jacqueline. "The Hovel Condemned: The Environmental Psychology of Place in Horror." In *Dark Forces at Work: Essays on Social Dynamics and Cinematic Horrors,* edited by Cynthia J. Miller and A. Bowdoin Van Riper, 267–278. Lanham, MD: Lexington Books, 2020.

Murphy, Bernice. "'It's Not the House That's Haunted': Demons, Debt, and the Family in Peril in Recent Horror Cinema." In *Cinematic Ghosts: Haunting Spectrality from Silent Cinema to the Digital Era,* edited by Murray Leeder, 235–252. New York: Bloomsbury, 2015.

Newit, Annalee, and Matt Wray, eds. *White Trash: Race and Class in America.* New York: Routledge, 1997.

Niemi, Nancy S. "Why Does the Public Distrust Higher Ed? Too Many Women." *Chronicle of Higher Education,* April 13, 2018. https://www.chronicle.com /article/Why-Does-the-Public-Distrust/243114?key=2K4N4HYtD2aA1V-c_T84p2lvrzcVrcnmYJrvzIw3tfUs3n48voHArlQJP7P-ah1PekkxTVRPc-m81SzU1MmlTLUlQaWRUSFFsYVBWU3ZJWkUyOUNMMGxtWUhtVQ.

Noble, Safiya Umoja. *Algorithms of Oppression: How Search Engines Reinforce Racism.* New York: NYU Press, 2018.

Oliver, Tracy. "Where Are All the POC in Horror Movies?" *Cosmopolitan,* October 29, 2018. https://www.cosmopolitan.com/entertainment/a24393125/tracy-oliver -survive-the-night-diversity-horror-movies/?fbclid=IwAR0a4LXmmIaiVPaAD DiODcPZi9IIiEyOOtGQagwPmhLNE1rlAR_YSUlqVHA.

Olszyk, Nick. "Pope Paul VI Makes a Horror Movie." *Catholic World Report,* April 14, 2015. http://www.catholicworldreport.com/2015/04/14/pope-paul-vi-makes -a-horror-movie/.

O'Neil, Cathy. *Weapons of Math Destruction: How Big Data Increases Inequality and Threatens Democracy.* New York: Crown, 2016.

Phillips, Kendall. *Projected Fears: Horror Films and American Culture.* Westport, CT: Praeger, 2005.

Pickert, Kate. "Russian Kids in America: When the Adopted Can't Adapt." *Time*, June 28, 2010. http://content.time.com/time/magazine/article/0,9171,1997439,00.html.

Prather, Cynthia, Taleria R. Fuller, William L. Jeffries IV, Khiya J. Marshall, A. Vyann Howell, Angela Belyue-Umole, and Winnifred King. "Racism, African American Women, and Their Sexual and Reproductive Health: A Review of Historical and Contemporary Evidence and Implications for Health Equity." *Health Equity* 2, no. 1 (2018): 249–259.

Prince, Stephen. "Introduction: The Dark Genre and Its Paradoxes." In *The Horror Film*, edited by Stephen Prince, 1–14. New Brunswick, NJ: Rutgers University Press, 2004.

Quinlan, Sean. "Demonizing the Sixties: Possession Stories and the Crisis of Religious and Medical Authority in Post-Sixties American Popular Culture." *Journal of American Culture* 37, no. 3 (2014): 314–330.

Rabin, Roni Caryn. "Huge Racial Disparities Found in Deaths Linked to Pregnancy." *New York Times*, May 7, 2019. https://www.nytimes.com/2019/05/07/health/pregnancy-deaths-.html?action=click&module=News&pgtype=Homepage.

Rayner, Alex. "Trapped in the Sunken Place: How *Get Out*'s Purgatory Engulfed Pop Culture." *The Guardian*, March 17, 2018. https://www.theguardian.com/film/2018/mar/17/trapped-in-the-sunken-place-how-get-outs-purgatory-engulfed-pop-culture.

Roche, David. *Making and Remaking Horror in the 1970s and 2000s: Why Don't They Do It Like They Used To?* Jackson: University of Mississippi Press, 2006.

Rodino-Colocino, Michelle. "The Great He-Cession: Why Feminists Should Rally for the End of White Supremacist Capitalist Patriarchy." *Feminist Media Studies* 14, no. 2 (2014): 343–347.

Romano, Aja. "*Us*'s Big Plot Twist, Explained." *Vox*, March 22, 2019. https://www.vox.com/2019/3/22/18277163/us-movie-ending-what-happened-adelaide-red-explained.

Rubin, Jennifer. "The Demographic Change Fueling the Angst of Trump's Base." *Washington Post*, September 6, 2017. https://www.washingtonpost.com/blogs/right-turn/wp/2017/09/06/the-demographic-change-fueling-the-angst-of-trumps-base/?utm_term=.6e751361b6c6.

Scahill, Andrew. *The Revolting Child in Horror Cinema: Youth Rebellion and Queer Spectatorship*. New York: Palgrave Macmillan, 2015.

Sharrett, Christopher. "The Horror Film as Social Allegory (And How It Comes Undone)." In *A Companion to the Horror Film*, edited by Harry Benshoff, 56–72. Malden, MA: Wiley Blackwell, 2017.

Siddique, Sophia, and Raphael Raphael, eds. *Transnational Horror Cinema: Bodies of Excess and the Global Grotesque*. London: Palgrave Macmillan, 2016.

Smith, David Norman, and Eric Hanley. "The Anger Games: Who Voted for Donald Trump in the 2016 Election, and Why?" *Critical Sociology* 44, no. 2 (2018): 195–212.

Snelson, Tim. "The (Re)possession of the American Home: Negative Equity, Gender Inequality, and the Housing Crisis Horror Story." In *Gendering the Recession: Media and Culture in an Age of Austerity*, edited by Diane Negra and Yvonne Tasker, 161–180. Durham, NC: Duke University Press, 2014.

Sobchack, Vivian. "Bringing It All Back Home: Family Exchange and Generic Exchange." In *American Horrors: Essays on the Modern American Horror Film*, edited by Gregory Waller, 175–194. Urbana: University of Illinois Press, 1987.

Soles, Carter. "Sympathy for the Devil: The Cannibalistic Hillbilly in 1970s Rural Slasher Films." In *Ecocinema Theory and Practice*, edited by Stephen Rust, Salma Monani, and Sean Cubitt, 233–250. New York: Routledge, 2013.

Szulkin, David A. *Wes Craven's Last House on the Left: The Making of a Cult Classic*. Guildford, UK: FAB Press, 2000.

Tensley, Brandon. "Horror Films Emerge as Best Political Commentary of Our Times." *CNN*, September 1, 2019. https://www.cnn.com/2019/09/01/politics /ready-or-not-horror-movies-trump-politics/index.html?fbclid=IwAR1EC _kEc_ziGWElPDec35ZZoE5b-XmZ9H9-E9_HcAKH0PA5EohjIruI3bs.

Tesler, Michael. *Post-Racial or Most-Racial? Race and Politics in the Obama Era*. Chicago: Chicago University Press, 2016.

Tobin, Jonathan S. "Other People's Babies and American Values." *National Review*, March 14, 2017. https://www.nationalreview.com/2017/03/steve-king-other -peoples-babies-tweet-undermines-conservative-american-values/.

Twenge, Jean M. *Generation Me—Revised and Updated: Why Today's Young Americans Are More Confident, Assertive, Entitled—and More Miserable Than Ever Before*. New York: Atria, 2014.

United States Census Bureau. "Projecting Majority-Minority: Non-Hispanic Whites May No Longer Comprise Over 50 Percent of the U.S. Population by 2044." Accessed May 11, 2021. https://www.census.gov/content/dam/Census /newsroom/releases/2015/cb15-tps16_graphic.pdf.

United States Department of Labor. "The African-American Labor Force." February 29, 2012. https://www.dol.gov/_sec/media/reports/BlackLaborForce /BlackLaborForce.pdf.

Unsell, Tyler. "In the Age of Trump, 'The Curse of La Llorona' Is Not Helpful." *Signal Horizon*, April 25, 2019. Accessed November 2019. https://www .signalhorizon.com/single-post/2019/04/24/In-the-Age-of-Trump-The-Curse -of-La-Llorona-is-Not-Helpful?fbclid=IwAR2IkBfDxK1XzyV2h7kscMk 9iH-Wei-kLjSwTJ9n_yYYBKojeXQCdty30NQ.

Valencia, Juan. "The House Settling: Race, Housing, and Wealth in the Post-Recession Horror Film." *Emergence*, November 25, 2017. http://emergencejournal

.english.ucsb.edu/index.php/2017/11/25/the-house-settling-race-housing-and
-wealth-in-the-post-recession-horror-film/.

Van Riper, A. Bowdoin. "All Against All: Dystopia, Dark Forces, and Hobbesian
Anarchy in the *Purge* Films." In *Dark Forces at Work: Essays on Social Dynamics
and Cinematic Horrors*, edited by Cynthia Miller and A. Bowdoin Van Riper,
115–130. Lanham, MD: Lexington Books, 2020.

Wang, Jackie. "'This Is a Story About Nerds and Cops': PredPol and Algorithmic
Policing." *E-Flux* 87 (December 2017). https://www.e-flux.com/journal
/87/169043/this-is-a-story-about-nerds-and-cops-predpol-and-algorithmic
-policing/.

Wang, Jessica. "The New Show 'Murder House Flip' Sounds Like 'Fixer Upper' for
True Crime Fans." *Bustle*, August 27, 2019. https://www.bustle.com/p/the-new
-show-murder-house-flip-sounds-like-fixer-upper-for-true-crime-fans-18704878.

Warner, Judith. *Perfect Madness: Motherhood in the Age of Anxiety*. New York: Riverhead Books, 2005.

Weissman, Jordan. "Student Debt Is Indeed Hurting Homeownership, Federal
Reserve Study Finds." *Slate*, January 17, 2019. https://slate.com/business/2019/01
/fed-estimates-college-loans-millenials-home-ownership.html.

Wilson, Natalie. *Willful Monstrosity: Gender and Race in 21st Century Horror*. Jefferson, NC: McFarland, 2020.

Wood, Robin. *Hollywood from Vietnam to Reagan . . . And Beyond*. New York:
Columbia University Press, 2003.

Zimmer, Catherine. *Surveillance Cinema*. New York: NYU Press, 2015.

INDEX

Page numbers in italics refer to illustrations.

RUSSELL MEEUF is Professor in the School of Journalism and Mass Media at the University of Idaho in Moscow. He is the author of *Rebellious Bodies: Stardom, Citizenship, and the New Body Politics* and *John Wayne's World: Transnational Masculinity in the Fifties.*